RAFE HUBRIS, BA (Oxon) is an advisor to the Conservative Party and thinks his career couldn't have gone better. Rafe was educated at Oxford University and is incapable of writing three sentences without mentioning it. Rafe spends most of his time not working so as not to get embroiled in something that will lead to more work. Rafe has no regrets.

JOSH BERRY is a comedian and writer and thinks his career really ought to have gone better. Josh was educated at Oxford University but only acknowledges it while looking apologetically at the floor if someone asks him three times. Josh spends most of his time working on being funny so he can have more opportunities to be funny which will allow him to continue working on being funny. Josh often regrets things even before he has done them.

STAGGERING
HUBRIS

Rafe Hubris BA (oxon)   **WITH
JOSH BERRY**

THE MEMOIR OF
BORIS JOHNSON'S

THE 'RONA YEARS, VOL.1

MOST CLASSIC SPAD

★ ★ ★

Lightning
Books

Published in 2021
by Lightning Books Ltd
Imprint of Eye Books Ltd
29A Barrow Street
Much Wenlock
Shropshire
TF13 6EN

www.lightning-books.com

Cover design by Ifan Bates
Cover picture by Blake Max
Typeset in Bembo and Arial

British Library Cataloguing in Publication Data
A catalogue record for this book is available from the British Library.

Printed by CPI Group (UK) Ltd, Croydon CR0 4YY

ISBN: 9781785633072

FSC
www.fsc.org
MIX
Paper from
responsible sources
FSC® C171272

Before we embark on the tier-one chat, it's important that I put in place some language to stop me from getting sued.

Though the following memoir may well provide a frighteningly plausible explanation of a lot of what went on in 2020, it is to be understood as a comical rendering, rather than a factual retelling. It is parody, not history.

None of what is said in the following pages amounts to an actual claim about someone's character or something that actually happened in government in 2020.

If it transpires that some of my comical imaginings happen to be true, that is purely coincidental.

JB

PROLOGUE

How are we? I do hope this finds you feeling positive but testing negative.

My name is RAFE HUBRIS, BA (Oxon) (I have a degree from Oxford University). Unless you're a woman on Tinder between the ages of nineteen and thirty swiping in the Clapham area, one of my 500+ connections on LinkedIn (which I like to think of as professional Tinder) or a high-end cocaine dealer operating in South West London, you won't have heard of me. Despite this, I am one of the most significant special advisors (spads) to the UK government working today and have been at the coalface (metaphorically speaking) throughout this coronavirus pandemic.

This, the first of what will be many memoirs as I inevitably ascend to the status of prime minister, documents my 2020 in its entirety (and iniquity). The memoir also offers an account of the pivotal role I played in the government's coronavirus response from when the virus first came to the UK, around mid to late March, to when the UK government skilfully and efficiently controlled and contained it for good by the close of *décembre*. This memoir really ought to be thought of as the first instalment of what will be many subsequent triumphs. The year 2020 for me is what Wimbledon 2003 was for Roger Federer: the beginning of a legacy.

As I imagine the educators of the future will use this as a cornerstone of the history syllabus, I've made a conscious effort to keep the language accessible. Where I fear my writing may be slightly too Oxbridge, I have endeavoured to clarify what I mean in language that is more comprehensible (easy to understand).

Before we begin, I must thank my alma mater: Exeter College, Oxford, and the small comprehensive just outside Slough where I received my secondary education, which some of you may know as Eton College. It's thanks to both these institutions that the majority of our political operatives act with such a robust and unwavering self-confidence as well as the sort of mind that just makes one better than everyone else. We all owe these institutions the ultimate debt, as without them we simply would not be able to find people clever enough to lead.

Enjoy.

I write vary, vary wall.

Floreat Etona!
Dominus Illuminatio Mea.
Classically,

Rafe Hubris BA (oxon)

Rafe Hubris, BA (Oxon)
31 December 2020
(Add me on LinkedIn)

JANUARY 2020

Wednesday 1 January

I wake up feeling more fucked than all of Boris's marriages.

The Spad New Year's Party last night, which I have already termed 'Chango Unchained' on our WhatsApp chat, was a masterclass in intoxication and debauchery. Everyone got stuck in, even Poppy, who can sometimes be a bit of a wetty. We skied across tables and drank till we were no longer able; I must have got through at least a whole bottle of Perrier-Jouët from the helmet of Lettie's family's suit of armour before we all piled into an enormous game of conjugation imbibition. For the uninitiated, conjugation imbibition is a drinking game where participants pick a Latin verb at random out of a hat and have to conjugate it within thirty seconds or face a punitive shot of port. It's my favourite of all the drinking games because in addition to infallibly ensuring that everyone gets absolutely binned, it also allows you to weed out and evict state school alumni who have sneakily infiltrated your social group but cannot conceal their lack of Latin.

In all my twenty-four classic years on this Earth I've never seen a group of people so collectively hammered. And who could blame us? 2019 was a year to celebrate!

We overcame Corbyn and his Bolshevik revolution and successfully duped the northerners into thinking we care about them (lol) to win an enormous election victory; Brexit is in the oven/defrosting/ready to be put in the microwave at some point and we have Boris at the helm.

Sadly, no Boris last night. He's off with some woman in the Caribbean; the man is incorrigible! But on a serious note, I can think of no one better to lead us into 2020. 2019 was excellent, but I get this feeling in my gut that 2020 will be even better and that I will inevitably play a pretty significant role (hence my decision to start this diary, which I imagine will act as a sort of political highlight reel, like the ones Sky Sports do but for the corridors of power).

I open my WhatsApp chat campaign for 2020 with the pithiest of zingers: 'I'm hanging more than the Sword of Damocles.' Sharp wit with an intellectual foundation in ancient Rome, I start the year as I intend to go on: vary wall.

Thursday 2 January

First day in work today.

There's a new spad in the office, Hugo, an old Harrovian (the Lidl of private schools) and alumnus of Regent's Park College (though part of Oxford, it's not technically speaking a proper college, it's merely a permanent private hall and therefore inferior; I was at Exeter College, which is consistently voted one of the best at Oxford). I would be surprised if he doesn't snap like a KitKat within the first fortnight.

Dominic Cummings (we all call him Big Daddy Cum Cum) welcomes all the spads back to work with a speech he makes in the Department for Business, Energy and Industrial Strategy.

He delivers the speech standing on top of a desk.

He keeps saying: 'We're turning up the flames under the cauldron to weed out the intellectual homunculi, guys.'

And: 'Operation recruit the worker bees has been activated.'

When he's finished, Big Daddy Cum Cum exits, leaving a completed Rubik's Cube with a note underneath saying, 'Conventional wisdom is for cunts (Dominic Cummings 2nd January 2020)' in his wake.

Matt Hancock, at the behest of no one, then gets up to say a few words.

Hancock has the natural authority of a man who's just been left by his girlfriend for his brother on the way into an end-of-year presentation he's written on the back of a cigarette packet, having forgotten to do any work for it. Practically no one is listening to anything he's saying, and he just gently tails off to a heavy, cement-like silence.

We all get a group email in the evening telling us to read Big Daddy Cum Cum's blog from 'osamabinladen@gov.uk' (the alias Dom uses to make us question conventional notions of offence). Like all things I get told are important reading, I skim the blog and see something about the importance of 'misfits and weirdos' and 'people from William Gibson novels' in government and no more 'public school bluffers'. I don't recall reading any William Gibson novels at Eton, but I'm sure I could spin something off the cuff to make it look like I had if I needed to.

I welcome Hugo to the spad WhatsApp chat before bed, telling everyone to 'be nice to Hugo, because Big Daddy Cum Cum has said it's out with public school bluffers, so he probably won't be around for very long'. Classic Rafe 'Big Dog' Hubris chat, you love to see it.

Friday 3 January

I'm sat on Boris's table at lunch.

He is genuinely an absolute riot.

He regales us with his cherry pie story, which I must have heard at least half a dozen times but somehow it gets funnier with every telling…the timing…the Thai accent he does…it's the platonic ideal of an anecdote.

Everyone starts drifting back to work leaving just me and Boris together. I still get a little nervous around him – he's so funny and charismatic and popular with women, I don't want to say anything that makes him think I'm not classic.

He sits trying to flick peas into the bras of female spads on nearby tables and I float the idea of trying to do something to mark getting Brexit done… I suggest a 'Bong for Brexit' on Big Ben.

This sets Boris off on a journey of plosive alliteration culminating in the words 'Bollocks', 'Boris' and 'Burst' and him humping the side of the table. I'm genuinely crying with laughter.

It's 3.23pm and everyone else, other than the staff, has gone. My Tinder flashes up as Boris polishes off his third Eton Mess. He effortlessly negotiates my phone out of my hand and before I know it is flicking through 'Tilly, 23' from Clapham's photos.

'Christ, those jugs… I'd dip my balls in a bath of acid just to be in the same room as them,' he comments, a droplet of drool falling from his open mouth onto the table.

Within five minutes he's arranged a date for me at Bluebird tomorrow night. He is a wizard.

'Bluebird to help mend your blue balls,' he chuckles.

'Right, I make that 3.30, weekend time. Good luck

tomorrow, old boy, get Sexit done.'

What an absolute top chap.

Saturday 4 January

Tilly arrives at Bluebird in a top the neckline of which has what I would call 'a strong gravitational pull'. I pray that my Milky Way ends up in her black hole. We get chatting, the Whispering Angel is flowing, I'm being my usual self-deprecating self and subtly slip into conversation that my flat is only a very short Addison Lee ride away in Clapham, just in case there's some sort of emergency and we desperately need to find a bedroom or something...a classic Hubris line.

The date is going wall, vary wall in fact.

I decide to take things to the next level when she comes back from the loo, and flick one of the peas from the plate of food in front of me into her bra. I launch the pea with the composure of Tiger Woods on the eighteenth of Augusta; it arcs elegantly through the air and settles definitively between her ample cleavage.

For some reason, Tilly does not join me in whooping to celebrate my short game; instead she looks at me with a mixture of disgust and confusion, as if I've been completely inappropriate.

I offer to fish out the pea but she tells me she doesn't think 'we're on the same page' and leaves!

The gall.

Women are genuinely a fucking enigma. They want affection and yet you give it to them and suddenly it's 'inappropriate'.

I'm also forced to cover the *entire* bill with my money. My own money. The money that belongs to me! I *always* split the bill on dates because I firmly believe in twenty-first-century feminism (where it can save me money) so she has literally stolen from me! I split the bill unless the girl is an absolute smoke show like Lily James or Susanna Reid who I would literally take out a high-interest rate loan and sell one of my kidneys to date.

As I'm paying seventy-three pounds fucking eighty, I clock Lettie and Poppy drinking at the far end of Bluebird. I can't bear to talk to them and acknowledge this grotesque failure.

I leave quietly before they manage to catch sight of me.

Sunday 5 January

I get a tasty email from Big Daddy Cum Cum in the evening. The email is simply a link to an unlisted YouTube video of him in a parka saying something I can't make sense of over some whiny guitar (presumably some sort of nod to Oasis??). On my third watch I realise the Big Daddy is using Pig Latin to convey a hidden message. Using all the power of my superior Oxbridge brain it takes me two minutes to decipher the message:

> The first ten spads who email me with the words 'Conventional wisdom is for cunts' will be promoted.

I fall on my laptop, almost breaking the keyboard in my zeal to send the email, which receives a reply from osamabinladen@gov.uk within seconds.

> Spad,
>
> You have successfully deciphered my hidden message

designed to make you think more deeply about language and unplug yourself from the Matrix.

You are now promoted from drone bee to the much more prestigious worker bee and will be working as an interviewer for the innovative spads of tomorrow.

You will receive your iPad and Rubik's Cube on arrival at Number 10.

Conventional wisdom is for cunts.

Classic Dom, Classic Dom,

Osama Bin Laden

This is hugely exciting news.

I change my Tinder bio to read: 'Very high up in government, but still willing to let you go down on me.'

No matches tonight.

Monday 6 January

I stroll into Number 10 with the swagger of the stockbroker and supposed felon Jordan Belfort from *The Wolf of Wall Street* (the greatest film of all time). My hair is perfect, I'm wearing a light-pink shirt with a light-blue tie (school colours, classic) and I'm holding a Pret coffee in my right hand. I absolutely fucking love Pret, it's one of the things that makes me incredibly proud to be British. I genuinely don't know what I'd do if that shop went under. I don't think any of us do...

Other things which stoke my British pride are: the King's Road, Embargo's, cocaine, the institution of the Royal Family, the rugby, Henley Regatta, Wimbledon, the Royal Borough of Hammersmith and Fulham, Barbour, Jaguar, Evian, Hugo Boss and of course Eton College and Oxford University (where I went).

I reach my desk in Number 10 and see, as promised, the Rubik's Cube and iPad with 'Worker Bee, Hubris, R' written on them in Post-it notes.

I scan the office to see who else has received one. Only Poppy in my immediate vicinity. She can sometimes be a wetty but she's vary good, Poppy; she's a vary good girl.

She mentions she thought she saw me on Friday in Bluebird. I reply that I was in fact on a successful date with a worldie elsewhere, though it's understandable to think she saw me in Bluebird – there are lots of tall, square-jawed, conventionally good-looking men in Chelsea on a Friday night. I don't mean this in a gay way – I've never even had a gay thought! I also actually scored zero on the Kinsey scale, which is the most heterosexual you can be.

The iPad, the six-digit passcode of which I correctly guess to be 032113 – 'cum' in a basic alphabet/number substitution cipher – has a grid of names and phone numbers along with possible questions:

What could a robot from Mars teach us about the future?

Can you build a bridge to the moon using the contents of a spark plug? If yes, why?

Is it genius because Dominic Cummings does it? Or does Dominic Cummings do it because it's genius?

The iPad doesn't specify where these interviews have to take place so I conduct them in Pret. Classic Rafe.

I manage to cleverly get the candidates to keep buying me coffees implying it might mean they're more likely to get the job if they do.

The first candidate is a misfit but not an intellect and completely freezes when I ask him to explain to me how he knows he is truly in Pret and not just a brain in a vat being tricked into thinking it's in Pret. He lasts about seven minutes before I thank him for his time and tell him 'We'll be in touch.' We won't (lol).

The second candidate, by contrast, is brilliant.

He catches the orange I throw at him on entry.

He aces the 'Is it genius because Dominic Cummings does it? Or does Dominic Cummings do it because it's genius?' question by correctly saying 'Both'.

He also nails the 'defence of something intuitively morally objectionable' section, making a surprisingly detailed, very statistically supported defence of eugenics. He must be an Oxford grad…I hire him on the spot.

Wednesday 8 January

The things worth having in this life are usually inherited (like money and land) or received (like pronunciation). Very occasionally, though, one must go out and claim them, like we did with Africa in the nineteenth century (Rafe Hubris, 2020). In this vein I decide to take mine and Boris's Brexit Bong chat to the next level and reach out to touch base about it via email:

Boris,

Flicking peas into Lettie's bra and making the girls go yah, no doubt. How are we?

I think we should jump on the back of this Brexit Bong stuff and ride it like a bull. It's sure to be a great Johnson legacy move, a huge one in fact, almost as big as the girl from Tinder's tits (no joy on Friday by the way, her chat was incredibly weak, so I sacked her off).

Let's lock in a time to chat about this; let me know when works for you.

Incorrigibly,
Rafe

Shortly after I press 'send', a blood-curdling screech pierces the air. It's Bully Patel on one of her trips from the Home Office. These trips are invariably bad news as they mean she's run out of people to butcher at 10 Marsham Street and is looking for prey in Downing Street.

I swiftly post on the WhatsApp: 'Popcorn-worthy spad butchery from Bully Patel in Number 10. T minus now.'

'*You lazy cunt!*' she screams at Hugo with an artistic savagery. 'Rewrite the whole fucking thing...*now*.'

She then throws to the floor the lever-arch file she's apparently prised from him and turns on her heel.

The most bizarre part of all of this is that Hugo doesn't even work for Bully Patel. She knows that; she just loves to fuck people up.

A silence falls in the office only for Lee Cain, Big Daddy

Cum Cum's number two, to emerge…he walks over to the lever-arch file Bully Patel has savaged with a terrifying calmness and then proceeds to stamp on the file with both feet repeatedly, all while pointing with two fingers to his own eyes and then back at Hugo. Poor chap, I did say this wasn't the place for a Harrovian…

Thursday 9 January

Nothing back from Boris. Every time I chase I get the same reply:

> I am currently on leave and won't be replying to emails.
>
> For urgent correspondence please contact osamabinladen@gov.uk.
>
> Yours,
> Boris Johnson

After lunch, though, Boris does get back to me.

> Rafe,
>
> I'm all over this like Jennifer Arcuri. Canteen. Tomorrow.
>
> Incorrigibly,
> BJ

I have to clench my conventionally attractive jaw extra hard to stop my mouth opening and letting out a giddy yelp of joy at

Boris using my email sign-off back to me. I can't stop smiling for the rest of the day.

Friday 10 January

Big Daddy Cum Cum has gone rogue and has started incessantly sending emails from his osamabinladen@gov.uk account, each one more bizarre than the last.

I receive one as I'm getting off the tube at Westminster with a picture of his face and the words:

Big Daddy Cum Cum is watching you

and underneath that:

DEAD CATS ARE ALIVE CATS

THE FUTURE IS THE PRESENT

UNCONVENTIONAL WISDOM IS CONVENTIONAL WISDOM
(WHICH IS FOR CUNTS).

The rumour on the spad Whatsapp chat is that he's banned all references to the 'pre-Cummings era' in politics and has started giving spads pop quizzes on his 'essential reading'. All spads are presented with a large folder of Cummings' key works (known colloquially as 'the Cum folder') on arrival in government so that they may enter the same 'cognitive universe' as him. There are many accounts from spads who've had to endure the Big Daddy's testing, but the problem with these is that they often cancel each other out.

For example, Felix claims to have been ambushed by the Big

Daddy in the Department of Health at 10am on Wednesday, but this was also supposedly when he was grilling Elizabeth on the essays of Warren Buffett in the Home Office. I briefly wonder whether he might be hiring a series of aggressive badly dressed bald men to create complete totalitarian confusion among the spads. What is certain in all this is that failure to pass Big Daddy Cum Cum's 'pop quiz' means 're-education' at the hands of Lee Cain. Having seen what Cain did to Hugo last week I decide to keep a very low profile and slide into lunch at 12.45.

Boris is a no-show; he pings me an email at 2.45 to say:

Rafe,

May have to bail on today, old boy. Currently in the middle of a *Telegraph* journalist.

Chat on Monday re: Brexit Bongs – Javid will never fund it, so we'll need to get the public to – good old charity – come to me on Monday with a zinger for Brexit Bongs that explains all that.

Incorrigibly,
BJ

I don't even feel annoyed that Boris bailed; I just want to make sure I can craft him the best zinger since language was invented (at Eton College).

I promptly leave the canteen and consign myself to coming up with the zingiest of zingers, but my mind is like cement. All I can think of is 'Boris's Blue Brexit Bollocks Bursting on Breasts', which, though vary funny, isn't right.

It's seven and still nothing. I'm back home and have invited a few of the chaps from school round for some chang: Rupert, a consultant who works in the City, Henry, a lawyer who works in the City and Dom, a banker who works in the City – a really interesting and diverse group. I've also invited Hugo; it's been a tough week for the old boy...

'The thing about politics,' I say to him, chopping up the Columbian snow with my Amex, 'is it's all about doing as little as you can but making it look as though you're doing loads... It's not about working hard; it's about someone else doing the work and then you claiming it was yours if it's good and theirs if it's shit. Do you follow?'

He nods.

'Perfect example: imagine hypothetically there was a hypothetical initiative to get the public to hypothetically put money to funding Big Ben going Bong on Brexit day. If I were clever I'd ask you to think of an alliterative pithy zinger to describe that initiative and if it's good, I'd claim it as my own... hypothetically.'

'A zinger like *Bung a Bob for Brexit Bongs*?' he says.

'No, obviously not that. That's crap,' I say.

It's not crap, it's fucking perfect and now it's mine to send to Boris. I'm pretty sure I came up with it. Even though it came from Hugo's mouth, he said it in my flat, which I own, which makes it intellect expressed in my property, which makes it my intellectual property.

'Just be mindful about this stuff, mate; trying to look out for you,' I say.

'I really appreciate it mate. Thank you,' says Hugo.

I rack up a couple of white caterpillars for us both, making sure I keep a mental tally of exactly how much Hugo owes me, and snort the larger of the two through my designated Sellotaped fifty-pound note.

Monday 13 January

Boris absolutely fucking loves the zinger and gives me the green light to announce the scheme. This is *grande*. This is Ariana Grande. I wonder if Hugo remembers he came up with it but I look over to the old chap and see he's got bigger problems to be thinking about…Bully Patel has returned from the Home Office and is heavily pasting him for the second time in five days! Normally she would only come over to Number 10 once a month but she must have developed a taste for savaging Hugo.

I sit down at my desk and see the brilliant spad I hired in Pret has arrived and is sat next to me. He's just as impressive today as I remember him being at interview. He absolutely aces his pop quiz, identifying a quote from page 13 of *Bismarck: The Man and the Statesman*, and correctly guessing what Big Daddy Cum Cum has hidden behind his back. He earns the name 'The Superprophet', a rank second only to Lee Cain. I book in a pint with him. As a Tory it's absolutely essential to stay close to those in power, like one of the greatest Tories of all time, Tony Blair, did with Rupert Murdoch.

The spad chat is blowing up about *Love Island*, which started last night. I load it up on my phone under the desk with my headphones in to make it look as if I'm working to music when I'm actually listening to all of them talk about which has the biggest mug and who is whose type on paper. Why the obsession with paper when none of these people know how to read or write?

They really do pick some absolute space cadets for this programme; there's one jolly good chap on it for a bit of diversity though, which is good. The women might be stupid but some of them are phenomenally fit. I decide to do a bit of horny Tinder swiping and Lettie pops up. Though it's undoubtedly vary delicate business shagging a colleague, being nothing if not a naughty boy, I swipe right like James Bond.

No match straight away, undoubtedly because she's yet to see me rather than because she doesn't want me. All women want me, I'm a male worldie.

Tuesday 14 January

I see on the tube into work that the bushfires in Australia are really bad, apocalyptic even. This is what happens when you ignore the early-warning signs: stuff spirals out of control and you're left with your cock in your hands apologising endlessly for needless death you've caused. Politics is like tennis: done well, it should be proactive not reactive.

I arrive at Number 10 at a 'gentleman's nine o'clock' (9.25) to a large Brexit dossier on my desk with a Post-it note and the word 'PROOFREAD' written on it. I decide this isn't work for someone of my stature and background so wait for Hugo to go to the loo and slip the dossier onto his desk.

The trick is to slip the folder onto someone's desk to make them think it's theirs and then take it back when the task is 95 per cent done. You then do the remaining 5 per cent of the work and pass the whole thing off as your own.

The Superprophet notices this move and wryly jokes, 'Proofreading is women's work – you should have given that to one of the females.' He does this with such deadpan delivery that if I didn't know better, I'd think he was being serious. It's brilliant. This guy is more than just a superprophet, he's a super-comedian too! Like Al Murray or something. Our pint can't come soon enough.

Wednesday 15 January

Another weirdo and misfit interview. This one is neither, he's just an arrogant cunt. I begin the interview as I begin practically every interaction.

'I was at Exeter; which college were you at?'

'Oh, Exeter. That's an Oxford college, right? Not bad... though it's hardly Trinity, Cambridge, is it?'

He smirks. I do not. What the fuck is even the point in saying something like that? I fucking hate one-upmanship, especially when it's from someone who is objectively not on my level. Irrefutably, Eton and PPE at Oxford has produced the most prime ministers, not fucking Cambridge. Prick.

I take an almost sexual pleasure in sending this chippy prick a rejection email as I'm shaking his inferior-signet-ring-wearing hand to signal the end of the interview.

Pint with the Superprophet. He's there early and has already got me a pint of San Miguel.

'How did you know San Miguel is my favourite?' I ask, thrilled about the antics to come.

He simply points at his temple indicating that he used his superforecasting abilities to deduce that that's what I'd want. Christ he's good.

The chat is scintillating. He embarks on this incredible

satirical monologue comparing the bubbles in a beer which rise to the top, unthinking and unfeeling, existing only to enhance the experience of our taste buds, to the working class in the UK. I guess it's kind of satire, but also kind of not because on a level the working class are vary much like that; this makes it even cleverer. After about ninety minutes, he tells me that there's a Jordan Peterson lecture he wants to watch before bed. We finish our pints and part ways.

I get home and flick on *Love Island* only to see the posh chap has gone. Classic BBC bias. Someone with a background to be proud of sticks their head above the parapet and suddenly they get fucking cancelled.

I try to watch for a few minutes but, without this chap on it, it's fucking intolerable. It's just a load of dead-eyed, half-naked poor people being exploited by executives for entertainment… If I wanted that, I could just watch *The X Factor*…or porn… At least in porn they actually take their clothes all the way off rather than this 'deepthroat the banana' challenge *Love Island* tease bullshit.

I decide to watch some porn.

Thursday 16 January

Lee Cain is having a bad day today. He's getting himself a cup of water from the water cooler in Number 10 but can't seem to keep his hands steady. He tries a couple of times and then screams '*Fuck!*' at the top of his lungs and storms off, causing several spads to visibly flinch and shudder as he departs.

I get another email from Boris.

Rafe,

I bring exciting news.

I have decided to put you in charge of delivering a Brexit Day party in Number 10 to put all hitherto organised debauchery to shame. I want the party to be so raucous you have to pull out all the stops the following day to keep ministers out of the tabloids. I want people to speak of this party like Roman nobility would have discussed the debauched forays of Caligula. No expense should be spared. This is your London 2012.

Take my number if you need a second opinion on which 'danger women' to invite, I've got a huge database with all the best ones.

077— ———

Incorrigibly,
BJ

PS Also, have had to sack off Brexit Bongs, old boy; would have loved to have backed it but my hands are tied (not for the first time) (woof).

I'm not even upset at all the work I did coming up with the Brexit Bong zinger going to waste. This is enormous. What an honour. I have Blojo's number. I can send him memes! The rise and rise of Rafe Hubris continues.

I reply:

Blojo,

Pulling out and not for the first time!

Mate, Zeus and Caligula will sit enviously in Elysium watching the party I will construct. I'm thinking of naming it: Britain Beyond Brexit Booze Bath and Bonanza. Thoughts?

I will not let you down, it will be iniquity in ubiquity, mate.

Incorrigibly,
Rafe

He responds immediately with:

Blojo, I like that. I like that a lot.

Incorrigibly,
Blojo

The feeling that Boris Johnson and I are now friends is so good it's not even topped by £100 gak.

Friday 17 January

Another weirdo and misfit interview.

This applicant, Henrietta, twenty-six, Westminster, Girton, is literally the most beautiful girl I've ever seen on and off the internet. She's what Blojo would call a 'principle snapper'. An hour before the interview is due to start I slide into her Instagram message requests to reschedule the ~~date~~ professional interview to Bluebird, Chelsea. Classic Rafe. Classic Rafe.

She arrives and I deliver a killer line I've been practising under my breath in the Uber Lux on the way in:

'Welcome to this "worldies and misfits" interview…sorry, "weirdos and misfits"; you are a worldie though.'

The genius of this is that it vary subtly plants the seed in her head that I find her attractive, but it's subtle enough for her to probably not even be consciously aware of it. I got this from *The Man's Guide to Women*, a must-read for anyone who wants to truly understand women written by a couple of incredibly intelligent men.

The conversation is flowing like the River Cherwell.

'The thing is, I'm the most powerful twenty-four-year-old in the UK right now. Everyone looks at Boris Johnson as the leader, but he always runs the big decisions past me. So what I'm saying is, if you impress me, you'll do just fine in government… The one thing is, if I do offer you the job, and as I say I do have that power, you probably wouldn't have time to have a boyfriend. So, you'd have to dump your current one.'

'Oh I don't have a boyfriend,' she says.

I try vary hard not to spontaneously burst into flames before her green eyes (I've even noticed the colour of her eyes, I might have to marry her) when she says this.

I offer her the job right there and then and formally end the interview but offer her a drink.

'It won't mean I take the job away if you say no, but it also will,' I say with a wink.

Before long, we're flirting. Before long, I'm ordering Whispering Angel on the government account. Before long, we're kissing. Before long, she's in my bed… I embark on the sex like the 600 horsemen in Tennyson's 'Charge of the Light Brigade': boldly, fiercely but with an inevitable futility. Before

29

long, I ejaculate nobly into her jaws of death.

From this moment, my mind and body is immediately awash with an overwhelming feeling of disgust towards this girl. I don't think I ever want to see her ever again. She keeps trying to rest her head on my chest, it's absolutely horrific. I tell her I'm really sorry, but I have to be up incredibly early in the morning and I find it absolutely impossible to sleep with someone next to me and given that I work for the government, she has a civic duty to leave. She gets dressed and slips out. I breathe an almighty sigh of relief as the door closes. I don't think we'll be getting married.

Sunday 19 January

Lunch at *el casa del* Mummy and my father in Virginia Water. Will, my older brother, is there with his wife Juliette, who is about seven and half months pregnant so isn't drinking (a bit wet if you ask me). Everyone's talking about how amazing Will is for starting a family, buying a house in Teddington and closing in on being made partner at Slaughter and May, all at just twenty-nine.

'Isn't Will wonderful?'

'We couldn't be prouder of our boy!'

'Wonderful Will keeps soaring.'

After a good half-hour of this, Mummy asks when they might be seeing a similar return on the investment they poured into my education.

'Things have been going really well, actually. I've been working personally with Boris Johnson to secure arrangements for the 31st of January,' I say.

'You've been working to finalise Brexit?' says my mother,

her eyebrow raised.

'Well, I've been arranging the party for when we've left,' I say. 'Boris has personally put me in charge of it and he's given me his phone number.'

'Sounds world-shattering,' says Will.

Juliette tries to stop her lip from curling but both Mummy and my father openly laugh.

Monday 20 January

Big Daddy Cum Cum is standing on top of a table in Number 10.

He's wearing a cloak this morning and is brandishing a wand (alluding to Voldemort?) to unveil 'the latest great success in the Classic Dom reign'. It's a proposed 'Move Boris's Chair' scheme (he loves a linguistic trio), where Boris would have to leave Number 10 and be stationed at Number 12 along with a small cadre of 'senior bees'. This, Big Daddy Cum Cum argues, would allow Blojo to focus 'much more ably on predicting the future'.

'It is known,' says Lee Cain after every few sentences in support of Big Daddy Cum Cum's propositions.

This evokes firm opposition from Blojo, who says moving him from Number 10 would be like moving the Queen out of Windsor Castle or Hugh Heffner out of the Playboy Mansion.

'I've always been a vociferous advocate of working in close proximity to prime Number 10 totty; I will not move to Number 12 for that reason, Dom. I've also got a jolly comfortable chair here which goes all tippy when I lean back on it.' He demonstrates this. 'No deal,' he concludes.

Big Daddy Cum Cum, perturbed, still on top of the desk,

paces around muttering something incomprehensible under his breath (possibly ancient Norse). I notice at this point he isn't wearing any shoes…After some ten seconds he says, 'It is the only way. It's a desk revolution or my departure.'

Boris comes back at him by saying, 'Look old boy, I'll give you funds to create the ant colony out of Lego you've been asking for, but my chair stays here.'

Cummings strides around muttering at the floor again and finally looks up and says:

'Very well, it shall be done.' He gently hops down from the desk assisted by Lee Cain and disappears off into his office. Lee Cain follows and kicks the water dispenser on his way through.

Wednesday 22 January

I hear Poppy and Hugo talking about some bloke who ate a bat in China or something over lunch. They are fucking bizarre over there.

I don't have time to dwell on the trivial, though. I have serious business to attend to like sorting a red wine shipment for the Brexit party (still nothing back from Blojo about whether the 'Britain Beyond Brexit Booze Bath and Bonanza' name is a goer yet). Sorting red wine is proving to be quite fucking difficult as all the good ones are from the EU, and we need to celebrate British culture with this party.

I do some googling and see our national dish is Chicken Tikka Masala so decide to get that and loads of Stella Artois, which I'm pretty sure is British too.

'Look at the new spad that's started today. She's so pretty,' says Poppy in that way girls do to try and show they're not jealous.

'She's so fit,' says Hugo.

I look up and see Henrietta and the dread nearly causes my stomach to drop out of my arsehole. As she approaches our table I briefly consider running away but before I can, I hear her say:

'Hi Rafe, nice to see you again.'

'Huh? Oh yeah, hey. Henrietta, right? Great to see you too,' I say.

I look at her and her beauty figuratively slaps me across the face. For some reason she looks like the most beautiful woman on and off the internet again. I decide to unleash the irresistible Hubris charm offensive again and say, sexily:

'This is Poppy and Hugo, a couple of spads I have the displeasure of working with on a regular basis…I hired Henrietta,' I say to Poppy and Hugo. I wonder how I could ever have been disgusted by her…she is an angel. Even her tray of food is fit, a fancy-looking salad with an Evian. I think I'm falling in love with her; I think the marriage might be back on.

We all get chatting and she seems to get vary engrossed in conversation with Hugo who is definitely, embarrassingly, trying it on with her. I'm not threatened, there's no way she'll go for him, he's a Harrovian from Regent's Park! Besides I'm much more senior; no one would choose the cub sat beside them when there's a lion sat across from them.

'Henrietta, why don't I show you back to your desk?' I say, rolling my sleeves up to just before the elbow, which I've read women fucking love.

'I know where my desk is; thanks, though,' she says.

It feels like she might be trying to neg me?

After lunch I decide to 'happen to be passing through the Department of Education' where Henrietta works, to lock in *une deuxième boisson* with the old girl: classic Rafe chivalry. I spot her still talking with fucking Hugo who has beaten me to it/her, the prick. My phone buzzes with a WhatsApp from Poppy which reads:

> Looks like Hugo doesn't hang about. Word on the grapevine is that he's taking her for a drink at Bluebird tonight.

It takes all my willpower not to launch my iPhone X into the cranium of the nervous-looking mousey spad ten feet in front of me. The wedding is fucking off. Hugo is a cunt. Henrietta is a bitch.

I go for a pint with the Superprophet and explain the whole thing.

'The thing you've got to remember about females,' he says sliding into a second San Miguel, 'is that they're more limited than us. Think about it. In the Garden of Eden, God made Adam out of Eve's rib, then who went and betrayed Adam and fed him the apple? Eve. Females are intellectually and morally stunted, mate, you'd be stupid to give your heart to one. That's why you have to keep them in their rightful place: the home. They're just about clever enough to manage a domain that small. Take them out of that and you start getting all these feminists you see now who want us to chop off our own dicks lest we make someone feel uncomfortable. Never forget that,' he says.

He's right. He's so right. I'm not sure about the chopping-off-our-own-dicks stuff but women are deceitful, spineless and stupid. As soon as Henrietta got what she wanted from me, she fucked off.

'Listen, mate, let me take care of this one for you. I've got an ingenious plan.'

'You'd do that for me?' I ask, genuinely touched.

'It has already been put into action,' he says, pointing at his temple with a look of sage certainty.

What a fucking great guy he is.

I drink just about enough to not think about Hugo and Henrietta at Bluebird and what they'll be doing to each other's forearms and/or orifices and drift off into a very drunken sleep.

Thursday 23 January

I arrive at my desk to find a note from the Superprophet.

R,

Everything sorted with the wench. I told Cummings I suspected her of conspiring against the machine. He disappeared her.

For the brotherhood,
TS (The Superprophet)

I feel a twinge of guilt but remember she was a horrible person so it's for the best she's gone.

I look up to see Hugo being monstered by Bully Patel, which wonderfully seems to be becoming an almost weekly fixture.

'You haven't done it properly. *Do it again, you cunt!*'

I feel an extinguishing inner peace. Harmony has been restored.

Friday 24 January

I sit at my desk and realise I have nothing to do. I say I have
nothing to do, there's plenty of work I could be doing, but I
don't want to do it, which means I have nothing to do. Having
run out of girls to swipe on Tinder (incredulously still nothing
from Lettie) I decide to browse the papers and start reading
about this 'SARS-like virus from China,' in the *Times*. By the
looks of it, it gives you a blocked-up nose and a dry throat... I
audibly snort. As a Claphamite I can proudly say I submit my
nasal cavity to extremely taxing alpine training at least three to
four times a week so I don't think some poxy virus is going to
touch me... I'm with Bupa anyway; we all are.

At this point Blojo sends me a WhatsApp:

Old boy,

I've been asked to chair a Cobra meeting and need to take
a working lunch (game of tennis at Queen's) to get out of it
pronto. Her Majesty's government requires your presence as a
matter of urgency...;)

Blojo

I don't need telling twice. I quietly and efficiently gather my
things, slip past Big Daddy Cum Cum's office and I'm on the
court with Blojo within the hour.

I have to stop myself falling about laughing as Blojo and I
play. He's such a natural comedian, stomping around, wooden
racket from the 1960s in hand, wearing a yellowed vest and
some vary questionably stained shorts. We play some points
and he's making me laugh so hard and doing underarm serves

when I'm not looking that I end up losing 7–5. We enjoy a couple of beers in the bar afterwards 'to rehydrate'.

'The warm-down is incredibly important, old boy,' says Blojo with a wink, sliding into an Estrella. 'Without that, everything falls apart. We must not forget the lessons learnt from the ancient Greeks,' he says, eyes wide, gesticulating with huge, magnetic energy.

He has such an incredible aura, Boris, he's like an amazing older brother. He's wise and funny and knowledgeable and women love him. I kind of wish he was my dad. Not in a gay way or anything; it's just I don't think my dad really likes talking to me, but with Boris I could chat for hours… He keeps giving the women at the bar the eyes and they love it.

We chat a little about this Chinese virus, or as I call it 'Kung Flu' (Blojo loves this).

'My policy on all viruses is the same, old boy: have a shot of penicillin and you'll be right as rain. You can't trust all this journalist nonsense anyway, the whole job is just making stuff up.'

We laugh at how he's sacked off a Cobra meeting about it to play tennis, imagining how much froth you'd see at the corners of the Lefties' mouths if they knew.

Saturday 25 January

I wake up with this awful feeling that I've been spending loads of money of late, but, on checking my Barclays account, see that my tenants in the flat I own have paid their rent and I'm a very tasty five thousand pounds in the black. You absolutely love to see it.

Monday 27 January

Weirdos and misfits interview. I'm enjoying a breakfast egg-and-cress baguette from Pret.

I get the candidate – young and vary impressionable – to sort some additional bits for the 'Britain Beyond Brexit Booze Bath and Bonanza' (Boris has given this name the green light), so I can head back to Number 10 and chill.

'Make sure the booze shipment arrives for Friday morning,' I say, coffee in one hand, *une petite baguette* in the other.

'Is this part of the interview?' he asks, confused. 'It's just I was expecting us to talk about data and stuff…?'

'And why on earth would you assume I'd be interviewing you on something you'd prepared for?' I wryly riposte. 'Sort this and send me the details when it's done and if you do well, we might hire you.'

As I wander back into the office, I think about Pret and how it's seemingly redefining cuisine. Normally for breakfast one might have a piece of toast and some orange juice and yet here they're offering baguette (which is French for a sandwich) at breakfast time! The mind boggles. Rather like Aristotle and his assassination of Plato's tripartite conception of the soul in favour of a binary model, Pret is shattering all that came before and paving the way for its own philosophical revolution. The other fascinating question Pret raises of course is, how might one define it? Is it a restaurant? Surely not; you don't need a reservation to dine there. Yet calling it fast food seems too crude for something of its level of sophistication…

I really don't know what I'd do if Pret went under.

I don't think any of us do.

Wednesday 29 January

Today is a big day in Number 10.

We're signing the Brexit withdrawal agreement and we've got a load of Chinese coming for a PR stunt with Blojo to celebrate Chinese New Year, which promises to be absolutely classic.

I spot Poppy on my way out of Westminster tube and we walk into work together.

'I can't believe Boris isn't going to the Cobra meeting today,' she says. 'That's the second he'll have missed about this virus.'

'Come on, Poppy,' I say, 'surely you've seen what the symptoms are? You get a blocked-up nose…big fucking deal. People get blocked-up noses all the time and they're fine. Also, if it really *was* a problem there'd be restrictions on people flying into the UK, but there aren't any, so it can't be.'

'I just think this is the sort of thing a prime minister should be taking an active role in rather than actively avoiding,' she says, lips pursed.

'I just think this is the sort of thing a prime minister should be taking an active role in rather than actively avoiding,' I mimic back. 'Look, Blojo is a top bloke and if he doesn't think it's important, then it probably isn't. Besides, he's committed to doing Chinese New Year and so he'll honour that commitment. Blojo's a good chap like that; he's not the sort to go back on a promise…unless it's marital, or one he doesn't want to keep…'

The outside of Number 10 is teeming with at least thirty little Chinese children (I mean, to be fair, they're all little – the Chinese, I mean – but in fairness children are as well…).

Hugo and I are stood among the journalists facing the door to Number 10, set to watch a master at work. These press rituals really are where Blojo comes into his own.

The atmosphere is like the moments before the first ball is struck in the Wimbledon final: heavy with anticipation. Roughly ninety seconds after he's due to arrive, Blojo comes bounding out, pelvis tilted forwards, hair messy, shirt untucked, tie askew, as if he's just emerged from the store cupboard with a married woman (perhaps he has?!). The Chinese fucking love it. Two of them are in a dragon costume and Blojo gets stuck into painting their eyes.

'Can you see what I've done?' he says to the children, pointing to his artwork.

They all cheer.

'Can you really?' he says, looking into the crowd with a look of playful cynicism on his face. I was hoping for this: a joke about them having squinty eyes, subtle enough that the mathematically adept but subtextually incapable Chinese would miss it, but the English speakers would understand it.

Both Hugo and I crack up. The *Telegraph* journalist at hand chuckles; the *Guardian* one looks like he's sucked a lemon, which is even funnier.

Then, with a flourish, Blojo's gone. Effortless talent and guile, well worth missing a fucking inconsequential Cobra meeting for.

Friday 31 January

It's 16:30 and everything is in place for the Britain Beyond Brexit Booze Bath and Bonanza (which as it transpires is a bit of a fucking nightmare to put up in bunting).

I get an email at 17:30 from Hancock, who tells me he 'might have to stay at the Department of Health a little longer because he's had an email about some European PPE we're being offered to fight off this virus'.

I reply telling him that the only place capable of offering PPE is Oxford University.

Within ten minutes he's at Number 10 heartily slapping me on the back, telling me he thought my joke was 'ruddy brill' and explaining that he's 'stuck European PPE on the later base'. He grabs a champagne flute and joins the throng.

Everything looks phenomenal (weirdo and misfit from Pret came through for me, you love to see it). There's heaps of food, booze; the only things missing are the midgets I'd planned to invite along to throw at a target with Ursula von der Lemon's face on it. Apparently this 'can't happen' because 'it would look bad if it got out', which is obviously ridiculous, as anyone who has ever seen a midget thrown onto a great big target will know (see *The Wolf of Wall Street*): it looks fucking hilarious.

The speeches are short. I say speeches – Big Daddy Cum Cum takes the opportunity to do an interpretive dance piece to the music of 'Bring Me to Life' by Evanescence, which I think is supposed to be some sort of metaphor for Britain's freedom from Belgian bureaucracy. Blojo follows up with a hysterical speech on how we will no longer have to tolerate the French women and their 'hairy *croque monsieurs*', which he finishes by opening a bottle of British champagne with a sword to signal the start of the party.

Within forty-five minutes, everyone is fucked; we peer-pressure Poppy into breaking dry Jan within the first two! Even Big Daddy Cum Cum looks like he's having a good time, a copy of his own printed blog in one hand, a pint of the beer he brews in his own basement in the other and something close to a smile on his face.

The only person who doesn't look happy is Lee Cain, who

is sat alone drinking from a brown paper bag. I go over to ask if he's okay but before I can speak, without looking up, he very clearly says: 'Don't fucking talk to me, you floppy-haired cunt flannel.'

I end up partaking in some late-night skiing with the spads back at mine. Poppy is drinking Sauvignon Blanc while Lettie, Hugo and I are on *le gak*. The batch we make our way through is from a delightful chap called Moped Ed who operates in the Fulham area and is sat on some absolute fucking rocket fuel. He's not literally sat on it, obviously; it hasn't gone up his arse…although apparently that is how it gets transported I understand…

We're all about four lines in at this point and we've started gushing about how great it is to work together.

'Whatever happened to that Henrietta girl?' I ask Hugo, my tongue continuously circuiting round the space between my teeth and the inside of my upper lip by this point.

'Oh yeah, she got fired, mate,' says Hugo, running his hands through his hair repeatedly.

'But, like, are you guys seeing each other?' I press.

'God no, mate. No…shagged her and lost interest,' Hugo says as he tucks into another line.

I suddenly gain a lot more respect for Hugo.

'You know, for a Harrovian, Hugo, you're actually quite classic.'

FEBRUARY

Monday 3 February

All the spads receive another erratic email from Big Daddy Cum Cum this morning following up on his previous:

DEAD CATS ARE ALIVE CATS

THE FUTURE IS THE PRESENT

UNCONVENTIONAL WISDOM IS CONVENTIONAL WISDOM
(WHICH IS FOR CUNTS)

Big Daddy Cum Cum has now added:

JOURNALISTS ARE ENEMIES OF THE GOVERNMENT.

ANY SPAD CAUGHT WITH A JOURNALIST OR RECEIVING
A LUNCH WITH A JOURNALIST WILL BE DISAPPEARED.

As I examine these words, I feel a hand gripping the back of my shirt. It's Big Daddy Cum Cum himself, breathing heavily, a manic look of giddy excitement across his face.

'Traitor! Heretic! Enemy of the state! You've been talking to journalists!'

'I haven't, I swear!'

'Yes you have, you've been going for coffees with them behind my back, haven't you? I can tell!'

'Dom, I promise, I only ever go and get coffee with ministers or other spads.'

'What do you all think?' he says, addressing Number 10, still gripping the back of my shirt. 'Have you seen him with journalists?'

Eventually Poppy breaks the silence: 'He hasn't been seeing any journalists, Dom. I would have reported him if he had.'

'Very well,' he says, begrudgingly relinquishing me from his grasp, 'you are spared, for now. But this is a lesson for all. Anyone breaking the rules will be disappeared. All traitors must be turned in!'

With that he scuttles back to his office muttering, 'Classic Dom, classic Dom' as he goes.

I look over to Poppy to thank her with my eyes but she is absorbed by her laptop, afraid to show any recognition lest she's reported for it.

I receive an email before clocking off for the day from osamabinladen@gov.uk:

Hubris, R,

I know you haven't been seeing journalists. I know everything.

I just wanted to see how you would react.

I'm a fucking genius.

Conventional wisdom is for cunts,

Classic Dom/Osama Bin Laden

Tuesday 4 February

I buy Poppy a flat white from Pret to thank her for yesterday. Poppy really is a vary good girl, even if she can sometimes be a bit of a wetty.

I'm not enormously looking forward to the prospect of being in work and potentially getting pegged by Big Daddy Cum Cum in front of the whole office again. I've also been getting quite a lot of chat about how I 'full on shat myself' from Hugo and some of the other spads on WhatsApp. I'm all for chat, just not when it gets really personal and directed at me, which is just in poor taste.

Just as I'm thinking up some really cutting wordplay around how, despite his ambition to be a chap, Hugo will always be a chav, I get a text from Blojo:

Rafe,

Another fucking Cobra meeting today. I'm going to be 'corporately indisposed' (at a corporate lunch). Come with, it will be a riot.

Incorrigibly,
Blojo

I do not need to be invited twice.
On my way out of the office I tip the cold remains of my Pret

flat white onto Hugo's chair. Prick.

The lunch *is* a riot.

Not only is the food and drink excellent, the company is scintillating.

I feel so lucky to be sat in such a diverse group of white chaps in their fifties…along with their accompanying secretary girls in their twenties, all of whom are absolute worldies and make for vary nice visual furniture around the table. It's like a snapshot into the future as I imagine I'll be accompanied by a girl of this sort at an event quite like this in thirty years' time.

At the table is a barrister who predominantly defends the *Daily Mail*, someone who works doing advertising for us, a couple of chaps from Morgan Stanley and a lord. What an amazing group!

They all spend most of the time chatting about how much money they have, which is absolutely fascinating. Just a lunch in their company makes me realise how much they all deserve it.

I try to make eyes at any/all of the secretaries but none of them look my way. Fucking women. They love Blojo, though. Everyone does. He tells his cherry pie anecdote, which has everyone in stitches; he even demonstrates the broom cupboard part with the most buxom secretary. Classic Blojo.

In the auction a game of tennis with him goes for 60K. This makes me feel particularly smug as I get to play with him for free. Not that 60K is vary much money in the grand scheme of things… I mean if that was my annual income I'd probably have to emigrate out of shame. For an hour's work, though, it's obviously vary good. And it goes to charity, which is the highest good of them all! I say this, of course, not because charity helps the vulnerable and other assorted wetties, but because Eton is one.

Thursday 6 February

The focus around this Kung Flu virus (official name the much less amusing 'Covid-19') is now becoming hysterical, pathetic even. Poppy has even bought a huge vat of hand sanitiser from the internet, for Christ's sake. This exact same hysteria happened with Swine Flu, SARS and Mad Cow Disease and they all came to nothing; this will be exactly the same.

Nonetheless, we all have to shuffle off to the Department of Health and sit through a chap called Chris Whitty, who looks rather like a sort of bald llama, explaining the science of the virus. He tells us how important it is to wash our hands. Really world-shattering stuff…

Whitty suggests it may be the case that women are affected by the virus less badly than men. At this, the Superprophet raises his hand and gets into a long discussion about the documented differences between male and female respiratory lining and how the latter is actually inferior. I can't help thinking that this isn't really the time for some Al Murray Pub Landlord-esque misogyny satire, but it is quite amusing, nonetheless.

Poppy and some of the other female spads seem less amused and glare at him while he continues to challenge Whitty.

Since Monday, Big Daddy Cum Cum has really been going all out on the accusation front.

He's 'disappearing' spads who are surely innocent left, right and centre on trumped-up 'thought crime' charges. His decree is then backed up by Lee Cain who long-arm-sweeps across the person's desk and tells them to 'fuck off' after they've retrieved their scattered possessions from the Number 10 carpet.

Cummings has even started having a go at ministers. The new chancellor, Javid, gets an earful from Cummings for refusing to implement the budget Dom has written for him.

'We can't just reallocate the funds for social care to "ant research", Dom,' says Javid, incredibly bemused. 'What even is ant research anyway?'

Big Daddy Cum Cum does not take this well and calls Javid 'a blue-pill normallo' and tells him, 'It's co-operation or extermination.'

It's all getting a little sour now; I think some people are starting to file formal complaints...

Friday 7 February

We all get pulled into a Big Daddy Cum Cum 'illumination session' just before the weekend break on Friday at 4pm. He enters to 'Jesus Walks' by Kanye West and seems to be wearing some sort of hooded gown, like a boxer might wear on the way into a fight. Lee Cain brings up the rear, brandishing a stapler and looking furious.

'Guys, I've bought you here today because it's come to my attention that we have a little bitch among us,' Dom says, pacing back and forth. 'This little bitch has accused me of being "paranoid", "aggressive" and "abusive".'

At this point Cain absolutely unloads on one of the newer spads.

'Oi! Fucking listen when he's talking, you stupid prick!'

The affected spad shudders.

'Imagine a beehive,' says Dom, still gently pacing, 'where all the bees are working together to make honey for the queen. But one bee, one bee wants to wreck everything for all the other hard-working bees. That one bee decides to tell on the queen bee, who just wants what's best for the hive. She cares about her bees more than anyone and it makes her *fucking angry when one stupid fucking bee tries to ruin it for everyone*.' Lee Cain launches a stapler at Fabian, St Paul's, Trinity (Oxford), as Dom screams at him.

Fabian ducks and the stapler hits the wall. A deathly silence falls over the room. As Fabian slowly brings his head back up, all the colour has completely drained from his face.

'Did you think I wouldn't find out, Fabian?' says Dom, a cold fury in his voice, his back to us now.

'Answer his fucking question,' screams Lee Cain.

'I…I…I'm sorry, Dom, for complaining. I just felt you'd been a bit heavy-handed with some of us lately. But I'm sorry for saying that. I don't mean it. I take it back.'

Dom, very slowly and purposefully walks up to Fabian, looks him square in the eyes and whispers, 'You are hereby banished from the hive. Fuck. Off.'

Within seconds, Lee Cain is gruffly escorting him out of the office.

'What have we learnt today, bees?' Cummings asks us.

'We've learnt that bitches get stitches. The hive is everything. If you hear even whispers of someone who is putting anything before the hive, you've seen what happens.' Then, in a high whiny voice, he says: 'Ooooooh, boohoo, Dom wasn't very nice to me… Toughen up or fuck off.'

And with that we're dismissed.

Saturday 8 February

Valentine's Day is in T minus *six jours*.

I spend most of the morning prepping my campaign for 14 February across Tinder, Raya, Bumble and LinkedIn.

I upgrade to Tinder Gold and update my bio to 'accepting applications for 14 February', to imply I'm extremely sought after, thus on a subconscious level attaching a vary high level of prestige to dating me.

I swipe a fair amount on Bumble and get lots of matches (obviously) but no worldies. I also slide into the LinkedIn message section of all the secretaries from the corporate dinner with Blojo. Nothing back from any of them. Shocking form.

Monday 10 February

The female spads are all crowded round a phone in the canteen at lunch.

I slide into the conversation with a classic Rafe line:

'If you want to watch *2 Girls 1 Cup*, shouldn't you do it outside office hours?' Classic Rafe, classic Rafe.

'This isn't *2 Girls 1 Cup*, you child, it's that Superprophet guy, the one that Cummings really likes,' says Poppy.

'What about him?'

'We've been reading this blog he wrote back in 2014…and like…it's pretty horrendous.'

'Some of the stuff he's written is actually not okay,' says Emily, sadly not fit at all…like at all… I'd be more attracted to a man than her. Not that I'm attracted to men at all. See above for my score on the Kinsey scale (it's zero).

'Yeah, but come on, is it actually not okay? Or is it just what women collectively decide is morally wrong with no men present to steer them in the right direction, like the MeToo movement?' I intelligently riposte.

'Look and see for yourself,' says Poppy, flinging the phone across the table.

Christ. It's not good. There's stuff arguing that black Americans are less intelligent than their white counterparts and a whole bit about the benefits of encouraging the working class not to reproduce.

'Yeah, no, that's not good,' I eventually concede to the girls, sheepishly running my hands through my hair.

I'm in shock. I thought he spent the whole time talking about eugenics as a sort of satirical commentary on the state of the twenty-first century, not because he actually thought it was a good idea! All those times I thought he was being outrageous for comic effect, those were actually his opinions! Obviously, there are parts of society that are superior – no one is debating that – but you can't just exterminate the bits you don't like (except possibly Slough; I just don't know if we need it with Eton and Windsor right by it – it just feels like it maybe lowers the tone of Eton's peripheral surroundings…). It all makes sense why he liked me now: I'd be a poster boy for the master race as I'm tall, square-jawed and frankly vary Aryan. Once again, I'm a victim of my own conventional attractiveness.

I try to keep interaction with the Superprophet to a minimum and pretend to be deeply immersed in work when I return to my desk.

Javid, on his way in from the Treasury for a meeting with Blojo, no doubt, appears to have been intercepted by Big Daddy Cum Cum, who is insisting Javid sit the ninety-minute exam paper he's written for him to prove his IQ is at the 'requisite level for a chancellor'.

Javid retorts that 'he doesn't need to prove himself' to Big Daddy Cum Cum and certainly doesn't need to sit an exam.

Big Daddy Cum Cum then resorts to throwing thought experiments at Javid, which Javid finds offensive and refuses to answer.

As Big Daddy Cum Cum is instructing Javid to solve and show his working to Dom's version of the chicken, fox and sack of grain maths problem (his version is the classic Dom, bees and honey problem), Javid storms out of the office.

Tuesday 11 February

The Javid–Cummings beef has not cooled off overnight.

If anything, it's got hotter.

Javid, attempting to get an audience with Blojo for the second time, is intercepted yet again by Big Daddy Cum Cum, who grabs Javid and tells him he suspects him of being 'a sub-intellect' and an 'enemy of unconventional wisdom'. Then, with the help of Lee Cain, Big Daddy Cum Cum tries to force-feed Javid 'brain pills' he's found on the dark web.

Lee Cain is so terrifying, none of us dare intervene. Instead, we all just watch agog as he tries to pinch Javid's nose so he'll have to eventually open his mouth to breathe and Dom can pop one of the pills in.

Cain succeeds at this and they make Javid swallow the pill.

Big Daddy Cum Cum and Cain depart, leaving Javid with 'some maths problems to be getting on with'.

I sit considering what's just happened.

It's obviously bad to force-feed someone something if it's against their will. But it can sometimes be quite classic to give people drugs without them knowing. Not Rohypnol, obviously!!! But like one of my mates Rupert always puts chang in the gravy at the Christmas lunch he throws with his flatmates every year. Obviously all the flatmates know this is what he's doing but, hilariously, none of the guests do. The best thing about this is that as soon as someone finds out they've had chang slipped into their food, they can't be angry with you, because they're on chang!! It's the perfect bit of naughtiness.

Javid, furious at what's just happened, storms into Blojo's office and, so the whole office can hear, screams: 'It's him or me! This is too far now, Boris. This is beyond a joke. He goes, or I go.'

We hear Blojo prevaricating and replying: 'Come on, old boy, be reasonable. I can't fire Dom. Who's going to do all the hard prime-minister bits like policy and stuff if he goes? Can't we all just get along?'

There's a short pause and very clearly Javid announces: 'I'm resigning.'

He then exits Number 10, holding a middle finger up to Big Daddy Cum Cum's office as he does.

And then he's gone.

As we return after lunch, the hunt for a new chancellor begins. It would obviously be great to get someone from the BAME (Black, Asian, Minority, Ethnic) community to step into the role because it's great for diversity and also because Asians do tend to be excellent at maths…

I do actually know quite a few Asians from university but sadly all the ones I know have gone down the other Asian career path: medicine.

Wednesday 12 February

Big Daddy Cum Cum has come through for us and found a BAME chancellor!

The guy's name is Rishi Sunak, a Winchester and Lincoln

College alumnus; though it's not Eton, given the turnaround time, this is really phenomenal work from Big Daddy Cum Cum.

He's also a serious upgrade on Javid, who was only an Exeter graduate, incredibly, not the college at Oxford (my alma mater). Apparently there's a town actually called Exeter with its own university…a polytechnic I believe.

Blojo uses Rishi's appointment to sack off the afternoon's work and hold a 'welcome drinks' in one of Number 10's side rooms. The room is grand with high ceilings and a considerable amount of female erotica on the walls, which is very tasteful and undoubtedly Blojo's touch.

I grab some champagne and talk briefly with Sunak. He's tiny and comes up to just beneath my chest and is dressed in a very expensive suit with a cashmere jumper underneath that, a bit like the child of an oligarch at a wedding. He's not drinking any of the champagne, port or Stella that's available, but instead seems to be ploughing into full-sugar Coca-Cola.

'I'm not allowed these at home except for on special occasions. I'm on my fourth!' he exclaims, looking absolutely ecstatic.

We speak a little more and he asks me to give him numbers, of which he calculates the square root on the spot. It's vary impressive, but also a little odd.

I manage to sneak a few moments with Blojo who tells me he's sacked off another Cobra meeting to be at these drinks. Classic Blojo.

He seems tired, though; subdued even. I ask if he's okay and he mumbles something about coming to a divorce settlement with his ex-wife, which is turning out to be a bit of a nightmare alongside all the hard work he's doing.

I tell him he should take time off if it's stressing him out too much.

'There's no point doing this job if you can't make it work for you, Blojo,' I say.

Blojo murmurs in agreement and drifts off. I catch Lettie's eye; she smiles and I smile back. Surely I'd have come up on her Tinder by now…

She's stood with Emily, who is just so not fit I'd rather not have to be in the same room as her, and the Superprophet, who I'm now very keen to avoid. I end up breaking off from the drinks early in order to do so…and to plough through the (now twelve) romantic apps on my phone as I'm still yet to secure a worldie for Friday. I remind myself it's just a numbers game and with enough legwork the right result will come in.

Friday 14 February

The right result has not come in.

In fact I have completely fucked myself vis-à-vis Valentine's Day. No worldies have been forthcoming despite what has been an all-out campaign to secure one. The problem I'm now facing as I turn to the less fit girls I had in reserve to plan for this eventuality is that they've now been reserved by other men. As has so often historically been the problem for Blojo, I have pulled out too late.

The prospect of spending Valentine's Day alone is truly appalling. I might be forced to get an escort.

The perfect storm of my love life has seemingly coincided with a perfect storm and mass flooding in the north. Personally I don't think it's worth doing anything about this; rather like with Noah's ark, God has clearly made his desire to drown a specific section of the population abundantly clear, and who are we to stand in the way? Despite this infallible reasoning, Lee Cain gruffly informs me that if I don't find a minister to go and visit the northern flooded areas, he will break me, so I set to.

These visits all tend to follow the same tedious script:

1. Minister goes to shithole location X that no one cares about.

2. Minister attempts to look sympathetic in a hard hat and a fluorescent vest as they desperately try to understand whatever primitive dialect is being aggressively vomited towards them out of the mouth of a disgruntled northerner.

3. Minister then waves at northerners from afar in order to 'boost morale'.

4. During some sort of PR photo attempt, usually involving a spade and some sandbags, some other northerner will call the minister a 'prick', or 'a twat', or 'a spineless dickhead who doesn't care about anything north of Watford Gap', which obviously looks terrible (not least because it's true).

5. The minister has to then work out how to deal with this while remaining professional, and normally does a pretty shoddy job.

6. After this exotic display of failure for the media, the minister returns to London with worse rep than when they left, only to see their toe-curlingly cringeworthy PR failures are all over the ten o' clock news.

It is for this very reason that such visits are extremely unpopular among ministers. I start by emailing Michael Gove in the hope he'll help, but within five minutes receive the following:

Rafe, Hi,

What an incredibly important issue this is. Let me say how grateful I am to you for drawing it to my attention! While I feel a real sense of moral duty to help, unfortunately I feel a greater sense of moral duty to stay here in London so can't do it.

I'll tell you who would be great for this though: Alok Sharma. Give him an email!

Michael

Things have become desperate on the Valentine's Day front. I've increased my age and distance limit to the maximum on Tinder and am trawling through Sharons in their fifties and Wendys in their sixties all in places I've never heard of like Coventry and Stratford-upon-Avon. Christ, this is bleak. Just as I'm about to google escort agencies, I hear:

'Rafe.'

'Yes,' I say, looking up to see Lettie. Shit. It's Lettie.

'I thought perhaps we should have a drink tonight…you know…considering…'

I try to mask my excitement at the fact that I've fucking done it again in the eleventh hour and play it extremely cool.

'Yeah, I was thinking the same thing, it felt like we'd inevitably end up doing that,' I say, tipping back on my chair.

'Great,' she says. 'My place at eight?'

'Great, catch you then,' I say.

I knew she wouldn't be able to resist my looks.

As the day and week is coming to a close, I drop Blojo a WhatsApp asking if he can help out with the northern floods but it transpires he's taking a working holiday at Chevening for the next fortnight 'to sort his fucking divorce'.

I send him my condolences and promise to send over pictures of any absolute babes that come into the office.

I arrive at Lettie's flat in Battersea. It's situated in a big high-rise complex but not in a sort of scummy council estate way, but rather in a sort of high-end 'like all the buildings in the City' way. It's so nice in fact it may be even better than *mi casa* on the Clapham Riviera…I'm dressed in a white shirt, indigo jeans and suede boots (the chap classic). Lettie opens the door and is dressed in a tracksuit.

'Oh my goodness you dressed up and I look like such a chav,' she says.

'Not at all,' I say, wandering in and taking a seat on her sofa. Her place is absolutely massive. I'd been a couple of times before for spad pre-drinks and stuff but had never quite appreciated how truly huge it is. She has one of those dead lion rugs in front of her sofa and an enormous wine rack full of Châteauneuf-du-Pape and other vintages. I get the feeling I'm in for the night of my life.

She pours me a glass and sits next to me on the sofa.

'That's Lennie,' she says, gesturing to the rug on the floor. 'I shot him in Africa… Isn't he beautiful? So, here we are, what a sorry state of affairs this is.'

'I don't think it's that sorry, in fact, I think we're a rather good match,' I say, flirtatiously resting my hand on her leg.

'Well, I'd rather have an actual date on Valentine's Day than have to ask a friend to help me drink through it,' she says.

I pause, looking slightly confused.

'Wait, you didn't think this was a date did you?! Oh my God, no. It just seemed so obvious that you hadn't found anyone so I thought we could spend it together as friends.'

Slowly and deliberately I reply: 'So you're saying you've invited me round on Valentine's Day but not to have sex?'

She nods and starts saying something about how she was hoping we could drink wine 'as friends', but by this point I've already told her 'something's come up' and am out of the door. What a fucking snake. Never before has a snake led someone astray this badly.

I use all my energy and effort to try to desperately salvage Valentine's Day for myself and message old Tinder matches and phone several escort agencies, but no one picks up. I return home, reflect on what a colossal failure of a Valentine's Day this has been and embark on perhaps the most furious wank of my life to date.

Monday 17 February

Blojo seems to have caught wind of the Superprophet's blog and he's not happy. He's had to break off divorce settlement arrangements to video-call Big Daddy Cum Cum from Chevening House, and is insisting that the Superprophet is gone 'by the end of the day'.

To be fair to Blojo, he is right, it *is* completely unreasonable to write masses of morally objectionable stuff online and expect to take public office afterwards…

Word on the grapevine though is that Big Daddy Cum Cum is aggressively backing the Superprophet who 'can see what lies ahead where other spads can only see what lies in front'. He also apparently thinks that the Superprophet is just busting through 'the prevailing moral fashion', that we shouldn't have a master race.

Blojo and Big Daddy Cum Cum eventually pick up the call again in the afternoon and, for perhaps the first time in his life outside the bedroom, Blojo holds firm. The Superprophet is ousted. I find the prospect of the awkwardness of having to say goodbye to him so incredibly uncomfortable that I decide to take refuge in the Number 10 loos so he'll leave and I'll never have to see him again.

Just as I'm browsing LinkedIn I notice a pair of brogues similar to mine stationed in the cubicle next to me. Ten minutes elapse and neither of us leave. I'm sure they're Hugo's brogues.

'Hugo?'

'Rafe?' he replies.

'What are you doing in here?'

'I could ask you the same thing.'

'Mate, Bully Patel has been fucking me so hard, sometimes I have to come here for a bit of time out,' he says.

The old tactical skive. A move straight out of the Rafe Hubris political handbook. I rate this from Hugo.

We talk for the next thirty minutes or so about Tinder, LinkedIn, money, girls and chang and before we know it, it's the end of the day.

We both return to the office to see that the Superprophet has gone and Bully Patel has returned to the Home Office.

People who tell you that you can't run from your problems certainly never worked in politics. You can do precisely that. You can even hide in a fridge if there's one available.

Tuesday 18 February

I wake up to two texts, one from the Superprophet explaining how even though he's been 'cancelled' by 'the fucking Marxists',we can 'still be really good mates'. There's a few links on his text as well – one to Joe Rogan's podcast with Ben Shapiro and another to an article entitled 'Skull circumference and its link to IQ: An apologist's defence'.

I decide to air it.

The other text is from Blojo telling me I need to minute the Cobra meeting on the virus that's happening today.

I tell him I'm 'all over this like scabies'; classic Rafe.

Rather than bothering to do it myself, I decide to take Hugo with me to minute this Cobra meeting; he gets to escape Bully Patel, I get to chill, it's win-win. Matt Hancock is also there, somehow managing to look nervous and cagey (as if he's just shat himself and is worried people will notice) and yet simultaneously stand-offish and arrogant.

We have to listen to Chris Whitty's hand-wringing neuroticism (I've started calling him Chris Wetty among the spads: classic Rafe). When Chris Wetty is done, some bloke called Jonathan tells us about 'possible death numbers' and 'the need for urgency'. Both Hancock and I find it a challenge to mask our scepticism. That's the thing about experts: they've always got an opinion, but who's to say it's right? I'm a bit sick and tired of them to be honest.

'The problem, chaps, with all this,' I say, cutting Chris Wetty off mid-sentence with the elegance of Tim Henman intercepting a volley on Wimbledon's centre court, 'is that it's all very well saying we need to stop travel and impose restrictions, but what about the real victim in all this – the economy? The economy needs to be loved and nurtured and nourished and if that means a few people have to die, that's for the greater good. Surely we'd be better to do nothing, see if this whole Kung Flu thing blows over and that way we get to protect the economy and everybody wins.'

Wetty comes back at me with some waffling answer about data and numbers but I'm not really listening. I'm mentally replaying how fucking intelligent I sounded destroying his argument.

Hancock and I laugh together afterwards about how depressing all the so-called 'experts' are. He's actually an alright bloke, Hancock, even if he is a bit awkward. We book in a networking coffee in Pret for later in the week.

I text Blojo to tell him:

Everything's chill. A lot of doom-mongering expert chat, but nothing to worry about old boy.

Friday 21 February

I walk into Number 10 to hear that Italy has had its first Kung Flu death. This divides the spads into two halves. One half, Poppy and most of the women, are incredibly panicky and have started sanitising their hands every thirty minutes and even (ridiculously) wearing masks. The other half, aka the sensible half, Hugo, me, etc., see this for what it is: Italian melodrama.

'I once shagged an Italian girl,' I amusingly recount to Hugo at the water cooler. 'She was vary passionate but also vary over-emotional when it turned out I'd slipped her sister my number when I'd 'gone to the loo', between pumps. They're all over-emotional over there, so I'd be pretty sceptical as to the truth of a lot of the stories you're hearing…they might even just be making it up for attention.' He nods in agreement as we sip the premium *agua*. Sadly, nothing came of *el slipping del nombre* to Italian girl's sister, which was a shame because she was much fitter. You win some, you lose some in the game of women.

Networking coffee with Hancock in Pret. (Where else? You love to see it.)

He greets me with a really big squeezy hug, which is definitely weird, but I go with it.

He's friendly though, and passionate, and when he's not put under pressure by a considerable audience he's actually a pretty cogent speaker. We talk about all kinds of things, from his enjoyment of my joke about how the only PPE worth having is the one you get from Oxford to his love of grime and the Cheltenham Races.

'I just think Skepta's got such a nasty flow,' he says, 'I love that one he does…"Shut up"…and "Vossi Bop". That's really dutty too. I love listening to it when I do parkour at the weekends,' he says, eyes wide, staring at me with a slightly disconcerting intensity.

I try to steer the conversation in the direction of his ambitions in politics so I can work out how best to position myself to rise up the political ladder in the future (ever the tactician) but he just seems to want to talk about the Cheltenham Races the whole time.

'I am so chuffing well excited for it,' he says, the same intense gaze searing through me. I'm now finding it a little too much and am having to blink and look around as I talk, to deal with it.

We spend a good half-hour looking at different horses and going through every minute detail of the Cheltenham site on

Google Street View.

'Let's just say I felt pretty wavey when I was here,' he says, pointing out a fairly anonymous bit of path. 'I'd had six shandies in just over two hours… I thought I might be sick!'

I smile vacantly, realising this guy is a fucking chopper.

'Do you want to come with me to the races…the ones at Cheltenham, I mean?' he clarifies, as if he hasn't just been talking about them for the last fucking half-hour. 'Please say you will, it will be so fun; we can have such larks.'

I pause.

'Pleeeeeeease,' he presses.

'Sure,' I say, regretting the word as soon as it leaves my mouth.

'Amazeballs,' says Hancock, looking like he might burst with excitement.

How the fuck am I going to get out of this…?

I get round to emailing Alok Sharma about going to visit the northern flooded areas but get the following reply:

Hi Rafe,

What an incredibly important issue this is. Let me say how grateful I am to you for drawing it to my attention! While I feel a real sense of moral duty to help, unfortunately I feel a greater sense of moral duty to stay here in London so can't do it.

I'll tell you who would be great for this though: Grant Shapps. Give him an email!

Alok

The hunt continues.

Monday 24 February

Blojo is back! This is vary good news.

He looks relieved and a little more upbeat than before, although when I ask him how the 'wanking holiday' was, he says 'costly' with a stern look on his face.

He's getting a lot of heat from some of the miserable civil servants who think he's 'absconding from his duties as prime minister' and that he should 'do his job', which I think is a really disrespectful thing to say to someone who's going through a divorce.

Wednesday 26 February

Hancock keeps emailing me about Cheltenham and I really don't want to fucking go. He sends over literally every fucking bit of press about it. Hopefully, if I just don't reply, he'll lose interest. My worry is he is vary much not the type of person to discern implicit social cues.

I catch Rishi at lunch and we end up discussing Hancock, who, it transpires, is trying to recruit him for Cheltenham as well. Hancock is like one of those fucking weird flirty fishing Christians who try and trap you into becoming one of them, yet unlike the flirty fishing Christians (who are mostly attractive women), Hancock has virtually no charm or vivacity. His energy reminds me of the child in everyone's year at junior school that would blow snot bubbles out of their nose and would speak to you, massively invading your personal space, with two dried rivers of the stuff connecting mouth and nostril. We both agree that airing Hancock's emails is for the best.

As we're sat talking, some of the female spads seem to be

giggling and pointing in our direction. They're all talking about how much they fancy me, no doubt. I apologise to Rishi explaining 'they're only human', with a wink.

He picks up the *Ultimate Mathematical Challenge* book he carries around with him and peels off to go to the loo, as he's absolutely ripping through the Diet Cokes (his wife has banned him from drinking the full-sugar stuff). For some strange reason, as soon as he leaves, the girls stop giggling... I don't have time to dwell on this though, as I'm distracted by my rent coming in. A wonderful 2K top-up. You love to see it. I really don't understand how people don't think money is the source of all happiness.

Thursday 27 February

I'm still trying to find a minister to go up north and make it look like we care about the floods.

On emailing Grant Shapps though, at Alok Sharma's recommendation, I receive the following:

Rafe,

What an incredibly important issue this is. Let me say how grateful I am to you for drawing it to my attention! While I feel a real sense of moral duty to help, unfortunately, I feel a greater sense of moral duty to stay here in London, so can't do it.

I'll tell you who would be great for this though: Oliver Dowden. Give him an email!

Grant

Fucking hell.

Saturday 29 February

Me and a few of the other sufficiently high-end spads are charging over to Chequers today to celebrate Blojo's announcement that he's got another woman pregnant! The man is an absolute machine.

Apparently she's twenty-three years younger than him. Cracking form from Blojo; you love to see it!

Rishi has also announced an economic scheme to deal with this virus (which I still think will probably blow over but you have to err on the side of caution when you're less than three weeks into the role). The scheme is called 'the furlough scheme' and sees the government pay 80 per cent of the wages of employees that can't work for companies because of Kung Flu shit. Sounds a bit socialist to me but everyone seems to love him so who am I to disagree?

I try to congratulate him on the scheme as we're all quaffing wine and chowing down on canapés but he's surrounded by a huge group of female spads who I can't penetrate (in the social sense – I wouldn't want to in the sexual sense – they are all butters). They're all twirling their hair and laughing too loudly at his jokes.

When Rishi leaves I slide into their group and learn they're all sexually obsessed with him. They all call him Dishy Susnacc. Suddenly the giggling and pointing at lunch makes sense; incredibly, they weren't marvelling at *my* looks, they were swooning at Rishi…

'He just looks like he'd make you such a delicious curry and is like so clever and good at maths. We could have such amazing children and they could become dentists or something,' says one spad.

'I bet he'd be into dressing up in bed, like I bet he'd make me wear a turban...so ethnic,' swoons another.

'I don't think he's a Sikh,' I say, slightly confused.

'Whatever he is, I want him,' says Emily, a look of fervent lust in her eyes.

I'm not quite sure what to make of this.

I listen to Blojo give a brief speech on welcoming a new life into the world, where it's pretty clear he's just hilariously recycled an old speech but changed the names.

As we're all mingling afterwards I get a chance to talk to his girlfriend, Carrie. She's fit and also seems like a vary good girl. I can really see myself settling down with a girl like her when I'm in my mid-fifties.

'A year ago I was laterally feeling so *tragique* about my love life, and now, here I am surrounded by gorg people, sipping Dommy P, about to have a little one with the most powerful man in the UK. Thank God for manifestation. I asked the universe for what I wanted and it answered,' she says genially. 'You should try it: laterally ask the universe for like anything and it gives you it. It's so perf!'

She then dashes off to go and make arrangements for the cake, telling me, 'It was laterally so nice to meet you, hun; you've got such good vibes.'

I stand pondering what she's just said. On the one hand the idea that the universe grants you things if you just ask for them sounds like the sort of complete bollocks that people with loads of money and opportunity tell themselves to make them feel like they've earned all the opportunities they've actually just been given by virtue of their place in the social strata. Yet on the other hand if it is true it could be an absolute game changer.

I decide to try it; at the very least, nothing will come of it.

I ask the universe for a shag. I'm currently in a spell of Saharan levels of dryness that needs breaking, and frankly I don't really give a fuck how.

As Carrie peels off I get chatting to Emily who keeps going on about how aroused Sunak has made her. She is really not fit though, so I find her talking about sex both unpleasant and irritating and make up an excuse to duck out of the conversation.

'I'm sure we'll run into each other later,' she says.

I think I'd rather kneecap myself than run into her later.

I feel incredibly drunk. In classic Rafe fashion I've gone out hard – vary hard – drinking the red wine the waiting staff continually pour into my glass with reckless abandon.

I drift outside to see Hugo enjoying a cig with Lettie.

'How are we, chaps?' I ask, shattering any potential awkwardness between Lettie and me re Valentine's Day by doubling down on my incredibly charismatic and charming nature.

'Vary, vary wall,' they reply.

I notice the classic white veneer around Hugo's nostril and it imbues me with an insatiable desire for a line.

'You two look like you've been snorting and cavorting,' I say, at which they both sheepishly grin.

'Can I get in on the next line?' I ask Hugo.

'Would love to, mate,' says Hugo, 'but Lettie and I went twos up on this one and there's only two lines left.'

I'm so desperate I end up bank-transferring Hugo an eye-watering £300 for what turns out to be one line of coke.

Giving him the money feels like handing over a piece of my soul, but needs must.

I must have had at least two bottles of wine by now. Though it's perked me up somewhat, the chang has mostly just made my heart beat like the bassline in a Prodigy song.

I'm fucked.

I'm now in what I call 'The Red Zone': I'm drinking booze like it's water. I'm doing shots with Emily. Emily tells me she has some coke. We end up doing the coke in the downstairs loo together.

About three minutes later we're going at it. As we repeatedly crash into each other, I catch my reflection in the bathroom mirror and experience two thoughts simultaneously:

1. I guess manifestation isn't such a load of shit after all.
2. No one must ever know about this. Ever.

MARCH

Sunday 1 March

Will's wife has given birth to a baby chap, Jonty Titus Hubris, and I've crawled to a small get-together of thirty or so people Will is having in Teddington to welcome him into the world. My head is still absolutely pulsing with the booze and drugs I fed it last night as well as, perhaps even more disturbingly, images of me railing Emily in the downstairs loo at Chequers.

As I lay eyes on Jonty for the first time, the unsettling possibility of me and Emily having a child flickers through my brain. I'm almost certain we were safe but you can obviously never absolutely know for sure. I banish this thought by remembering that even if the worst did happen, I could always just get legal in to sort the whole thing out (both my godfathers are QCs) and carry on as if nothing had happened, or NDA and *continuer*.

Even though he's only a baby I can tell that Jonty is going to be absolutely classic; he's already starting to develop the Hubris jawline, perfect for picking up many a worldie and discussing PPE. I wonder which Oxford college the old chap will end up at. I congratulate Juliette and go to pick up some orange juice.

'Here he is,' says Will, enmeshed in a large group of his

school mates from five years above me at Eton (even though we're all much older now, they're still a bit intimidating).

'Juliette gives birth on Wednesday and Rafe doesn't even acknowledge it until Sunday. Great start as an uncle, mate, really strong.' All his school mates chuckle at this.

'Mate, I've been unbelievably busy with work at Number 10,' I say.

'Busy doing what?' he replies. 'Come on,' he says clicking his fingers repeatedly as he does, 'it can't be helping to stop the spread of Covid-19 because no one seems to be doing that in the government, so what was it, Rafe, that was so important you couldn't give five seconds to acknowledge Jonty?'

He stands smiling as I look back aggressively at him for ten seconds before giving up because I know I've got nothing. It's just like all my childhood arguments with him all over again where he'd know more words than I did and would always make me look stupid. I decide to just leave.

For some weird reason I can't work out why I feel really fucking angry on the way home, but then some dormant chang dislodges itself from my nasal passage and I start to feel quite classic again.

Thank God for chang.

Monday 2 March

I'm still trying to sort a minister for the fucking northern floods.

On emailing Oliver Dowden at Grant Shapps' recommendation this morning I get the same fucking reply as I've had back from everyone:

Hi Rafe,

What an incredibly important issue this is. Let me say how grateful I am to you for drawing it to my attention! While I feel a real sense of moral duty to help, unfortunately I feel a greater sense of moral duty to stay here in London, so can't do it.

I'll tell you who would be great for this though: Matt Hancock. Give him an email!

Oliver

This is obviously a dead end as, with Cheltenham Races looming, I'm trying to avoid Hancock at all costs.

The old chap has finally been pressured into giving a speech on this fucking virus by the hand-wringers and doom-mongers. Though I think the hysteria and the call to give a speech are ridiculous, I'm fucking pumped that Blojo has asked me to write it. The rise and rise of Rafe Hubris continues!

It is here, in the domain of penmanship and oratory, that Rafe 'Big Dog' Hubris really comes into his own. I used to write a weekly column summarising the debauched antics that took place at Oxford Uni Golf Club's weekly socials.[1] I ponder over what sort of tone to strike, whether to go hard on the jokes, how much boring information to impart and how many references to ancient Greece there ought to be.

I've been told to spin it according to the following paragraph Blojo has slung me via email:

1 The weekly column was called 'A Hole in One' and was described as 'a veritable tour de force' by Henry Harrington (Balliol) and 'as enthralling as it is enjoyable' by Alex Pembersley (Christchurch). As chance would have it, both these chaps now work for Merrill Lynch. How mad is that!! Two guys in the same golf team at Oxford now both working at the same bank, what a crazy coincidence!

> Emphasise everything will be fine, but also there will be loads
> of cases, but really there's nothing to worry about, getting it
> won't be a big deal, so just keep doing everything as usual, but
> also wash your hands, but it'll all totally be fine.

This all sounds pretty clear and coherent to me. I set to, weaving all the central points together into a speech for Blojo in no time. As a little Easter Egg, I write that people should wash their hands for the amount of time it takes Blojo to inseminate a woman or to sing 'Happy Birthday' twice (the insemination gag will obviously never get used but Blojo will definitely find it vary classic and for that reason alone it is worth including).

Tuesday 3 March

Hugo and I are enjoying a couple of mid-morning double espressos (each) in Pret and he's telling me about some civil servant who's had a 25K payout after allegedly taking an overdose because Bully Patel allegedly bullied them.

'That's fucking mental,' I say.

'I mean what a load of cack,' says Hugo, downing his first coffee. 'We've all been a bit palpy after one too many white runs across some of Clapham's premium alps, but it doesn't mean it's a fucking overdose. Think about it: she's basically been paid 25K to go and have a fat night out. She's literally been paid to take drugs.'

'Yeah, like Liam Gallagher or something,' I murmur in agreement. 'I guess it's not just her though is it, with the Bully Patel stuff? Poppy told me apparently the head Home Office civil service honcho is resigning and there's going to be a meaty enquiry.'

'Seriously?' Hugo says, shocked.

'Yeah mate, it's serious shit. To be honest I've seen her come down quite hard on you a few times, old boy. Are you not thinking of saying something?'

'Yeah mate, I have been getting fucked quite hard by Patel of late, you're not wrong. The problem is when she shouts at me and stuff, it's not nice, but at the same time there's something about it that's kind of...

'Hot?' I say.

'So I'm not the only one who thinks it?' Hugo says, leaning in towards me, a mixture of discomfort, excitement and abashment on his face, like a Nineties Hugh Grant.

'No. For some reason there is something vary sexy about an attractive woman being incredibly horrible to you,' I say.

He nods in agreement.

We head back to the office.

I catch Blojo's speech that evening. He does vary, vary wall. (Although he did have an excellent speech writer...) Sadly, no inclusion of the insemination joke, but as ever he's on cracking form.

He even ad-libs about how he went to a hospital recently and was 'shaking hands with everybody', including some patients who had Kung Flu. Good on him, that's exactly the sort of fearless attitude we need from a prime minister unafraid to go against the reckless media narrative about how 'dangerous' this whole thing is. I imagine if he hadn't said words to that effect, that's the sort of thing that would age really badly when this whole thing has blown over.

Thursday 5 March

I'm about to give up on securing a minister to go up north. In a last-ditch attempt I message Blojo for the second time to ask if he'll do it. To my surprise he replies saying he will.

Anything to avoid having to do more work on this fucking virus.

Thank Christ for that.

I'm sat at lunch with Poppy who is pretty much continuously sanitising her hands at this point.

She drops into conversation that Lettie has been furloughed.

'Lettie's been furloughed?' I say in disbelief.

'Yeah, they put her on furlough from Monday,' says Poppy matter-of-factly. 'They can't get rid of her because her dad donates like more money to the party than anyone in the world[2] and they're really good friends with Rees-Mogg, but like she doesn't do anything all day. She just smokes and occasionally says really racist stuff that we all pretend not to have heard.'

'Shit…do you think this means she won't be coming to the rugby on Saturday?

'I don't know…but I'm definitely not going. Big sporting events like that are literally going to be hot houses for Covid-19, Rafe. I've been watching some of the videos coming out of Italy and it's scary. I don't think you should go, it's a stupid idea.'

Before I have time to explain to Poppy how she's being an enormous wet lettuce about this whole thing and that my membership of Bupa means I don't have to worry about anything to do with my health ever, I spot Hancock walking into the canteen and am forced to duck out lest he sees and

2 I can't imagine he donates as much as Rupert ;)

harasses me further about fucking Cheltenham.

She a vary good girl, Poppy, but she can be a bit of a fucking wetty sometimes.

Saturday 7 March

Twickenham is absolutely fucking packed.

It's a veritable sea of tweed, Barbours and glinting signet rings, and the smell of Guinness and cigarette smoke sits heavy on the air. You absolutely love to see and smell it. Quite a few chaps seem to be coughing quite heavily…it's an odd cough, too, a sort of dry, substanceless cough… There must be some cold getting passed around the upper middle classes – nothing a colourful handkerchief from Pringle won't catch!

I fucking love the rugby. I think it's such a good advert for the UK. It's just like the football, except everyone has good manners, better teeth and knows who Chaucer is.

We're playing Wales so I've already workshopped a couple of sheep-shagging joke zingers before arriving, to impress women.

I link up with Hugo, who's with a couple of his friends from Oxford (University – which is where I also studied), and we sink into a couple of pints *de la* Guinness 'so as not to pull a muscle'.

Anna, one of Hugo's friends, is fit and I learn that she studied Theology. With the ease and slickness of James Bond I reply: 'And are you a fully fledged member of the God squad? Or are you an irredeemable sinner?' I wink at her as I say 'sinner'. Timing is everything in the game of women.

She looks a little confused at this so I pull back my rep with one of the sheep jokes I'd workshopped earlier: 'What do you call a Welshman who likes lamb? A paedophile.'

With this, incredibly, I've lost her.

Her face contorts to what I would call a *Guardian* level of sourness and she coldly replies:

'I am Welshwe don't shag sheep. Also why would you joke about paedophiles like that? That's not a funny thing to joke about.'

I accept that I have completely fucked any chance I may have had with her and we tacitly agree not to speak to each other for the rest of the day.

I've been drinking quite heavily to assuage some of the chronic awkwardness around Anna who, by some bitter twist of fate, I've had to sit next to. By the time half-time comes I'm pretty boozed. I manage to talk my way into VIP by slipping the bouncer fifty quid and telling him I work for the government.

I make my way to the bar to order my fifth San Miguel of the afternoon. It's teeming with large, gravelly voiced men with faces like enormous whoopee cushions. As I'm queuing I hear someone call my name.

'Rafe, Rafe, over here!'

I turn round and see it's Michael Gove. Before I know it, he's worked his way through the queue, explaining to everyone I was just holding his place, and slides in just in front of me.

He tells me how all the ministers like to talk to each other about how great they think I am and orders five drinks before I get a chance to order my beer, which is absolutely unbelievable... I can't believe all the ministers love talking to each other about me!!!

He takes his tray of drinks over to his friends asking if I might hold his place until he gets back 'in just a wee minute'.

I order and start work on my San Miguel but Govey is nowhere to be seen. I look around and he seems to have disappeared.

'Look, if your friend isn't coming back, you're going to have to pay for his drinks,' the disgruntled barwoman barks at me.

'Just give him five more minutes, I'm sure he's on his way,' I reply.

Five minutes elapse and still no Govey. He's done a runner. Michael Gove has snaked me! Under duress I settle the bar tab for £65.80 and go to return to my seat to catch what's left of the match, but it's fucking finished!

I can't believe he's done a fucking runner. What a prick!

As I'm leaving the ground I'm sure I see Govey walking out.

'Mate!' I shout. 'You owe me £65.80.'

He locks eyes with me and says:

'Sorry, I won't be making any public comment at this time,' and disappears into the crowd.

I've been played. I've been played like a jazz piano at a wine mixer.

Sunday 8 March

I'm still incredibly fucked off about the £65.80 that has been stolen from me. I catch Blojo bumbling around on the news though and that cheers me up. He's in Bewsley or Bewsford or Didsbury or somewhere where they haven't discovered Pret… or fire.

Despite arriving nearly a month after the floods started, Blojo has managed to come up smelling of roses. I just don't know how the old chap does it, it's remarkable. Obviously there are a few lemon Leftie journalists calling him a 'traitor', and saying 'he's too late'[3] to visit the flooded area, but these attacks are no

---

3 Perhaps they should try getting a minister to go up north and being knocked back and forth like a tennis ball over email for three fucking weeks.

match for his avuncular, bumbling persona. I really can't stress enough how grateful we are at the Conservative party to the chaps over at *Have I Got News for You* for helping Blojo develop this persona back in the Nineties. The best thing about the persona is that it accounts for failure just as well as it does for success. In making it look like you're pretending not to know what you're doing, people will never know when you actually don't. It's bulletproof.

Monday 9 March

I enjoy a pretty chilled day at work today. Not that much on since I finished the northern floods stuff so I've been reading the *FT* in detail. I also decide to mix up my Pret order today and go rogue with one of their falafel and halloumi wraps. Normally I wouldn't go for something like this because I'm not a virtue-signalling wetty who thinks eating meat involves violence, but to be fair to Pret they've done vary wall here. They are just so consistently excellent in all domains. I wonder if there's a way to give an OBE to an organisation…

There are now 298 confirmed Kung Flu cases in the UK, which is roughly the size of a small Oxford college like St Peter's. In other words, rather like St Peter's, the cases are pretty meaningless. Thankfully, Big Daddy Cum Cum is seeing sense and ignoring the hysterical calls from scientists to have a 'lockdown'. He's instead putting the finishing touches on the ant village he got funding for from Blojo back in January. It's vary impressive, there's a whole system of trams and a Lego cathedral and everything.

Before I go to bed Hancock sends me a barrage of texts.

> Hey my dude Cheltenham tomoz! So excited, can't wait to see you. You're still coming right? It looks like you haven't taken the next three days off? Bit worried :/ xxxxx

I just don't reply. I've learnt with clingy girls that if you just don't reply to something for long enough it eventually goes away. I'm in too deep now anyway, he's sent me too many messages, I can't just reply now as if I've only just seen them. This would only ever happen to Rafe Hubris; my problem is I'm fundamentally just a bit too likeable for my own good…

Tuesday 10 March

I wake up to Hancock calling me.

I let it go to voicemail.

Fucking hell.

He phones me several times throughout the day and sends me pictures of him stood at various points on the Cheltenham course with variations on:

> Where are you? I'm stood right here, come and find me, we can have some larks!

In several pictures he appears to be accompanied by the backbencher John Penrose's wife, Dido Harding; the poor girl appears to be yet another victim of Hancock's cloying insistence.

> I've been telling Dido all about you and she'd love to meet you.

Don't let Dido down, Rafe.

Dido is sad now, Rafe :(She wants to meet her new buddy Rafe.

This continues at thirty-minute intervals for the rest of the day.

Wednesday 11 March

I wake up to more missed calls from Hancock (I've never known someone this clingy in all my life) and an email from osamabinladen@gov.uk sent at 03:30 in the morning.

Bee,

Illumination session tomorrow at 9 sharp. All bees must attend.

Find attached a 'Diabolical' (the hardest level there is) Sudoku puzzle to prepare your mind for the meeting.

Conventional wisdom is for cunts,

Classic Dom,
Osama.

Today Big Daddy Cum Cum has a stethoscope around his neck and is wearing a set of green scrubs under a white lab coat. I think this is him satirising the medical industry and getting us to question why we would trust people with medical degrees.

As ever, Lee Cain stands threateningly in the background by a roughly six-foot-wide object covered by a drape.

'Bees, I have concocted a genius plan,' Big Daddy Cum Cum says, speaking with a feverish energy. 'In an attempt to throw their conventional wisdom onto us like a blanket made of shit, the experts have told us to lock down all of the UK. To fuck the experts in their brains along with their conventional wisdom…'

'…which is for cunts,' Lee Cain chips in.

'…I have created "Herd Immunity",' says Dom pulling the drape away to reveal a completely different Lego configuration from the one I'd seen just a few days ago.

The cathedral, the transport system and all of the ants have gone; instead there's just a large block of green Lego and on that a huge number of Lego cows, all packed in very close proximity.

'Classic Dom, classic Dom,' he whispers to himself. 'This is the population of the UK. They are not geniuses like me. They are the herd, they are cattle, unthinking and mostly unfeeling. We need the herd to do all the stupid-people jobs. Without them society wouldn't function…at least until we can replace them all with robots,' he murmurs gleefully as an aside. 'But, the members of the herd are only valuable to us insofar as they are strong. Some of the herd are weak. For the good of the herd as a whole, they must be the ones who perish.'

As Big Daddy Cum Cum says this, Lee Cain long-arm-sweeps a third of the Lego cattle onto the floor and proceeds to stamp on them with his thick Dr Martens.

'Surely you're not saying we should just keep everything open and let the virus work through the population Dom?' says a spad with an apparent death wish. 'You'd just be sentencing thousands of people to needless death, that's a crazy ide—'

Before he's able to even finish his sentence Lee Cain is screaming into this poor spad's face:

'IT'S A FUCKING GOOD IDEA, YOU LITTLE PRICK. IF YOU DON'T LIKE IT YOU CAN FUCKING FUCK OFF.'

As we're dismissed I can't help but agree with Lee Cain. I think it *is* a good idea, an excellent idea in fact, it basically gives us a basis to not have to change anything or do any work… and if that means a few old people who would have died soon anyway have to die a little bit earlier then that's a shame but sadly unavoidable.

After my linguistically swashbuckling performance with Blojo's previous speech, I've been asked to write the one he's doing tomorrow, which I imagine will probably be the last Kung Flu conference we have to do.

I have *Shrek* on in the background while I'm writing the speech. I fucking love *Shrek*. I've been told to include loads of serious shite about how this is now a 'global pandemic', which sounds scary but is really just semantic nonsense. I make sure I explain how there's no good reason to stop sporting events or close schools, which would be a fucking ball ache to organise.

I also chuck in something about us having a plan that we're really working through which we absolutely don't. A few more lovely vague statements that repurpose something that seems credibly truthful and I'm done in forty-five minutes. I really am a master in spin, I'm the king of spin. In fact, I'm RAFEal Nadal.

Game set and match.

I clock off at a gentleman's five o'clock…4.30…you love to see it.

By the looks of it Hancock has finally got the message and has stopped texting me. Today is a good day.

Thursday 12 March

I wake up in the early hours of the morning. This quite often happens when I have a brilliant idea like a review system for Tinder or a series of hyper-elite private-private schools.

I'd been chewing on the idea that everyone's hammering us on our 'failures' to 'test for Covid', and by the looks of it this is only going to get worse. It was only as my brilliant brain whirred while I slept that the answer came to me: just stop testing altogether.

The more we test, the more Covid we're going to see and the worse we're going to look. If, however, we stop testing altogether then the cases will drop down to zero so we won't have to worry.

It's fucking genius.

I fire off an email to osamabinladen@gov.uk at 3.47am suggesting we enact this policy.

I get a reply back from him within five minutes.

Hubris, R,

This is an idea I thought of just before you sent me your email.

Like all my ideas, it's genius.
It has already been put in place.

Well done for challenging the narrative.

Read The Sacred and the Profane by Mercia Eliade before I next see you.

Conventional wisdom is for cunts,

Classic Dom,
Osama

That evening I sit watching my penmanship come to life through the mouth of Blojo.[4] He duly delivers my line: 'Many more families are going to lose loved ones before their time.'

It seems oddly familiar, but I can't quite place where it's from.

Right before I'm about to go to sleep it hits me. The line is just like that bit in *Shrek* where Lord Farquaad talking to his subjects says: 'Some of you may die, but it's a sacrifice I'm willing to make.'

I must have been watching that bit when I wrote it. Ha! That is absolutely fucking classic.

This is just like when I tried to get *Wolf of Wall Street* quotes into my finals at Oxford.

Rafe Hubris, part-time spad, full-time comedian, is alive and wall. Vary wall in fact.

Friday 13 March

I wake up to see a few articles have been written about Blojo's comment and the parallel with *Shrek*. This is absolutely huge.

I tell Hugo about what's happened and he agrees it is 'extremely classic'.

Big Daddy Cum Cum pulls us all in for another meeting. Today

4 As opposed to watching his pen come alive in the mouths of others as it so often does – classic!

he's wearing a blue wig arranged into two ponytails, knee-high boots, fishnet tights and a T-shirt that says 'Silence is Violence'.

I'm not initially sure what he's satirising with this outfit but as I hear him say, 'Herd immunity is cancelled,' it becomes clear it's a satire of the authoritarian Left on Twitter.

The Big Daddy tells us that herd immunity was just a ploy and was never part of the real plan anyway and that the more astute spads would have already worked this out.

I'm not sure this was Big Daddy Cum Cum's plan all along; there's a report going round the office that suggests the herd immunity strategy would lead to 500K deaths. The report is also from a guy called Neil Ferguson at Imperial College which, though not Oxford, is actually pretty respectable so should be trusted.

500K really is a lot of people, that's not good. Obviously everyone dies ultimately so 500K people dead isn't really any skin off my nose, but if that all happened quickly the media shitstorm would be fucking intolerable. So while there's no good moral reason to do anything about it, for the purposes of politics we probably ought to implement some sort of lockdown.

I'm not saying we should be wetties about it. Obviously you'd want to keep the King's Road, Pret, GAIL's, Embargo's and Infernos (if you're after a less sophisticated woman) open, but the rest of the comparatively low-end stuff has surely got to shut...

I sit eating lunch with Hugo. We'd normally be joined by Poppy but she's so uptight about Covid she's refusing to sit with anyone at lunch to 'decrease likelihood of contamination'.

Hugo tells me that he's spent most of yesterday briefing Peston that the government strategy *was* herd immunity. 'I can't go back on it today I'll look a fucking chief,' he says.

I sit puzzling over this for a few moments. I ask myself how Big Daddy Cum Cum, in all his genius, might approach this conundrum. Within seconds my brain comes up with something vary good.

'Mate, you know what gaslighting is, right?'[5]

'Mate, I invented gaslighting,' he replies.

'Well, what if it wasn't just applied to women but in the field of politics as wall? So Peston will make out you said herd immunity was the government policy and you can just say "that conversation never happened".'

'So I don't have to do anything about it?' Hugo says.

'Exactly,' I say. 'Never be afraid to apply your skill *avec* women to work, I always find there's a surprising amount of crossover.'

Saturday 14 March

It's the biannual pub trip with some of the chaps from school to the White Horse in Parsons Green, aka the Sloaney Pony.

Some people in the office (three guesses who) have actually cancelled their weekend plans because of Covid. Christ alive. I'm all for remaining cautious, which is why I'll be washing my hands every time I use the bathroom for urination or inhalation (;-)), but we cannot succumb to neuroticism and wettiness here. If we stay inside, the virus wins. We must fight it

5 For the uninitiated, gaslighting is a crafty psychological technique utilised by many a wily fox in the romantic domain that makes its subjects question their memory judgement or perception.

E.g.

Girl: You shagged my sister, I saw you!

Chap: No I didn't and you don't even have a sister.

Girl: Yes I do, why are you saying this?

Chap: Saying what? We haven't been talking.

in the South West London pubs and in the Mayfair members-only clubs, we must fight it in the Uber Execs, in other girls' beds and we sure as hell must fight it in the Pret a Mangers the morning after the night before.[6]

The event has been referred to historically as 'The search for white whores in the White Horse,' and is absolutely classic. These nights tend to play out as follows:

3pm: Chaps arrive
3:15pm–5:30pm: Pints
5:30pm–6:00pm: Cigs
6:00pm–6:45pm: Pints and more chat
6:45pm–7:30pm: Pints with food
7:30pm: Gak
7:33pm: Gak
7:46pm: Gak and a G&T
8:20pm: Cig
8:30pm: Gak and a shot
8:35pm–late: Women

The pub is packed to the rafters.

Henrys, Archies and Tabbys desperately jostle for space at the bar all vying to secure their drinks first with the sort of ruthless competitiveness boarding school alumni know all too wall.

I locate the chaps, Rupert, Henry and Dom, and we get aggressively stuck in.

By 8.20 I'm absolutely fucked, chewing the ear off some girl in the Sloaney Pony smoking area.

'I'm pretty high up in the government,' I say, 'I guess you could say I'm the alpha dog in Number 10. Check me out on

6 Here, Rafe Hubris is amusingly adapting the famous speech by Winston Churchill which included the line 'we shall fight on the beaches,' but is applying it to the modern day.[§]

§ Here, Hubris is amusingly referring to himself in the third person for comic effect.

LinkedIn.'

I pass her my phone with my LinkedIn profile on it and take a drag from my cigarette only to realise it's from the wrong fucking end. The pain is horrific. I have to retreat inside to get water and run cold water into my mouth for ten minutes and when I return, she's gone.

We're all doing chang at mine. It just didn't feel like I'd had quite enough at the pub. I just feel like I need one more line and I'll be right as rain.

As it transpires one line wasn't enough and I've done another four and now I can't feel the inside of my mouth, which is handy because I imagine it's like the inside of a fucking barbecue thanks to the cigarette incident.

The chaps all start drifting off.

I feel extremely awake still.

I pace furiously around my flat and do another couple of lines just to tide me over.

I find myself texting Emily. I don't really feel as though this is a very good idea but my fingers seem to have already sent the ominous two words all single pringles know vary wall.

U up? x

No one knew the first time it happened, I'm sure no one will know the second.

We say nothing to each other after the sex, I just walk her to the door and close it after her. I lie in bed physically incapable of closing my eyes for a good four hours. I eventually manage to drift off as the fingers of morning light creep through the cracks in my curtains.

Sunday 15 March

The inside of my mouth feels like an enormous blister and my brain feels as though it's shrunk to the size of a raisin, I'm so dehydrated.

I'm also getting this really odd feeling like there's no point in doing anything any more. Not in an interesting Albert Camus in *L'Étranger* kind of way, more in a sort of 'you'll fail at everything you try so just stay in bed forever' kind of way.

I squirt some water up my left nostril to cleanse myself but this seems to dislodge some dormant chang and makes me feel even more awake but also simultaneously dead.

You hate to feel it.

I may have to give up drugs.

I mean obviously I won't…but it's just what you say…

Monday 16 March

We're keeping on with the tactic of gaslighting the UK by now encouraging them to limit social contact as if that was the message all along and we haven't, in the words of Dua Lipa, 'done a full 180'.

I'm sure the press will accuse us of U-turning here but rather like one might ask, 'If a tree falls in a forest but there's no one there to hear it does it make a sound?' you might also ask, 'If the government does a 180 on policy but doesn't acknowledge it, is it really a U-turn?' These are all fascinating academic debates and wonderfully distract from us being scrutinised ;-).

Once more I'm asked to write Blojo's speech for this evening. Obviously that puts some time pressure on the whole thing but I'm not worried about the deadline: I once did all the reading and wrote an entire essay for my Plato's *Republic* tutorial at Ox in three hours. I think I've got this covered.

I skim the briefing notes and see we're toeing the perfect line as a government here. We're telling people they shouldn't mix but also not closing any of the pubs so as not to infringe on the public's crucial libertarian freedoms. This means people will still be going out and propping up the economy (essential) and if they do die we're not to blame because we did warn them. Also it will probably be the less clever state school people who don't follow the advice and go out and get it, so in a sense this guidance also provides a neat solution for the social care crisis too, as there's a lot of staties in social care and you don't have to pay for someone's social care if they're dead...

Wednesday 18 March

Things are all starting to get a little panicky in the office.

There's a video going round on the spad WhatsApp of Hancock coming back to work at the Department of Health for the first time since Cheltenham and getting absolutely bollocked by Lee Cain.

'Why the fuck haven't you sorted PPE, Hancock? That's YOUR fucking job. You're the minister for fucking health and you've been off fannying around at fucking Cheltenham,' Cain screams.

Hancock then replies with the fluidity of a man trying to get to the end of a sentence while also trying not to cum:

'I thought we weren't worrying about PPE. We were all joking about it being a degree from Oxford and I th-th-th—'

'Do your job, you nonce-faced toddler,' Cain kicks the

water cooler on his way through. He really does not like water coolers.

He also raises an interesting point with that insult. Hancock *does* somehow manage to look like a paedophile and a paedophile's victim at the same time.

Blojo is being visited by a practically endless procession of civil servants urging him to lock the UK down.

It's like a twenty-first-century *Christmas Carol*.

The interactions I manage to catch all seem to follow an almost identical script:

Civil servant: Prime Minister, we must act. We can radically reduce death numbers if we take action and lock down now.

Boris: You're absolutely right. I really must jolly well get round to that…although what if things start getting better? Then a lockdown will have been a waste of time…

Civil servant: Prime Minister, I wouldn't say it unless I wholeheartedly believed this was essential to preserving the prosperity of the United Kingdom moving forward. Boris, what are you doing?

Boris: Sorry old chap, I'm reading about how the great Marcus Aurelius dealt with the Antonine Plague in ancient Rome, perhaps the answer is there…

Civil servant: Prime Minister, we cannot delay any further, you must lock down.

Boris: Yes, yes, old boy you're right, I really must do it. Thank you.

Ten minutes will pass, he won't take steps to actively put a lockdown in place and he'll be visited by another civil servant and the conversation repeats.

Thursday 19 March

Hancock really is absolutely woeful.

He's told doctors they shouldn't wear PPE unless they're in 'really dangerous situations'.

'What on earth *is* a dangerous situation, Health Secretary, if not in a ward surrounded by Covid patients?' says one furious-looking senior civil servant. 'Should you only wear it if you're crossing a motorway on foot? Or if you're thrown into a lion sanctuary?! Is *then* the time to wear it, Health Secretary?!'

His counter-examples aren't as funny as they could have been[7] but you can't argue with his point. Hancock is just covering over for abject failure by pretending the necessary thing he hasn't ordered isn't necessary, which is only going to lead to more death and make him look even worse than he already does when it comes out that it is necessary after all!

He's also absolutely shit at taking criticism. According to the spad WhatsApp, every time someone suggests he maybe ought

7 I would have gone for: 'Should you only wear it if you look a bit foreign around Bully Patel? Or if you're a conventionally good-looking man like Rafe Hubris and picking up soap on the prison shower floor?!'[†]

† Obviously if it were me delivering this line I'd just point to my face after saying 'conventionally good-looking man' rather than saying 'like Rafe Hubris'. These are all things that people without my comic delivery and experience might not totally appreciate.

to try and source some PPE, he'll say: 'Look, I'm not bloody superman, okay? I can't just *Wingardium Leviosa* PPE out of the sky.'

If he gets really pushed with, say, two bits of negative feedback in the same hour he'll aggressively clench his fists, shake slightly and say: 'I'm getting really angry with the way you're talking to me right now.'

The problem is, we can't fire him.

You could not pay anyone else to do this job… I certainly wouldn't… Not even for 150 mill.

I get another text from Hancock this evening. By the looks of it, it's a group text.

Hey guys,

Firstly, Cheltenham was absolutely bonkers, I had such an amazing time. I don't remember much of it though. Let's just say it was a pretty heavy one…by this I mean alcoholically… I drank lots of alcohol so can't remember what happened lol.

Anyway, could really do with any of your help with this whole virus thing.

Does anyone know or know anyone who knows how to manufacture PPE?

Really need this done ASAP or I'm gonna be in serious troubs. Can pay big dollar.

Love you guys so much,
Mazzle xoxoxoxox

Christ. I really do fucking hope he's friends with the bosses at enormous medical equipment companies and not just a load of management consultants from Oxford.

Friday 20 March

They're closing the fucking pubs.

What the fuck? Why the fuck didn't we act sooner to stop this from happening?

This is Hancock's fault. This is all Hancock's half-arsed, pissing-around-at-Cheltenham, reactive, nonce-faced fucking fault.

I have a brief moment of existential crisis as I genuinely can't think how I'm going to entice women back to my flat without a neutral sexually non-threatening setting that serves alcohol. Am I expected to just invite them into my flat straight away now, like some sort of fucking American?!? Or even worse, am I going to have to have sex with women in parks during our 'allocated exercise period' like some sort of working-class teenager catapulted into the plot of *1984*!? My shags per week are going to plummet and it's because Hancock didn't act. Then what? What on earth will my life be then?

I end up having to host a drinks at my flat with Hugo and a few other fun spads.

We have a great time.

This, however, is not the point. The fact that I've had to go to the effort of offering up my home as a social environment when in a different possible world I could have just done this in a pub is completely unacceptable and it's all because of Hancock.

I get quite boozed and end up texting Hancock.

I don't even scroll to the top of our messages, there's too many (I've had to stop WhatsApp automatically downloading the pictures people send me as I literally had about seventy of Hancock in various different locations from Cheltenham).

I tell him that he'd better fucking sort some fucking PPE or we're fucking fucked and it'll be his head on a spike.

I see him typing as soon as I've sent the message.

For some reason he doesn't react like he does to the civil servants who nail him. He seems to think he and I are involved in one great big joke:

LOL great chat, great bants, my dude.

It's all under wraps, don't worry, that group text I sent round has a few pretty tasty hombres of mine in the management consultant and pub-owning game sorting the PPE.

I've paid them extra money too which will mean they'll do it extra fast and well.

He then follows up with some horrifically wet chat about how 'he misses me' and 'we should hang out some time'.

I air this text.

This had better fucking come off.

I refuse to live in a world without Bluebird.

Saturday 21 March

Mummy phones me up. I wonder if my father has died…

It transpires he has not died and that she's phoning about

Mother's Day.

We agree that having me as well as Will and his mob on Mother's Day will make the place too crowded, so we agree for me to stay in Clapham. I tell her I've got super-important stuff at the government to be organising so I'd have had to cancel anyway.

'More event planning to do?' she says dryly.

I chuckle. She tells me to 'take care' and puts the phone down.

Sunday 22 March

We get an email mid-afternoon telling us that the UK *will* be going into lockdown as of tomorrow.

Minutes later I learn that Pret is going to be shutting its doors for the time being as well. My phone drops from my hand and I stand dumbfounded. For a moment I genuinely have no idea what I'm going to do with myself. What is life without Pret? I briefly contemplate ending it all right there and then, putting my head in an oven or taking a le Creuset knife to my wrists, but decide against it; it would be a disservice to the UK for me to deprive it of a future prime minister by killing myself.

I push Pret from my mind for the time being and instead turn my attention to the dating apps with the work ethic of a Chinese factory worker in the hope of securing one last hurrah pre-lockdown. I've changed my name to 'Last tango in Clapham', which is a reference to the erotic film *Last Tango in Paris* from the 1970s. It's a pretty left-field reference but if any group of women are going to understand references to *le ciné basé en Paris*, it's the women of Clapham.

Within moments I secure a girl ('Alexis, 24') who is a solid

8.5 and is apparently a French film enthusiast. You love to see it. Sunday is an elite time to play the game of women.

We get chatting and she suggests meeting next weekend for a 'rendezvous'. I tell her it has to be *ce soir* as the inside scoop is we're all getting locked down from tomorrow.

She agrees and we book in tonight at eight (*on aime le voir*[8]).

I realise that all this anxiety I'd experienced about remodelling myself on an American, inviting women into my flat rather than the pub before sex was misplaced. I don't have to be American about sex now, I can be Parisian about the whole thing!

I decide to light myself a cigarette and pour myself a glass of red wine and look out over my balcony in Clapham, contemplating how meaningless everything is.

As I'm doing so I get a buzz through on my phone from 'Lizzie' on Tinder.

Boff! I think to myself as I open the app to see what could have been but now won't be.

My jaw nearly drops all three flights of stairs to the floor on seeing this girl.

She is quite possibly the most beautiful girl I've seen on and off the internet.

I have to have sex with her.

We get chatting and somehow I manage to book in an encounter tonight at eight…which obviously leaves me in something of a conundrum…

I put out the cigarette and pour the red wine down the sink and pace around my flat contemplating how best to deal with this predicament.

It seems I have three options:

8   Here Rafe has used his world-class education to translate 'you love to see it' into French and is once more referring to himself in the third person for comic effect.

1 Do nothing and wait for them both to arrive at eight and pluckily propose a threesome.

2 Cancel one of the dates.

3 Stagger one date forward by half an hour, shag the first girl then briskly bid her goodbye to make way for the second girl, who I'll have sex with for pudding.

I definitely am not going to settle for option 2. You have to dream big to achieve big and option 2 is low-ball stuff. Option 1, by contrast, is a little too plucky for the situation. While this is definitely something I would do if we weren't on the brink of an indefinite lockdown, given that this could be my last shag for some time the only viable option seems like option 3.

I message the worldie and manage to pull the date forward by half an hour to 7.30.

It gets to 7.30 and Lizzie is yet to arrive.

Fuck. I hadn't considered all the social code shit of being 'fashionably late' so as 'not to appear too keen'.

Shit.

It gets to 7.40 and I hear a knock on the door.

It's Alexis. She's fucking early. Fuck.

This has literally fucked everything.

I take two moments to formulate how to play this in my head and decide on the following plan.

I shag Alexis vary quickly, I quickly usher her out to make way for Lizzie who is fitter than her anyway, so actually it makes more sense to do her second. Badabang, badaboom.

At 7.52 my plan is not going to plan.

This Alexis keeps wanting to talk about French film and do all the fucking flirty will-we-won't-we stuff before sex.

I hear an ominous knock on the door.

It's Lizzie, of course it fucking is.

And she looks world-shatteringly beautiful. Fuck. I would break all my teeth to be with her.

As she enters I try to usher her into the bedroom but before I can fucking Alexis pipes up with:

'Who is that, Rafe?'

I freeze. Lizzie looks at me confused, replying:

'Who is *that*, Rafe?'

Within moments they are looking each other up and down and working out what's going on here.

I look sheepishly at the ground and garble: 'I'm up for it if you both are.'

Within ninety seconds I'm womanless.

I'm forced to 'negotiate my own Brexit deal' to see off the day.

I feel like Roger Federer must have felt after squandering the 2019 Wimbledon final despite having two match points at 8–7 in the fifth set.

This is literally a case of one bird in the hand, two in the bush.

Monday 23 March

First day of lockdown today.

Poppy is working from home like a massive wetty.

Given all the essential work I do for the UK, I'm still going into the office.

I take the BMW in like the alpha dog I am, doing my absolute best to ignore the now derelict roadside Prets, which sit empty like abandoned homes in an apocalypse.

I slide into the private room I've been allocated in the Department of Health to stop the spread of the virus. The wonderful advantage of this set-up is that it's incredibly hard for one's productivity to be surveilled. I take advantage of this and absolutely rip through all of *Tiger King* on Netflix in seven hours, by which point it's time to go home.

The show is vary good, though sadly no fit girls, which is surely a must for any piece of entertainment.

I drop Blojo a line to tell him about my foiled escapades last night but get nothing back. This is odd, he normally loves hearing stories like this…

Tuesday 24 March

As Pret is closed I'm having to brew my own coffee in an enormous flask and carry it around with me like some sort of paedophile.

My attempt isn't even a patch on the magicians that make Pret coffee.

We need to beat this virus – and fast.

I still haven't heard anything from Blojo, which is concerning. I send him a couple of photos of Susanna Reid looking phenomenal and *still* nothing. Something must be wrong.

I decide to text Hugo about it.

'Didn't you hear, mate? He's got Covid. He, Hancock and Big Daddy Cum Cum have got it. It's serious shit mate,' he texts me.

I'm so shocked I let out an audible gasp.

I can't believe Blojo's got the virus. I wonder briefly whether shaking hands with all those Covid patients might have had something to do with it. Probably not: it's respiratory so I can't imagine it could travel from hand to hand...

I really hope he's alright though. I'm not sure how the country will run without him and he's also a real top bloke.

Wednesday 25 March

I'm having to stay at home because of the risk of contamination. I'm being forced to stay somewhere against my will like a northerner or a member of the working class. This simply isn't the sort of thing that someone like me should have to put up with.

By 9.30am I'm so phenomenally bored I actually decide to do some work. I've been tasked with trying to sort PPE for the NHS's front line thanks to Hancock's massive fucking failure to plan ahead of time. The problem is, all the other countries have pretty much bled the PPE manufacturing companies dry, even the fucking British ones. If I'm going to nail this – and I will – I'll need to be creative. Luckily, I went to Oxford and have more than enough mental agility to save the day.

I decide to go really off the wall and into my junk mail folder. There's a lot of stuff on penis enlargement which – and I cannot stress this enough – I absolutely do not need. There's a few Nigerian princes with 'unique business opportunities' for me, which I scroll past. I then stumble on something interesting: an email which seems to be from a Turkish T-shirt and tracksuit salesman promising me 'he do me good deal on big man T-shirt'.

I've always had a vary good rapport with the Turkish. In fact, when I was at Oxford University I'd always stop off by the Turkish kebab van on the way back from a night out at Bridge or, if I was feeling particularly rogue, Cellar. We used to chat about what sauce I wanted with my chips or whether I wanted salad and they would frequently call me 'boss man'.

I decide to book in a phone call with this Turkish chap and within twenty minutes I've ordered 400K PPE gowns on behalf of the UK government. I'm fairly sure he understood what PPE was – his English wasn't amazing. I'm sure it'll all be fine though Turkey is good. You always hear of people going there to get hair transplants or have their teeth done, and having a really good experiences, so I think this will work vary wall.

Rafe Hubris does it again.

Given that I'm unable to celebrate my excellent work in the pub, I briefly participate in some sort of group Facetime thing called 'Zoom' with some of the other spads, which is absolutely awful.

Before I go to sleep I lie in bed and reflect that I might be starting to go insane. I'm shaking slightly, which must be withdrawal from Pret. I also have absolutely no way of telling what time it is or how much has elapsed, other than the clock in my room, but I start to think that might be lying to me. I make a mental note never to become embroiled in high-profile tax evasion, which leads to imprisonment. I'm simply not cut out for this.

Thursday 26 March

I order some Waitrose smoked salmon to my flat on Deliveroo and eat it in a baguette; it's no Pret baguette but it does restore some of my sanity and stop the shakes.

In the evening everyone seems to be taking part in this 'clap for carers' initiative where people stand out on their doorsteps and applaud the NHS. I think this is great. Not because I think the NHS deserves praise. Far from it. I like it because in applauding them it means we don't have to pay them any more money. It's really excellent economics.

I've got nothing against the NHS. Obviously I've never used it…but I'm sure a lot of the work they do is great. I'm just not convinced that people should get healthcare for free. The last thing we want is people taking coronary bypasses for granted.

I decide to go out and bellow for Bupa at the slightly later time of 20:15. Classic Rafe.

Before bed, I see images of Blojo pretending to clap for carers outside Number 10. He looks rough as shit, like he's had a dodgy festival pill.

I really hope he feels better by the morning.

I wonder if Carrie might be able to manifest Blojo out of this situation. I text her and ask.

Friday 27 March

Carrie's manifestation hasn't worked and Blojo is apparently even worse this morning. We announce to the press that he has Covid.

At about 3.30pm my phone rings from a withheld number.

When I pick up all I can hear is a rattling, wheezing breath, which sounds just like Big Daddy Cum Cum's.

'Dom?'

'Ah, Rafe,' says Cummings, 'you have worked out the clues I've left for you to find me.'

'The clues of you phoning me?' I reply, confused.

'I have been infected with the virus by journalists, Rafe,' he says as if I hadn't spoken. 'The solution to this pandemic lies, as it does with so many things, in Viking culture. I must go and find the ancient Norse scriptures with all the answers we need. Legend has it the scriptures are buried off the M1. I am going now, but in the meantime my spiritual voice will project to Lee Cain. He will be the acting Queen Bee. Look to my coming when I return. You won't know when I'll be back but when I am you'll know. Translate the Nicene Creed into Celtic before I next see you,' he says, and with that he puts down the phone.

Shortly after my phone call with Big Daddy Cum Cum, images of him running from Downing Street pop up on Twitter. The Big Daddy looks panicked, paranoid and a long way from the assured presence I just spoke with. A lot of the spads are absolutely thrilled he's gone and hope he never comes back. Both Poppy and Felix say he's an unelected bully undermining the very foundations of democracy. Others argue his is exactly the sort of radical genius mind we need to overcome bureaucratic inaction. Others still think he's not a genius at all, but rather just an eccentric intellectual narcissist with no ability of enforcing or doing anything that doesn't pique his interest and a penchant for enacting dangerous policies like herd immunity. Whether he's a force for good or not, Number 10 is certainly going to be very different without Big Daddy Cum Cum in it.

In the evening I fall into a deep depression at my imprisonment and Pret's ill health and I drink and smoke while contemplating how unfair it is that this health pandemic has happened to me. I decide to open my bank account, which always cheers me up, but I log on and nearly drop my glass of wine. There's only fucking 5K in there. Where the fuck is the money from my tenants that should have been paid on the 19th!?!? This is a disgrace.

I send a very strongly worded text to my tenants, informing them that if they don't pay their rent by the end of the weekend, the bailiffs will be coming to take away everything that matters to them, including their children.

I get a whingy reply about how they've been 'furloughed' and 'can't afford the whole rent'.

I tell them I don't give a fuck how it gets paid but if it doesn't they're getting evicted.

Before I go to bed I get a text from Hancock:

I know we haven't spoken that much or whatever, but I just wanted to let you know that if I do die, you're my best friend,

Matt

This makes me cringe horrifically. Even in a moment of existential terror, Hancock manages to be a massive fucking wetty.

What a terrible evening.

Sunday 29 March

I'm enjoying some particularly nice smoked salmon and eggs and get pinged to inform me that someone has paid me some money. As ever when I receive one of these notifications, the dopamine is palpable. On closer examination, though, I'm appalled to see the money is only a portion of what I'm owed from my tenants.

This robbery is accompanied by a long pathetic text about how they're 'financially pressed' by Covid and that they 'have friends' 'whose landlord' 'agreed' 'to' 'them' 'paying' 'partial' 'rent'.

I nearly spit smoked salmon all over my French press as I finish reading this audacious bilge. They're treating me as if I'm some kind of charity!

I sit pondering this injustice and think about how we might take action to protect the rights of landlords being exploited by their tenants.

I've never really cared about social justice before but this is important and calls for urgent action. If not me, who? If not now, when?

That evening I realise that I was wrong about my tenant situation. In reality, if someone can't pay the full rent, you shouldn't confiscate their children and throw them out on the street...especially when you can set them up with a debt they won't ever be able to clear which brings in even more money in the long run ;) I message my tenants and very kindly tell them not to worry about settling the whole rent and that I can just set up repayments at a very (un)reasonable rate. Classic Rafe strikes again.

Monday 30 March

Wonderfully, I'm allowed to return to the office this morning and hereby end my lockdown. It's obviously fine for the people that do it, but personally for someone as important as me it's kind of like abuse so simply can't happen.

UK government is in complete disarray.

I go to Number 10 but there's no one in.

I then go to the Department of Health and see Lee Cain,

who seems to have reached a new level of anger and emotional volatility in the absence of Big Daddy Cum Cum. As I enter the office I see papers strewn all over the floor and the water cooler lying on its side in a pool of its own fluid, a bit like a dead body. He's sat in the corner of the office frantically and indiscriminately rifling through folders, occasionally pausing to scream the word 'fuck' generally into the ether. He seems to have very little idea of what he's supposed to be doing, which makes him angry. He then tries to educate himself by going through the random assortment of folders he's found, which make him realise he still has very little idea of what he should be doing, which makes him even more angry and the cycle repeats.

He catches sight of me and tells me he'll rip out my eyes and bollocks and mash them into a paste and make me eat it if I don't find him some PPE. I don't need to be told twice and charge back to Number 10 but as soon as I return to my desk I get a group email from Govey telling everyone to focus on testing, so I shift my attention to that. Then Dominic Raab texts all the spads to say we should probably look into people coming in from foreign countries, so I shift my focus to that.

After forty-five minutes, I'm forced to log off and watch *Wolf of Wall Street* for my mental health.

APRIL

Wednesday 1 April

I'm sat on a Zoom meeting with Poppy (still working from home like a wetty), Govey and Dido Harding. Govey and Poppy arrive on time, but Dido Harding keeps emailing me to say she 'can't work out how to make a profile on this website'. I use the ten minutes it takes for her to log on to change my display name to 'Rafe "Big Dog" Hubris' and the background to a picture of the Sack of Rome: classic Rafe. What I'm doing here is vary entertainingly exaggerating for comic effect to add a bit of levity to the situation and the now 2,000 dead. This is the sort of classic joke that someone like Blojo would have loved if he were here, but Govey doesn't even acknowledge it.

Dido Harding eventually joins us, though for a good five minutes has the camera pointed at her forehead and doesn't work out how to unmute.

Finally we get going and Govey explains the importance of sorting a Test and Trace system and app to nip this virus in the bud.

'Now Rafe,' he says, cheeks bulbous, fishy lips twitching as he speaks, 'I've thought long and hard about this and I really think you're the man to take steps to get this process started.

Why don't you compile some profiles on different companies that might be able to sort this for us and present them to Dido and me tomorrow morning?'

I see what he's doing here: he's trying to get me to do all the work. Spotting this and with the grace of an Eton-educated swan, I explain that the undertaking really needs to be done properly rather than quickly and it would be better to have a small team of spads on the case rather than just one and have a week-long deadline rather than a day.

Quite some time before I come to the end of this speech I hear Govey say: 'That's great. Thanks Rafe. See you tomorrow.'

Accompanied by a 'Thanks Rafe' from Dido Harding soon after.

It's only when the Zoom call has ended and all three of them have logged off that I realise Govey had fucking muted me so I couldn't talk myself out of the work. He's snaked me again! This is Twickenham 2.0! I email him several times but keep getting an out-of-office bounce-back! The fucking snake!

I begrudgingly google how to get in contact with Google to develop an app but every time you google 'Google Email' the entries you get are for setting up a Google mail account. The task is impossible. My saviour from it is perhaps the most unlikely of saviours in the entire gamut of fictional and non-fictional history: Matt Hancock.

At 16:15 he texts me to say:

Hey buddy. Guess who's coming back? Back again. Matty's back! Tell a friend! Get it? It's Eminem LOL. I'm back in action, Rafe, and I've sorted it out so we get to work together on speeches and everything from tomoz. Can't wait for it. This is such good news.

For once, the prospect of spending more time with Matt Hancock actually is good news.

I gleefully email Govey to tell him I've been pulled in by Hancock to write speeches so will have to delegate the task to Poppy.

Take that, you slithery prick.

Thursday 2 April

Matt insists that he and I spend an entire day in a room together in the Department of Health which, though slightly weird, does protect me from Lee Cain, who has now taken to throwing lever-arch folders at civil servants, aided and abetted by Bully Patel. Matt has had Mrs Hancock make us both packed lunches, which he presents to me with his somehow simultaneously vacant and intense gaze. He opens his packed lunch and looks furious:

'I told her I wanted cheese not ham. She's always getting it wrong, that stupid idiot,' he mutters to himself.

Rather than ponder whether this seems like a good way to talk about one's wife, I plough on with the meeting agenda. We decide not to worry about telling the people of the UK to wear masks. Fundamentally, only wetties like Poppy wear one and I just don't see how something that covers your mouth and nose is going to protect you from a respiratory virus, so we sack them off in favour of really nailing testing, which, if you think about it, makes absolute sense.

'How many tests can we commit to doing a day?' I say, mouth half-full of Mrs Hancock's ham sandwich. 'The thing is we need the number to look significant to the media but not be unattainable for us by any stretch.'

Hancock stares aggressively at the table in thought, his head reddening and shaking slightly as he does, like a baby doing a poo.

'Let me put this another way,' I say, now enjoying a Walker's Baked ready salted crisp. 'If your mate told you he had a new job, what salary would he have to say he was getting paid for you to think it was significant but eminently achievable? Like you'd say, "Well done", but you'd still look down on him a bit.'

Hancock, not having to strain this time, fires back immediately: '100K.'

'Perfect,' I say.

Hancock goes to give me a high five. If anyone else was around I'd ignore it, but seeing as it's just us, I high-five him, which he absolutely loves.

'It would also be completely awful to artificially hit our testing target by double-counting tests and just counting the number of tests we've mailed out rather than carried out,' I continue, a look of mischievous glee across my conventionally good-looking face.

I decide to work up an incredibly complicated speech around our testing pledge to make it vary hard for the mostly non-Oxbridge media to scrutinise us if we potentially don't deliver on our promises.

Hancock is so thrilled at this he exclaims: 'We should go on a double date with some of the girls in the office to celebrate.' This is so weird I decide to pretend not to have heard it and crack on with writing Hancock a speech.

Though I'd normally include the jokes in a speech for someone like Blojo, I decide in Hancock's case it's best not to try and sprint before he can crawl.

We run through the speech a couple of times and Hancock's delivery is diabolical. Going from working with Blojo to working with Hancock, from an oratory perspective, is like going from driving a Range Rover to driving a Nissan Micra without any tyres on. This is what happens when you get ministers who don't have oratory as part of the syllabus at school; it's a fucking nightmare.

A lot of the afternoon is spent coaching Hancock to reassure the public with his voice, rather than making them feel as if they're about to be molested then murdered. We try everything to make him seem more at ease: a cool tie, no tie, one button undone, two buttons undone; we try different accents; Matt starting the conference with the word 'Howdy', but nothing seems to work. I eventually have to end up lying and tell him he's 'absolutely smashed it', as he fails at everything I suggest. We're just going to have to hope it'll be alright on the night.

He goes in and delivers the speech, which goes as well as it could. Are there moments where he looks like a beta-male serial killer? Yes, of course there are. Is he at any point in the speech a good speaker? Of course not,. He's not even at the level of a 'poor' speaker. But does he get through it? Yes he does and I think that's all we can expect from the old chap.

Moments afterwards he tells me he thought it went really well and that he could really see himself raking it in on the old public-speaking circuit after he's done with politics.

I suppose that's not completely wrong; the speech did go 'well' – just 'well' in the same sense that Prince Andrew's interview with Emily Maitlis went 'well'.

I smile politely and say something that makes it seem like I don't think that's the most ludicrous thing I've ever heard.

We need Blojo back – and fast.

Saturday 4 April

It's been an extremely stressful week, so, for my mental health, I decide to visit a garden centre in Battersea which, it transpires, serves alcohol in an indoor setting. Does this make it a pub? That's not for me to say. What is for me to say is that if I'm not able to drink in an indoor setting surrounded by women with names that sound like exotic sexual diseases I will surely develop chronic depression which, given my status as a public servant, is not an option. I've also been through a really tough time with all the Pret stuff recently so deserve an opportunity to let my conventionally good-looking hair down.

I tell the chap on the door the code (that I'm 'looking for some weed killer') and charge inside. The place is packed and wonderfully full of loads of great guys and girls from great schools, all seemingly plagued by similar mental health conditions to my own. I spot Hugo, who happens to be there as well, and we get stuck into *el pintos* straight away.

'Delicious, this weed killer isn't it, mate?' I say, my third San Miguel sliding down the ol' gullet like nectar.

'Mate, it goes down very well,' he agrees.

Just as we're discussing Poppy's insistence on wearing a mask all the time at work and how neurotic the old girl is, my phone buzzes in my pocket.

I check my emails and see that Blojo is being taken to A&E for persistent Covid symptoms.

Fucking hell. I hope the old boy's okay. This is really awful. What if he's not alright?

Although I suppose this is probably some clever PR stunt to show how robust the NHS is, so all will be fine… I realise there's no reason to worry.

I mention the whole thing to Hugo, who seems similarly

unconcerned.

'Yeah, Blojo will be fine, mate. I'm sure. The number of venereal diseases legend has it he's bounced back from over the years – the old chap will throw it off like a ladyboy in a Thai brothel.'

We laugh.

I decide to send Blojo some of the pictures of Matt Hancock playing football to cheer him up. I'm sure he'll be fine.

I see, hilariously, that Labour has elected a new leader. After the most crushing election defeat since the Thatcher years, owing in part to a complete alienation of the northern working classes, the Labour party has decided that the antidote is a lawyer from Islington. This is the wonderful thing about the Left: the chaps beat themselves for us. We could be the most lazy, self-satisfied, nepotistic, arrogant, incompetent government ever to exist and we'd still be better than Labour. Obviously, we're not any of those things as a government (I was making an ironic joke). All I'm saying is, we could be and it would be fine.

Monday 6 April

An emergency cabinet meeting is held in Number 10 to sort out the Boris predicament. As a big name, I've naturally been drafted in.

The atmosphere is tense. Everyone knows the top spot is up for grabs and to put even a toe wrong could be fatal.

Govey speaks first: 'My esteemed friends and colleagues, I'm sure like me you are completely overcome with grief at our dear friend Boris's condition; in fact, let us all have a moment of silence to wish him a full recovery.' Govey then pauses for a few milliseconds short of empathy and continues. 'Now is the time to focus on the present and we must think about what, or perhaps I should say *who,* Boris might have wanted at the helm. Now I'd just like to stress that I have absolutely no ambition to be prime minister at all. I'm just saying this because my conscience is telling me that's the right thing to do. Does anyone, unlike me, want to stand in as prime minister?'

No one says anything for about ten seconds, then something incredible happens. Matt Hancock breaks the silence and says: 'I'd like to put myself forward.'

There's a very brief pause before we all fall about laughing. It has to be the funniest thing I've ever heard, It actually makes my eyes water – obviously not with tears: I'm not a wetty.

'Any serious suggestions?' asks Govey.

Eventually, Raab and then Rishi put themselves forward.

Just as everyone is about to vote, Govey sits up abruptly as if pretending to steel himself and says: 'Hang on a second, everyone, my conscience is telling me something.' He then taps his temple, tries to look grave and says, 'I'm afraid my conscience has told me I need to put myself forward to be leader of the party. I absolutely don't want to do it, but it would be remiss of me to ignore the weight of moral duty. Begrudgingly, I will run to occupy the most powerful office in the United Kingdom and Northern Ireland and become the fifty-sixth prime minister.'

All the ministers write down who they're voting for and place them in a hat and I'm called on to count the votes. It's a tie between Raab and Gove but I notice when counting there are two identical scraps of paper, both with the name Michael Gove on them.

'It looks like someone's voted twice,' I say, confused. 'If we discount that vote the winner and interim prime minister is

Dominic Raab.'

I see Govey react to the news; for a fraction of a second he looks as though he might be about to pick up a biro from the table and stab Raab in the eye, but then he smiles and stands up and congratulates Raab saying: 'I'm so pleased you're in charge, Dom. I really didn't want the job anyway so it's all worked out brilliantly.'

I haven't had masses of interaction with Raab, though I have seen a video online where he says he doesn't believe in the Human Rights Act and doesn't support economic or social rights, so it's fair to say he seems like a pretty good bloke to be given most of the prime minister's powers.

Still no word from Big Daddy Cum Cum. No one has any idea where the fuck he is. The stuff he mentioned to me about the M1 could potentially be true, but then he might also have been saying it to test me as part of one of his many cognitive assessments. There are a few rumours from civil servants that he's gone to work for the Chinese government. He hasn't been seen on WhatsApp since Friday 27 March, when he ran out of Downing Street. Perhaps the virus has killed him...

Tuesday 7 April

Shit. Boris has gone into intensive care.

We all find out in the morning from Raab. Boris could actually die. If he goes, he'll leave behind ~~a family~~ several families and God knows how many children without a dad. Carrie will be without a boyfriend, their unborn son will never meet its father, the nation will be without a prime minister. I'll also really miss him. I really like Boris, not in a gay way or anything. I'm not gay; see above for my score on the Kinsey scale. I just really hope he doesn't die.

I sit in the canteen with Hugo. I don't want to sound like a wetty but I can't stop thinking about this Boris stuff.

'Mate, do you want to eat any slower?' says Hugo, chowing down on lasagne.

'Mate, I just can't stop thinking about Boris.'

'Why are you dwelling on that like some sort of woman?' he says, wiping garlic bread round his plate now. 'Mate, just don't think about it. It'll be fine. Stop being gay.'

'Mate, obviously I'm not upset. It's just there was this girl with massive tits on the street I saw earlier and Blojo would have loved her; that's all I was thinking about.'

We get talking about the Test and Trace system Hugo has taken the reins on.

'Yeah mate, I had a Zoom with some of the people at Google. They were choppers[9], mate,' he says.

'What did they say?'

'Well I went in with classic meeting energy: put them on the back foot, show them that you're boss. So I explained the situation and reminded them of how much tax we save them every year and basically said, "What can you do for us?"'

'Right.'

'And they came back with all this bullshit about how these things take a long time and require a lot of time and money spent on them and infrastructure and all that bollocks, so I sacked it off, mate. There's no way I can't learn to code and sort the app quicker than some techie freak at Google who didn't even go to Oxford. How hard can it be?'

9 As anyone who attended private school will know, a chopper means a complete idiot.

'I guess it's just reversing the premise of the Tinder algorithm isn't it? Nail that and you're away.'

'Exactly mate, exactly.'

Wednesday 8 April

I'm feeling particularly good today as I've started to get much better at brewing Pret-like coffee. Obviously I'm never going to be able to brew one as well as the baristas that work there in non-Covid times. Fundamentally my upper-middle-class brain has evolved to be more suited to excel at higher tasks like leading and networking, rather than the menial ones like making a flat white or operating the till at a Majestic Wine. That's not to say the people that do these things aren't important – they're essential – it's just this work is obviously not right for someone like me as I'm too talented for it so would doubtless become rapidly disillusioned if, by some quirk of fate, society were flipped on its head and I were forced to do it.

I have a meeting about PPE with Hancock, this time at his house.

There's a great big portrait of the Queen in his office and instead of an office chair Matt sits in one of those Hollywood director's chairs with the words 'Big Matt' written on the back. He offers me a Mikado biscuit; I decline.

Matt then goes to sit on his chair backwards but soon realises there won't be enough space for his legs so turns the chair back around.

'The word on the street is, the NHS is chomping up PPE at the rate the sort of families on Jeremy Kyle chomp through fast food,' he says, delighting in his garbled punchline as he delivers it, which ruins it. 'But seriously, we do need to sort some or Lee Cain is going to crush my nads.'

'Did you not get any from that massive group text you sent out?' I ask.

'Oh yeah, the owner of my local got back to me about it… oh and also my sister, so they're pitching in and having a go, but we need more, Rafe, we need way more. We need to be drowning in PPE. I want us to have more PPE than we have IPA when we go to Cheltenham next year,' he says, smiling at me like a freak.

He has a great big list of names he's printed out of people who are 'friends of the Conservative Party'. We work through it over the course of the afternoon. It's like telethon.[10]

The conversations tend to go as follows:

Hello Sir/Madam, how are you? It's Rafe from Number 10.

They speak.

Vary wall, thank you. Listen, I'm just getting in touch because we need someone to help manufacture PPE – no not the degree at Oxford, hahaha – yes I know, we thought that's what it was for a good six weeks. Vary easy mistake to make. Anyway, I know how incredibly loyal you've been to us in the past so I thought why not call you first to ask if you'd like first dibs.

They speak.

I know, we're nothing if not decent.

10 Telethon is where Oxford undergrads phone up alumni and ask them for money on behalf of the college. It's just the sort of charity I love, the sort that funds people who were already rich to begin with.

They speak.

Great. So you have a go at making some, we'll just write you a blank cheque and you can take as much as you like. Brilliant. We'll be in touch vary soon. Cheers.

With a good five people keen to manufacture for us, I tell Hancock I have to slip out as I'm meeting a friend and don't want to overwork myself and burn out.

He asks if it's 'a sexy lady' and if he can come for some 'larks'.

I tactfully explain that if he was seen breaking the rules it might cause a bit of a shitstorm; he reluctantly agrees and vows to stay home.

Another day, another delicious pint of weed killer…;) The pub is even more packed than before. I spot Henry, the chap from school I've arranged to meet, and I head over to his table. Henry has incidentally just left BCG and is looking for work.

I tell him how, if he's looking to make some next-level bank, PPE contracts are going like hot cakes at the moment. I explain the dynamics of the whole thing and we sign the deal there and then.

I am genuinely fucking excellent at my job.

It's one thing to do work while at work, but to do work while not at work – that, my friends, is genius, higher-plane stuff.[11]

Shortly after Henry leaves I get a text to tell me my PPE from Turkey will be with me in five to six working days.

Hancock is going to shit.

11 The only thing cleverer than this is not doing work while at work, which you may have noticed I do *souvent*…;) (*souvent* means often in French).

You love to see it.[12]

Thursday 9 April

I wake up and still nothing on the Boris front. I feel like I want to text him and say all this stuff and spend half an hour drafting something but I think about what Hugo would say and decide to sack it off.

In the evening all the spads get an email from osamabinladen@ gov.uk.

It's just pages and pages of zeros and ones, which I don't have the energy to try and decode. What's clear though is that Big Daddy Cum Cum is alive. This email infuriates a lot of spads, most notably Felix, who angrily complains that while the old chap is intellectually masturbating over email we're all on the front line having to do actual fucking work. This is a bold move; for all Felix knows, the Big Daddy could have infiltrated our WhatsApp and will punish him on his return.

Friday 10 April

It's Good Friday so no one is in work, but Bully Patel has still sent round an email to all the civil servants, joking that she'll crucify them like the Romans did Jesus if they don't keep working from home. At least I think it's a joke; the problem with Bully Patel is you're never quite sure as to whether she'd actually do it in practice or not. It's completely

12 You love to see my success, I mean. I would not love to see Hancock shitting, though, from his general facial expression, I do, regrettably, have a very accurate perception of how this might look.

unacceptable – abusive behaviour – and yet there remains something resolutely hot about the whole thing...

I'm looking sharp today. I have a date at the 'garden centre' with 'Verity, 27', St Paul's Girls', St John's, who I met on Hinge, which up until recently I had thought was only for gays.

She owns a business and I've told her there are some pretty tasty private contracts going for the right kind of ladies ;)

Just as *j'arrive* at the garden centre my phone goes off and I learn that:

BLOJO IS OUT OF INTENSIVE CARE. HE'S DONE IT. THE OLD BOY HAS ONLY GONE AND FUCKING GOT AWAY WITH IT AGAIN. I KNEW HE'D DO IT I JUST KNEW IT.

I'm so happy about this I could literally buy Verity a drink and not expect her to pay me back.

My evening gets even better when Verity arrives. She is a worldie. You always absolutely love to see a girl who looks just as good in real life as online. It's such a relief because so often you see girls who use dark magic to make themselves look phenomenal but in reality look offensively ugly. When this happens I normally try to slide out of the back entrance before they see me.[13] No need for such tactics tonight.

We get talking and she is incredibly sexy. She keeps doing this thing where she runs her finger round the top of her wine glass as we talk and goes 'Mmmhhhmmm' when I'm saying stuff. I think it might be the most erotic thing I've ever experienced.

I decide to deploy my 'my bedroom's only a short Addison Lee ride away' line.

'Well maybe if you can hook me up with a PPE contract we'll have to go there,' she says.

13   I don't mean anus.

124

Fucking hell.

We agree a PPE contract for her to sign right there and then for 15 or 50 million. I don't know which; I'm not really conscious at this point.

Within seconds her lips are inches from mine. I haven't been this excited since, well, Blojo getting released earlier today, but before then I haven't experienced this level since Bullingdon acceptance. Right as I'm about to get a load of the good stuff she pulls away and tells me she has to pop to the loo.

I'm literally prepared to smash my head through the table in excitement at this point.

After fifteen minutes she's not back.

After twenty-five I get a text from her telling me:

One of my girlfriends has had a bit of a crisis so I've had to go and sort her out. Let's link up at some point next week and pick up where we left off…;)

Oh. My. Jesus. College. Oxford.

Girlfriends…

One of her girlfriends…

One of…

There are multiple girlfriends!!!!

I'm going to have an orgy with her and her girlfriends and it's going to happen 'at some point next week'.

This might be the best day of my life.

Sunday 12 April

Blojo is out of hospital. I repeat, he is out of hospital. We have symbolically broken the back of this virus. This is our Battle of Britain.

On the day we celebrate Jesus rising from the dead, Britain's Jesus has done the same.

You love to see it.

I drop Blojo a text in the evening to say:

> Blojo, back from the dead and ready to receive some head, no doubt, how are we? Mate, I heard you only stayed in hospital for so long so you could have more time with the nurses. Fucking great to have you back, old boy. Lots to catch up on

He responds with a GIF of Dominic Cummings coming out of a coffin to imply resurrection. Classic Blojo.

I decide to follow up with Verity and drop her a message to say that perhaps we should link up, along with her 'girlfriends'[14] next Friday, same place, same time.

She does possibly the hottest thing she could possibly do and leaves me on 'Read'.

I check to see if she's typing at thirty-second intervals for the next hour. The longer she leaves it, the more unbelievably erotic it is.

Monday 13 April

I'm actually fucking loving lockdown.

The best thing is all the people from major public schools – aka my social group – are still going out, while the riff-raff from the minor public schools and below are following the

14 Holy fucking shit.

advice and staying inside. We've effectively effected[15] a social cleansing, which I personally hope remains after lockdown is over.

Then we can enter into a golden age where Prets are open everywhere and pubs are closed to the riff-raff. It'll be a land of milk and honey... Or oat milk and honey, I should say. I don't think they do dairy in Pret. God, I fucking miss Pret.

It's for this reason that I heartily welcome the three-week lockdown extension from Raab. Although he says it's to 'reduce the R rate', we all know it's for the chaps.

Still nothing back from Verity. I might have to ask her to marry me.

Tuesday 14 April

I've just been reading about the ninety-nine-year-old Tom Moore's fundraising efforts. What an amazing chap. He's been doing lengths of his garden to raise money for the NHS and has made nearly £30 mill! That's nearly as much as the average amount of money we're giving our mates for a PPE contract. Phenomenal.

I really think chaps like Tom Moore epitomise how great the UK is, where we, as the government, don't have to give to the NHS because we can rely on a ninety-nine-year-old to pull on people's heart strings enough to get them to pay for it for us. That right there is what Britain is all about.

As I sit at my desk, I feel so patriotic and just can't stop thinking about all the parallels between Covid and the Blitz. There are so many: in both instances Britain has been affected by something foreign, America hasn't really done anything

15   Non-Oxbridge writers might have erroneously put 'affected' here.

about it…loads. Obviously, there's more than that, I just can't think of them right now, but there are loads; that's demonstrable. I just can't demonstrate it.

I decide to make sure to get loads of Blitz imagery in the next speech I'm asked to do.

Thursday 16 April

In the morning I'm blessed with quite possibly the greatest news in the history of Western civilisation. Pret. Pret returns! Pret is coming back. Of course it's in a reduced capacity and only in a limited number of places, but Pret is back. I feel like the Israelites must have felt in the Old Testament when manna fell from heaven for them. Except rather than manna, I have an array of delicious hot drinks and delightful snacks to preside over.

I and a large group of other chaps and chapettes who have heard the gospel flock to leave Number 10. All the usual Westminster Prets appear to be shut and I'm instead forced to travel to Islington. When I arrive, it's unsurprisingly absolutely packed with other very important professional people, and also some NHS staff, which I think is a real shame and lowers the tone. I go slightly overboard with my order and get two different types of chocolate rice cakes, a flat white and an espresso, as well as two different types of baguette (Chicken Caesar, and bacon and Italian prosciutto). As I sit drinking my coffees and methodically ploughing through sandwich after sandwich, I start to feel a wonderful, elevating hope, like nature is healing and all the bad stuff in the world has simply evaporated away.

On the way back to the office, I get a text.

It's from Verity.

It reads:

Hey Rafe, I've got something planned with the girls on Friday night.Let's do Friday next week instead…;)

For the rest of the day my brain is absolutely riven with images of the lesbian escapades Verity and 'the girls' will be embroiled in.

I reply straight away to say it's booked in. Friday 24 April at seven o'clock. She sends me a wink in reply; this girl is amazing.

I return to my desk, slightly aroused still from Verity's text and slightly drowsy from my Pret feast, to a scrap of paper with 'Hubris, R. Stationery cupboard. T – now' written on it.

I duly follow the instruction and open the stationery cupboard door and am almost blinded by the light.

'Rafe,' calls out a voice I recognise as Big Daddy Cum Cum's. 'I knew you would come here.'

My eyes focus and I see the Big Daddy is dressed in a white robe, with a long, sleek white wig parted in the middle and a white staff in his right hand (which is surely a reference to Gandalf the White).

'Great to see you've recovered from Covid,' I say, still squinting slightly in the glare of the light.

'I fought it day and night, Rafe. From the first light of day to the fading of the light at dusk. The darkness took me and I strayed out of thought and time and every day was as long as a life age of the Earth…but it was not the end… I felt life in me again… I've been sent back to kill off all conventional wisdom for good.'

'Dom, I'm not really sure what you're talk—'

'Dom?' he interjects looking into the middle distance with a serious pensiveness. 'Yes,' he says, a look of recognition spreading across his face, 'that was what they used to call me… Dom Cummings.'

'Yes, Dom.'

'I am Dom the unconventional,' he says, staring intently at me, 'and I come back to you now.'

I don't really know what to make of this so say politely: 'It's great to have you back, mate,' and quietly close the stationery door as I leave.

Friday 17 April

Everyone except Blojo, who is still 'recovering' in bed, gets pulled into a big meeting at the Department of Health on securing more PPE. Despite all the tasty contracts I've now given out to five of my mates, it's not enough; the NHS front line seems to have even more of an appetite than Blojo for married women at a wine mixer.

Poppy is now back at work but is insisting people leave a chair between her and them and is still washing her hands with sanitiser every few minutes.

Hancock gets up and tells us it's absolutely imperative to 'message round friends' and see if anyone can make the PPE for us.

'Yes, great idea, Matt. Let's all just rely on friends who have never manufactured PPE before rather than the actual companies who know how to make it whose emails you were too lazy to reply to in March, and who are now too busy to take our orders,' says Govey snidely.

A silence falls on the office as no one wants to stand up for

Hancock, who looks for a moment as if he's going to cry. He then catches himself and, like a child implementing coping tactics from its parents to deal with bullies, says: 'I see what you're doing there with the sarcasm, Michael. Good one, but actually we didn't know we needed PPE in March because we all thought it meant Philosophy, Politics and Economics from Oxford University, and nearly all of us have that anyway. As soon as I'd realised it didn't mean that, I was straight on the case.'

Gove mutters something under his breath that sounds like 'Fuck off you wet prick' but isn't loud enough for it to be clear.

'What sort of budget have we got for this?' asks Hugo.

'That doesn't matter at this point,' says Hancock. 'We just need it to be done. Pay as much as you have to.'

'I suppose the best thing is, this isn't our money anyway,' says Hugo. 'It's the taxpayers', so it's not like it matters,' which is an excellent point.

Just as we're about to bring the meeting to a close, Letty, who has now been taken off furlough, pipes up: 'I don't understand why we need to protect everyone in the UK. The poor are like animals – they don't feel pain. Surely we should just let them die?'

I return to my desk after lunch to see that Lettie's desk is empty and learn she's been re-furloughed.

I'm slightly concerned that my Turkish PPE hasn't arrived yet, so I phone up the chap I ordered it from.

It takes a good five minutes to get him to realise I'm not trying to buy a tracksuit and that I just want to see where my PPE is.

He tells me the order is 'coming right up' and puts down

the phone.

From my extensive knowledge of Turkish kebab vans, when they say, 'coming right up', they mean max five minutes wait, so I announce on behalf of the government that it'll arrive tomorrow.

Monday 20 April

I arrive at work to learn that the Turkish PPE still hasn't come. I don't let it get me down too much though, as I know it'll arrive at some point and, to be honest ,most of the doctors on the front line have probably already caught and got over the virus, so actually probably won't need it anyway. I might try and chase it up later if I can remember and don't have something more important to do.

We start the week with a GM, which stands for General Meeting, but in this case probably more appropriately denotes the words 'Garotte Matt (Hancock)'. Everyone takes a turn at unloading on him. It's like Hancock Bukkake.[16] Not only is Govey ripping him, so too are Big Daddy Cum Cum, Lee Cain and Bully Patel.

'Why are we hitting our 100K testing target but the cases are still rocketing up?' asks Govey waspishly.

Hancock, forehead covered in sweat and shining under the light like a waxy apple, tries to start three different sentences across a thirty-second period but bails out of each of them. I'm acutely aware that the reason for this disparity is, technically speaking, me, as I may have suggested artificially hitting our testing pledge to make ourselves look better, which possibly

16 Bukkake is where several men ejaculate on one individual.

has had a role to play in the rise in death numbers. That said, I'm just a lowly advisor; I'm hardly to blame if ministers follow advice which I may or may not have given…

'Answer his question,' barks Lee Cain, slamming his fist down on the table as he does so.

Surely Hancock wouldn't betray me?

'Well,' he says, the sweat starting to drip onto the table before him, 'we thought it was best to double-count some of the tests and mail all of them out to meet the target.'

'Who is we?' asks Big Daddy Cum Cum.

Fuck.

Hancock looks conflicted:

'Me, I meant me,' he says, with the sort of resignation of a man who has just bailed out of masturbation.

Thank fuck for that.

Hancock's eyes are now darting round the room, desperate for some way out; they find mine and he splutters: 'But we're getting loads of PPE. Young Rafe over there has secured lots from Turkey, which I believe has already arrived.'

'Don't try and shift attention to me, Matt Cock-in-his-Hands,' I say, distracting from the fact it hasn't yet arrived and in the process unleashing perhaps one of the greatest pieces of wordplay known to man.

I'd been sitting on this zinger for a while, waiting for the right moment to unleash it. That's the thing about politics: it's all about timing.

Everyone laughs – even Big Daddy Cum Cum.

We all spend a good twenty minutes piling in on Hancock and the meeting ends.

The spad WhatsApp is absolutely exploding with praise for 'Matt Cock-in-his-Hands,' afterwards and you absolutely love to see it.

I get a text from Matt Cock-in-his-Hands just before home time around 3.45.

> Hey buddy,
>
> I just wanted to say really sorry for mentioning you in the meeting. I don't want you to think I'd ever put you under the bus. I've always got your back, man. I love you. Always here for you, man. I hope we're still best friends. You're definitely my best friend.
>
> Really sorry.
>
> Let's go for an IPA soon.
>
> Matt Cock-in-his-Hands
>
> (Great joke by the way. Really funny, really made me lol) xxxxxx

Only Matt Cock-in-his-Hands would respond to me publicly humiliating him by apologising.

I air the text.

Tuesday 21 April

Blojo is sliding back into work today. We're easing him in with a phone call with Donald Trump. These are usually quite easy and involve just listening to whatever ridiculous bollocks comes out of Trump's mouth and agreeing sympathetically, like you might with someone who is mentally ill.

I connect the call. They start their conversation, as is tradition, with a spot of 'locker-room talk'. Boris tells Trump about one particularly attractive nurse who he kept telling he had groin pain while in hospital. Trump responds with an anecdote about an air hostess he propositioned twelve times on a flight in the Eighties. It's all classic stuff. Trump then starts going off on one about bleach. It's bizarre, he keeps telling Boris: 'You absolutely should have drunk bleach, Boris. It kills the virus, believe me. You shine a light on it and the virus goes "ah" and it dies. It dies so much, believe me.'

At this point my phone buzzes in my pocket.

It's a message from Verity.

Holy shit.

It's a picture of her legs in tights sat at a desk somewhere.

Jesus Christ.

I'm so aggressively aroused that I don't have the headspace to ask about how her PPE manufacturing is going.

God she's amazing.

I show Hugo and Poppy the photo at lunch and explain how I'm embroiled in possibly the hottest erotic scenario of anyone ever. Poppy has seemingly overcome her wetty neuroticism despite the cases being at an all-time high and the deaths being 20,000 (40,000 if you don't discount every other person) and is sat with us without a mask.

'That's just a photo of a girl's legs,' Poppy says ignorantly. 'It sounds like this girl has just used her charm to get what she wants from you and is going to keep pushing back your dates indefinitely until you eventually lose interest.'

I explain to Poppy that this is an absolutely appalling take and that if she actually understood women she'd know what she's just said is moronic.

I check in with Hugo about the whole Test and Trace situation and he tells me: 'It's actually turned out to be *très difficile* to code, mate. I thought I could just pull a couple of all-nighters and do it but it turns out it takes a really long time to learn. We've got a fuck-tonne of people coming to contact trace for us though, so that's a definite plus.'

'But what are you going to do when they turn up, mate? If you haven't got a system in place, how are they going to know what to do?'

He looks slightly stumped here but quickly responds, 'I reckon we'll be able to get them to just wing it, mate.'

Just as I'm finishing a granola pot (not even in the same galaxy as the Pret ones in quality terms), I'm struck by a genius idea.

'Hugo, how many contact tracers do you have?'

'15K, mate, but to be honest, the more the merrier.'

I explain my tenant situation and the debt, and within a couple of minutes I've agreed on their behalf to make them contact tracers with all the profits going to *moi* to pay for their debt. What an absolutely incredible piece of Politics, Economics and I suppose also Philosophy if you think about it.[17]

Wednesday 22 April

I stride into work to learn that, rather than 400K PPE gowns, I've been delivered 32K tracksuits. I can't believe this has happened. In all my life to date I have never had a Turkish kebab chef get my order wrong and yet here the Turks have absolutely fucked me. I said PPE to the guy on the phone so

17 Here I'm referring to the degree I have from Oxford in Philosophy, Politics and Economics from Oxford University.

many fucking times. I mean obviously this doesn't affect me so it's not a huge problem but nonetheless they've wasted my time, which isn't really on. I think I'm going to have to stop eating kebabs on principle.

I decide to tell Matt Cock-in-his-Hands that the PPE arrived but 'simply was not up to the sort of health and safety standards that I, as a public servant, would insist on for the UK'.

He tells me he's 'so pleased I could open up to him about stuff' and tells me it's 'no problemo'.

Thursday 23 April

Another text from Verity. I pray it's another picture, but sadly this time just a paragraph of text.

> Hey Rafe ;) Something's come up on Friday so I'm going to set you up on a blind date with my girlfriend. I think you two will really get on...;) xxxxx

I ask her when she and I will be having our date. She replies:

> Soon ;) xxxxxx

I feel like she might be lying to me. Do incredibly sexy women lie? Intuitively, I feel like the answer to this question is 'no'.

Friday 24 April

It's Friday at seven. I'm sat nursing a gin and tonic in the garden centre waiting for my blind date to turn up. I hope she's not actually blind…as in a date that's blind on a blind date… Not that I wouldn't find a blind girl attractive, if she was attractive; it's just they do tend to speak a bit weirdly, which is a turn-off…or is that deaf women? I can't recall. I suppose one advantage of dating a blind woman is that if you did want to break up with her, you could just leave one day and she wouldn't ever be able to find and have a go at you.

I spot Henrietta of all people, the spad I interviewed to become a weirdo/misfit and slept with before firing because (if I remember correctly – and I think the faculty of my Oxbridge memory always does) she caught feels and became vary clingy. I wonder who she's meeting for a drink? She looks done up; very fit actually.

I sit and check my emails.

'Rafe?'

Fuck, she's stood right in front of me. I realise what has happened.

'Henrietta! Welcome to this not-so-blind date.'

She laughs.

We get chatting. It's just like old times. The Whispering Angel is flowing, the flirting begins. We're edging closer to each other.

As I top up both of our glasses with some more Whispering Angel, I seductively mutter: 'You know, when you look like you do tonight, it makes me regret having had you fired.'

It's like the atmosphere has totally drained of colour before my eyes.

'Sorry, what?' she says.

Fuck.

'I was just joking,' I stammer.

'It was you. *You* were the one! You absolute bastard. I can't believe you'd try to sleep with me after that.'

She picks up about £12.37 of Whispering Angel and throws it over my face. I feel like I'm in an episode of *Made in Chelsea* except for people with above-average IQs.

After a couple of failed attempts to try and ingratiate myself into groups of women sat together in the garden centre, I end up at home.

I'm so desperate for sex that I message Emily, whom I haven't spoken to since mid-March, and repeat my 'U up? x' text to her.

She doesn't reply.

What new depths of shame are these?

I feel like the time has come for Rafe Hubris to get a girlfriend.

Monday 27 April

Blojo is back in *Numero* 10. It's the return of the king.

Govey has bought a cake as well as a banner which says: 'Welcome back Boris'.

'We missed you so much, Boris,' he says in front of the whole office. 'We just have no idea what we would have done without you. Thank goodness, if you'd gone I might have had to have been prime minister; imagine how awful that would be. That's not worth thinking about and let me stress: I absolutely don't ever…'

Blojo says a few words about how, inches from death, he thought of Number 10 totty and it gave him the will to live and come back from the brink.

I start a chorus of 'He's a jolly good Blojo'. Hugo and a

couple of the other more classic spads get involved while champagne flutes are handed round and the civil servants look on disapprovingly. It's a really excellent affair, which incidentally are two words I can't think of anyone better to attribute to than Blojo.

After lunch, Blojo and I get stuck into his resurrection speech.

I cannot even begin to express how much better it is to be working with him rather than Hancock on speeches – and in general.

As a protection tactic we decide to boycott *Good Morning Britain* so Piers Morgan can't slaughter Hancock week in week out. It's undoubtedly for the best.

We spin the roughly 45K dead as an excellent triumph and a sign that we've come to the end of the first phase of fighting the virus, even though the daily cases are at just below 5,000…

The advantage with Blojo is that, even though we don't really have this virus under control and he's just emerged from intensive care, he has this remarkable ability to assert mistruth with such high levels of certainty that it makes you feel inclined to believe him; he's like the anti-Hancock. I chuck in some Blitz imagery which, as I've clarified above, really does uncannily parallel Covid, and given that we know this speech needs to be a biggie, I make sure I throw in some references to 'If' by Rudyard Kipling (one of my favourite white supremacists) for good measure. In a master stroke I manage to weave Captain Tom Moore into allusions to 'If' like some sort of nationalistic linguistic god, and write the line:

And if we as a country can show the same spirit of optimism and energy as was shown by Captain Tom Moore, who turns 100 this week…

It's classic Rafe stuff, combining the classical with the

contemporary. Blojo loves it and goes and smashes the speech out of the park.

We are back.

Thursday 30 April

Blojo and I are enjoying a spot of tennis.

Obviously clubs haven't reopened, but one of Blojo's mates has a court in central London so we pile in there. It's amazing; just like old times.

He casually mentions in the warm-up that he's having a baby today.

'Christ, are you sure you've got time to play tennis?' I reply, taken aback as I brush up the back of a forehand.

'Well old chap, if I was at the birth of all of my children, I wouldn't have time to do anything,' he says, an outrageous glint in his eye as he arcs his wooden racket through the air. 'You never want to be there for the birth,' he continues. 'I did it once and never again.'

'What was it like?' I ask.

'Worse than a Cobra meeting,' he says forlornly.

We play for about twenty minutes before Blojo has to stop for shortness of breath. He really doesn't look his best. His skin is pale and seems to hang off his face, and he's unable to get through a sentence without gulping desperately for air.

'You've got to do this job on your own terms, Rafe,' Blojo gasps from the floor, eyes still closed. 'It's like a relationship, old boy. It's there to make you feel good. Never forget that.'

'I won't,' I say, half smiling, confident that when I become prime minister, I'll be a prime minister just like Blojo.

MAY

Friday 1 May

The word on the Number 10 grapevine is that there's growing anger and discontent among the senior Tories re lockdown. Senior Tories spluttering indignation is common, and indeed, without it the harmony of the Conservative Party would be lost. This indignation, however, must be kept below a certain level, lest it bubbles over and brings the entire party into disrepute. If a senior Tory becomes too agitated they may say something 'choice' in an interview with a journalist, or even worse on Twitter…or worst of all, on LBC (Rees-Mogg, Grenfell, 2020). If this happens you have to go through the farce of writing a public statement where it's made to look like a public apology but actually just subtly blames the public for being outraged (see Patel 'I'm sorry if people feel there have been failings', April 2020). In essence, it's a lot of work that someone like me will be forced to do, so we need to try and avoid it.

Normally, you can appease one of the grumbling senior Tories with a tax cut for the consultancy firm they work for on the side, but annoyingly this is much bigger than that; the senior Tories have formed a group – 'the libertarian squadron' – and are insisting that lockdown ends with immediate effect.

Luckily, Blojo has promised to meet 'the libertarian squadron's' leader and 'sort this whole mess out'.

Blojo has palmed me off with meeting the 'libertarian squadron's' leader and 'sorting this whole mess out'.

The squadron leader and I meet in a vacated Number 10 office. On seeing Blojo isn't present he furiously demands to know when the prime minister will be attending. I tell him that I'll be taking the meeting, which causes him to blanche and say, 'But you look like you're still in short trousers,' brandishing his cane, monocle threatening to pop out of his left eye socket. He reels off a great list of demands, including one about 'reintroducing workhouses for the most impoverished 10 per cent', the reading of which makes him even more angry and red in the face. As soon as I start speaking to try and methodically address each of these demands he screams, 'I'm being silenced, I'm being silenced!' and storms out of the office.

I sincerely hope he doesn't work out how to use Twitter over the weekend…

Monday 4 May

Another Garotte Matt session this morning in the Department of Health.

Hancock really has aged horrifically over the last few weeks. I'm fairly sure he had a full head of hair in March…

The savagery is even worse this week, as we've all learnt that Matt Cock-in-his-Hands stood by while Covid patients were sent to care homes without adequate testing or PPE and predictably there has been mass death.

Hancock has adopted a new tactic to cope with mass scorn

and derision from the other ministers. Rather than looking like he's about to cry and then steeling himself and trying to diffuse the tension, he's now trying to assert his authority – a bit like one of those candidates on *The Apprentice* whose team lost masses of money but who tells Lord Sugar they've actually done loads of work and the task failure 'was absolutely nothing to do with' them.

'So, what would you have had me do?' says Matt, hands on hips (I can't work out whether he's gone to see a professional 'assertiveness coach' or his mum has given him this tactic. Either way, it's appalling).

'We'd have had you do the exact opposite of everything you've done, you stupid twat,' snipes Govey.

Just as Big Daddy Cum Cum and Lee Cain look set to feed Matt the brain pills they fed Javid, Blojo flaps into the office. He enters in a state of incomplete dress, tie askew, shirt untucked.

'Sorry about that, chaps,' he says, still looking flustered.

'So great to see you, prime minister. You're looking so great,' says Govey.

'We're in a bit of a pickle, chaps. Neil Ferguson has been caught breaking lockdown for a spot of "how's your father",' Blojo says.

I have to stifle my squawk of mirth and disguise it as a minor coughing fit. I find this so classic.

'This obviously looks very bad, chaps. I mean it's simply not the sort of behaviour someone this high up can be seen to be doing.'

Personally, I think Ferguson's extra-curricular activities make him precisely the sort of chap we need in government, but Blojo won't have it. We agree we'll be able to perform just as well at managing this virus as a government without him; he's only a 'leading expert' in virology and, as both Govey and Big Daddy Cum Cum correctly say, we don't need the experts any more. Besides, I got an A star in Biology IGCSE[18] and I'm pretty sure Big Daddy Cum Cum has done loads of experiments on dead cats' genes, so we can handle this; no problem. Blojo gets Bully Patel to phone Ferguson to tell him he's out and that's that.

Tuesday 5 May

I'm sat with Big Daddy Cum Cum discussing strategy now that Neil Ferguson is gone. I say, 'discussing strategy'; Big Daddy Cum Cum has made it a little more like an assessment test. He'll invite me to read something by Robespierre, then the poem 'Invictus', then a recent report on virology, then he'll get me to stack Jenga blocks on top of each other while we discuss the 'thematic relationship' between each of the pieces. When I say something the Big Daddy likes he'll reward me with some trail mix, which I don't really like the taste of but, equally, I don't want to get a low score on the assessment, so I eat it.

We begin discussing a report from some stats academic, David Spiegelhalter, which asserts that it's difficult to adequately compare different death rates in different countries owing to divergence in factors like population density and average age and given that different countries have different methods for counting death numbers.

'If this is so, Rafe, what broader implications might this have for Covid and conventional wisdom?' he says, shoving a Cummings–made crossword in front of me.

'Well,' I say, correctly guessing 'Genius, 8 across' to be

18 Along with all my other fifteen GCSEs, I also got five A stars at A Level in Classics, Ancient Greek, Latin, English and Economics.

'Cummings', 'doesn't this mean that if no comparisons can be made, we can effectively use this report to justify the death count in the UK as not really our fault, which would shatter the conventional wisdom that the government is a bit shit?' I say. He smiles and gently slinks off, a large pile of trail mix on the table behind him, which I think means I've done vary wall. I duly eat the rest of the trail mix after he's gone. Just because Big Daddy Cum Cum isn't still there, doesn't mean he's not still testing me.

On the way home Hugo sends me a clip of Cock-in-his-Hands still implementing his new-found 'assertiveness', telling some GP woman taking him to task on Test and Trace in Parliament to 'watch her tone'. It's getting absolutely torn to shreds on Twitter. The problem with Hancock is that, on a level, one does feel intuitively sorry for him, and yet everything he does seems to ignite a correspondingly overwhelming desire to bully him, like one of those kids at school it just made sense to savage recreationally: it's a stress reliever and vital for the mental health. Not theirs, obviously, but that of the group as a whole.

I wonder whatever happened to Test and Trace...

Wednesday 6 May

I decide to get an Uber Lux into the office because I'm nothing if not high-end. I've also slept in too long to get the tube... classic Rafe.

My driver is a real talker. They always love yammering on, Uber drivers, usually about Brexit and what a bastard Sadiq Khan is. This morning though he's talking about how he thinks the government have mismanaged the virus.

146

'The thing is, they can't seem to bloody sort out the testing. How on earth can we control the virus if they can't test whether or not people have it? They're just bloody arrogant and out of touch, d'you know what I mean?' he says.

I just nod and let his incorrect, boring, tired takes wash over me as I think about whether to have a flat white with oat milk or almond milk from Pret this morning.

'How do you think Boris Johnson is going to do in this debate with this new Starmer guy?'

Fuck.

PMQs. Today is Blojo's first PMQs back with Starmer, the lawyer. The forensic, cross-examining, detail-obsessed lawyer.

Shit.

I text Blojo right away

'Mate, have you done any prep for today's PMQs?'

'Old chap, I'm about as prepared as Matt Cock-in-his-Hands' wife is to have sex with him. We're going to have to bash this out pronto the hour before. Oxford-tutorial style.'

By the time Blojo shows up, it's fifteen minutes before PMQs are due to start.

'Sorry, old chap I was waylaid getting *très* laid,' he says sniggering.

We agree that the best thing from here is for him to just go in and wing it.

'Make sure you keep that Churchillian intonation and if you get really stuck you can always fall back on Latin or Ancient Greek,' I say, massaging the top of his back.

'Yap,' he says, shifting around like a boxer about to step into the ring.

'Oh, and Spiegelhalter. Do not forget to mention Spiegelhalter to justify the death numbers. His whole thing is saying you can't make comparisons with other countries so the death toll doesn't count.'

'Spiegelhalter,' repeats Blojo.

And with that he charges in.

Starmer goes straight in with the death numbers.

Blojo parries wonderfully, throwing Spiegelhalter out like a flaxen-haired God, saying that international comparisons just really can't be made.

Starmer comes straight back by showing us graphs we've produced comparing international death numbers for the last few weeks. Shit. He's got a whole folder full of fucking graphs.

Starmer has all the facts at his fingertips and reels them off one after another after another. He's like if Paxman had credible intellect and didn't just loudly bulldoze people. He doesn't raise his voice at all; he just coldly slaps Blojo across the face with the wet fish of his facts. This cannot end soon enough.

Blojo by comparison has no facts, numbers or stats and tries to refute Starmer by saying things like: 'Actually the Right Honourable gentleman is wrong when he says things have been bad, because actually recently they became good actually…so there…'

It's not good.

Starmer covers all the areas we're fucking: PPE (40 per cent of doctors have had to pay for it), Test and Trace (testing is falling below 100K) and care home deaths (Hancock, you stupid prick).

Blojo goes wildly off-piste in an attempt to save face and says the government will aim to do 200K tests a day, which would mean we're surely going to have to start triple-counting tests. There's even a moment where he totally stutters to a halt before restarting; this is bad.

Mercifully, the cross-examination ends and Blojo takes questions from the other MPs.

On his way out, he looks shaken and cross and I'm sure I hear him mutter something that sounds like 'Queer Starmer' and 'Not in the spirit of the fucking Blitz'.

I'm in another Uber Lux on the way home and even Farage on LBC is saying things haven't gone well for Blojo. As I'm listening to this, I get forwarded an email from David Spiegelhalter telling us not to use his study in favour of wriggling out of scrutiny, as that's not what he meant or said. This has not been our finest day.

Thursday 7 May

I go rogue and grab a Swedish meatball hot wrap for lunch today. Normally I'd have something cold for lunch but this wrap is actually *très* strong; Pret never misses.

I catch wind on the spad WhatsApp that Dido Harding is to be made head of Test and Trace. I wonder whether giving her such a prestigious role in technology when a few weeks ago she literally took half an hour to log onto a Zoom is a good idea. She's also not very popular among a lot of spads, who say she's about as useful at formulating policy as a marital aid. On reading this I write on the spad WhatsApp that perhaps we should all call her Dildo Harding, which is an absolutely classic bit of Hubris wordplay and goes down vary, vary wall.

Saturday 9 May

I wake up to learn that the garden centre has had to close down. I fall into a deep depression at this news. It's been a shit week at work with Starmer being a prick to us and now my one source of joy in the world has had to close down. Deep in existential self-analysis I start to worry that maybe I'm not the most conventionally good-looking and talented twenty-four-year-old in the UK; maybe I'm just a public-school bluffer… After a few seconds I snap out of this, realising it's precisely because I'm a public school bluffer that I am the most conventionally good-looking and talented twenty-four-year-old in the UK. I start to feel a bit less down. I think I just need a good shag; there's nothing in life a good shag can't fix.

I've been dragged into doing a spad Zoom quiz by Poppy, which is every bit as horrific as it sounds. I'm in a team with Poppy and Hugo, which I have hilariously named 'The Spadstics' (classic Rafe). As we're halfway through a round where each team must name as many colours on the Farrow and Ball paint chart as possible, I spot Emily (she's on a team called 'The Whitewhores', which I think is a pun on Whitehall and the White Horse. If so, vary good stuff). I've crushed about five pints by this point and am so desperate for a shag I decide to privately message her on the Zoom chat asking if she wants to come to mine after 'for something without strings attached'.

Moments later Felix comes off mute to say: 'Rafe, can't you at least take me for dinner first?'

Then Hugo pipes up: 'I'd rather it *was* strings attached, Rafe. I really like you.'

I realise I've messaged the entire Zoom group rather than Emily privately. The excruciating shame is annihilating, and the following shaming is annihilating and excruciating. This is like a lesser version of how Hancock must feel every day. It lasts for about twenty minutes and involves me briefly considering leaving the quiz to drown myself in the Thames. Mercifully, I hold strong and neither Emily nor I break the bond of secrecy.

When we win the quiz, I'm subject to another round of pile-on; Hugo tells me he's going to give the winning £50 in Deliveroo vouchers to me to enjoy recovering from my 'no strings attached' fun.

Sunday 10 May

I'm in work on a Sunday, which normally I'd find absolutely appalling as a prospect, but with all the chat I'm getting on WhatsApp at the moment I welcome the distraction.

We're sat in a Cobra meeting on ending lockdown in the cabinet room and poor Blojo seems to be stuck between hand-wringing scientists who say unlocking now could cause 100K deaths so we shouldn't, on one hand, and then on the other, spluttering red-faced senior Tories and members of the libertarian squadron who say we should unlock right away.

I pipe up to say we appear to be stuck between an unlock and a hard place, but no one enjoys my comic artistry.

Each side seems to be playing policy tennis with Blojo. First the scientists say, 'We should save every human life and the human race as a whole,' to which Blojo says, 'Yes, alright, then that's what we'll do,' then a senior Tory pipes up, 'We must save every job at JP Morgan, and JP Morgan as a whole,' to which Blojo replies, 'Yes, alright, then that's what we'll do.' This continues for about fifteen minutes. I decide to raise the eminently reasonable point that 100K people dead would be bad – but if these people are dead then they no longer exist, so surely we ought to prioritise the happiness of the people who would exist and unlock now, which is a vary good point.

Once everyone has made their points they all file out, leaving Blojo and me to work out his speech. Blojo is insistent that if we unlock it'll fuck us long-term, so we decide to effectively keep the lockdown in place. However, we slide a lot of conditional penmanship (courtesy of *moi*) into the speech to:

- Make sure we can get the working class to go back to work to get the economy firing again.
- Give enough loopholes for the chaps to still link up and socialise so as to preserve our mental health (crucial).
- Make things vague enough for the media, the senior Tories and Starmer not to be able to have a proper go at us (you can't attack a policy if it doesn't really exist).

I throw out some absolutely world-class conditional tense work including the line:

Work from home if you can, but you should go to work if you can't work from home.

We also tell people to go to work by car rather than public transport, which I had thought didn't really make sense when applied to the mostly working-class audience that it's addressed to, but of course I'd completely forgotten that tradespeople can just get Ubers to work every morning, so they'll be fine.

We also chuck out that we'll be increasing the fines for people who break social distancing, which of course won't be widely enforced but it's enough to dissuade people with budget incomes from leaving the house, to ensure there isn't any sort of drop-off in the quality of the sort of chap or chapette you'll see on the 'rona social scene. This, along with the realisation that I can still just go to loads of house parties, makes me feel a lot less annoyed about the garden-centre situation.

We also introduce a five-stage method to determine how bad Covid is in the UK. I say 'we' introduce this; we actually just steal it from the South Africans, who came up with it a month ago.

We fashion a cracking slogan:

Stay alert, control the virus, save lives

Which obviously doesn't mean anything, which is precisely the point. Keep it incomprehensible so you can't be held responsible: the Blojo special!

As Blojo destroys the speech with Churchillian flair, I check my WhatsApp to see the 'no strings attached' piss-taking has pretty much fizzled out, as they haven't been able to ascertain who the message was intended for. Today is a good day.

Monday 11 May

I'm slightly late for the GM this morning and the only seat left is next to Emily. I take it without looking at her.

We all set about the usual Hancock butchery, which is hugely enjoyable, as ever. During the meeting, though, the spad chat goes off about forty times, all with the same words:

'Mrs Emily Charming.'

I have no idea what this means; the spad chat really can be bizarre sometimes…

At about 11.30 I get a text from Poppy.

'You do know this Emily Charming stuff is directed at you?'

'What?' I reply, bemused.

'Everyone knows you and Emily have been getting together and they all think you're like the poser character in *Shrek 2* who thinks he's really hot but is really entitled and gross.'

'Prince Charming?' I reply.

'*Yes*. Prince Charming. All the spads say it behind your back so they keep saying Mrs Emily Charming as if you two are getting married and going to live happily ever after.'

I feel several emotions all mixed into a vile cocktail of angst: fury, betrayal, disgust, stupidity and slight flattery at the spads collectively noticing my charm.

What the fuck am I supposed to do now!? Do I deny on the spad WhatsApp that me and Emily have been shagging? Do I explain that it doesn't count because she's butters? Do I sue?

I decide eventually to say nothing in the hope that this will pass.

I get absolutely pelted with *Shrek*-related memes all afternoon, mostly of my face superimposed onto Prince Charming's. There are also a few with the caption 'When she says she's fucking a handsome prince' with a picture of me and the meme of Chloe Goes to Disney underneath.

This is vile.

My key gets stuck in the lock of my front door on my way back from work. I'm so angry at this that I smash my hand into the door until I draw blood.

Tuesday 12 May

If anything, the public pile-on that Emily and I were subject to yesterday has intensified today. I'm wearing a plaster on my index and middle finger after the door incident, a picture of which finds its way onto the spad WhatsApp along with the caption: 'A vigorous sex injury sustained last night with Emily Charming.'

I try to ignore it, just like the man boob stuff at school, and pile into a meeting in Blojo's office ahead of tomorrow's PMQs with Starmer, but even Blojo references it.

'Heard about Emily, old boy. Sounds like a paper bag job if ever I heard one,' he says, sniggering.

I grimace.

We start prep for Starmer.

Blojo is insistent that it cannot go as badly as last week and says several times: 'I will not let that slimy-haired prick fuck me again this week.'

We agree ahead of tomorrow that the more data we publish, the more ammunition Starmer has. To get round this, and the fact that other countries' death numbers are making us look shit, we decide to take the international death number comparison charts off our public briefings. You can't start a fire if you haven't got any kindling.

Amid the endless tsunami of piss-taking, I receive a text from Matt Cock-in-his-Hands saying:

Hey Buddy,

Heard about you and Emily Lol. Lol. Rofl. Roflcopter. You're such a playaaaaa. Let's go for a coffee. I wanna hear all the dirty deets. Has she got any fit mates?

Matt xoxoxox

Evidently the only thing worse than public shame is Hancock's approval, which makes me wish I had long Covid.

Wednesday 13 May

PMQs with Starmer, round two.

He starts with care homes (surely, he should have fucking moved on by now?) claiming that in mid-March we said, 'It remains very unlikely that people receiving care in a care home will become infected,' and yet apparently 40 per cent of national deaths were in care homes.

Blojo straight up denies that we ever said that.

Shit, Starmer has produced a piece of paper showing that we did say that on the government website (surely there should be a limit on the amount of paper you can bring into the chamber?).

Fucking hell.

Starmer then reads out a quote from some cardiologist saying that hospitals discharged known Covid cases into care homes in full knowledge that the homes weren't prepared.

Blojo tries to save face by stating that, in actuality, discharges from hospitals to care homes went down in March and April and that we had a system of testing in place in care homes, which is complete bollocks, but hopefully Starmer lets it pass.

He hasn't let it pass.

He pushes Blojo to explain why the average number of deaths in care homes in April for the last five years was 8K and yet in 2020 it was 26K. On the government's figures there were only 8K Covid deaths, leaving 10K unaccounted for (this is like doing the maths after a chaps' night out on the King's Road). 'How can this be?' he asks.

Blojo, sensing that any admission of truth might lead to a cross-examination of the old 'only every other one counts' method we've been using to record deaths, decides simply not to acknowledge the question.

This is huge from Blojo and surely an excellent tactic to employ moving forward. From here it feels like there's a huge momentum shift.

Starmer pushes Blojo again, but he holds firm and doesn't answer. Incredible integrity from Blojo.

Finally, Starmer asks why we've stopped producing graphs comparing death numbers, but Blojo comes up with another strong li(n)e about how 'the data isn't ready yet', which I'm sure people watching will believe.

I think Blojo's come away with this one; after a slow start he's rallied back, exquisitely repurposing the truth to beat Starmer.

I clap him on the back as he leaves the chamber.

'Top work, Blojo,' I say. 'The slimy-haired prick can't subject us to scrutiny if you opt out of speaking truthfully.'

He jumps up to give me a chest bump while shouting, 'Buller, Buller, Buller.'

You love to see it.

Thursday 14 May

I'm sat alone at lunch as I can't face sitting with the rest of the spads, who continue their *Shrek 2*-themed assault on my dignity.

On the table across from me is a man I haven't seen before around Number 10. He appears to be playing on a Nintendo DS and is drinking from a carton of Frijj strawberry milk. I watch him for about twenty minutes. Every eighth minute, he'll pause his game and pick up his phone and say something like: 'Hello AQA, it's Gavin Williamson. Have it done by Monday.'

He'll then put the phone down, but I can see from his screen that he's just pretending. He's not on the phone at all...

He also has the strangest voice I think I've ever heard. It's like he's tried to correct a northern accent to make it RP (which is obviously a move any self-respecting individual would do) but he's made a pig's ear of it and has ended up sounding like Frank Spencer.

I don't think I've ever heard the name Gavin Williamson before, but from a quick google, I see he's the education secretary...

I've literally never seen the man before.

On my way back through the canteen at 5pm, Gavin Williamson is still there, this time napping...

He's either the most efficient man in the world who has totally sorted a way of coming up with assessing Britain's schoolchildren ahead of the summer and is now just chilling, or he's set to receive the greatest fucking, the likes of which not even Matt Cock-in-his-Hands has had to endure. If that happens, I wouldn't wish being his spad on even my worst enemy...

Monday 18 May

Mercifully the Emily stuff has pretty much died down now. I'm still getting a few comments here and there on it but it has mostly blown over. That's the thing about public scandal: you've just got to keep your head down, weather the shitstorm and eventually everyone will forget, and you can go on as before – a bit like the Leveson Inquiry.

I'm sat in the canteen with Hugo, who tells me he really should be teaching the new cohort of contact tracers how to do their jobs but he's a bit fucked from last night, as he went 'Columbian nose diving' with a girl from Tinder and didn't get much sleep.

'I guess it's part of the job for them to have to work stuff out anyway so that seems like good policy,' I say, chugging my third double espresso of the day. Incidentally, I think this is woefully lazy, but as long as my tenants stay employed and can keep transferring *moi* their rent every month I really couldn't give a fuck.

Hugo starts going on about how he's got some techy weirdo or misfit to develop a tracing app and it's being trialled on the Isle of Wight this week and that when it's a success he can take all the credit. I'm not really listening though. I'm deep in the throes of analysing why I'm in such a dry spell (a period of no sex coming up to two months). For some reason women aren't lining up to have sex with me at the moment and I literally have no idea why…

Wednesday 20 May

We've all been assembled in the Department of Health for some fucking lecture by Chris Wetty about 'second waves', which supposedly tend to be 'worse' than the first waves. I'm vary cynical about this as we've definitely got enough things in place to stop the virus flaring up again, but listening to him burble on is still better than doing work. I'm supposed to be helping Blojo prep for Starmer's PMQs again but I find the work is really intense and therefore not very good for my mental health, so I take the opportunity to sack it.

Just as Wetty's working his way through his third tedious slide, Lee Cain confiscates his flow chart and forces him to sit down. Moments later, the lights and all our computers cut out, bathing the room in darkness. In the centre of the room, from the top of a desk, a torch is switched on pointing upwards, illuminating the face of Big Daddy Cum Cum. It's hard to tell with the lack of light, but from the faint rustling as he moves, the Big Daddy appears to be dressed in a bin bag (I'm really not sure what this is supposed to be a satire of – possibly the way we conceive of waste?).

'Bees,' he says, striding barefoot (again) over desk space.

'The time has come to reveal the wisdom… As the more able among you will have guessed, it is unconventional.'

A muffled banging sound can be heard in the corner of the office as Lee Cain takes a phone from a nearby spad who was evidently texting, and stamps on it. At this moment I realise Big Daddy Cum Cum's bin bag is satirising the concept of fashion.

'As all the spads who pay attention and aren't idiots will know, I sent you all an email in April in code explaining that back in March I went up to Durham to find an intellectual cure for this virus. As I lay in bed battling the virus and listening to

160

The Art of War by Sun Tzu, I was visited by the ghost of myself who told me the solution to this situation lay among the ruins of Barnard Castle, some thirty miles away from me. I was so consumed foraging among the ruins that I forgot to predict the future and see that I would be photographed by an ally of the media and conventional wisdom. There have been plenty of journalists sniffing around my pilgrimage.' (As Big Daddy Cum Cum says 'journalists', Lee Cain erupts in fury and punctures the water cooler with a metal ruler.)

'Bees, we must not let the media get hold of this. We must live by the principle of omerta.'[19]

He then gets us all to repeat 'loyalty cum, silent cum' three times.

When the lights come on, Cummings and Lee Cain are gone, with only the now completely destroyed water cooler remaining.

This is crazy – I had no idea people actually lived in Durham. I thought it was just a university…

This revelation about Big Daddy Cum Cum sets the spad WhatsApp alight. About 80 per cent of the spads are absolutely furious that he broke lockdown and think it's appalling that he was swanning around ignoring the rules when everyone else wasn't allowed to see their families. I think this is a bit of a shit take, as only choppers actually followed the rules anyway and it's a bit wet to need to hug your family like some sort of child. You don't need to do that sort of thing – I haven't hugged my mother since 2014 and I'm fine. I decide not to express this opinion on the chat though. I don't need to be told by all the girls that I'm a shit person; if I wanted to hear that I'd simply phone up every girl I've ever slept with.

19 A mafia term meaning not to rat out.

In a very clever attempt to distract the media, Big Daddy Cum Cum and Blojo agree to stop making foreign NHS workers pay to use the service. I personally view this as a necessity but obviously don't endorse it. We need to get money for the NHS from somewhere and I feel like if we just give foreign front-line NHS workers free healthcare, they might become addicted to things like dialysis machines and chemotherapy and need to be weaned off them. Be that as it may, given that here it benefits us, in this instance it's the right thing to do.

I sit at home watching the highlights of PMQs and see Blojo land a sarcastic zinger on Starmer claiming he's just reading pre-prepared answers. I think this is an excellent thing to mock: if there's one thing to hammer a politician for, it's erring on the side of being over-prepared, which invariably gets in the way of all the essential stuff like long lunches and staying in private houses.

Starmer keeps going on about testing and whether we have a system, which obviously is a fucking stupid question because fundamentally we don't know. Why on earth would you ask someone a question which they don't know the answer to? That's not scrutiny, it's just asinine.[20] Blojo promises we'll have a world-beating testing system in place by 1 June, which is certainly possible... I don't know how likely it is because Hugo and Dildo Harding are on the case, but it seems like a sensible thing for Blojo to promise.

A straight sets win for Blojo this week. I think the old chap has Starmer's number now. Strong, *très* strong.

20 For non-Oxbridge readers, 'asinine' means stupid or foolish.

Friday 22 May

Some fucking journalist has written an article about how we've been double-counting some of the Covid tests, which is a fucking outrage. Obviously we have been doing it, so I don't mean it's an outrage in that sense – I mean it's an outrage in that I'm going to have to find another fucking way to jimmy the numbers to make us look like we're adhering to our promises, for fuck's sake. At least Big Daddy Cum Cum hasn't been rumbled though.

Shit. Big Daddy Cum Cum has been rumbled.

The *Mirror* and the fucking *Guardian* (Leftie tossers) have broken the story that Big Daddy Cum Cum travelled up to Durham.

We decide the best thing to do is label the story Fake News and hope that by the end of the weekend it's blown over. No one important reads those shitty papers anyway...

Saturday 23 May

The situation has considerably worsened overnight. The people of Twitter are LIVID. I scroll through for about thirty seconds and see someone called #BeKind has said:

We must crucify #Cummings and his children and his wife in the street for this.

I decide that's enough Twitter for today.

My phone is exploding with emails and texts from various ministers about what should be done.

We eventually get pulled into a Zoom, where Blojo talks about the seriousness of the situation. His serious tone is however somewhat undermined by the fact he's forgotten to change his Zoom name from 'Captain Big Dick'.

People keep saying, 'We can't have the population think it's one rule for us and one for everybody else,' which I find confusing as that's exactly how the world works...

After a few minutes Blojo says definitively: 'Dom stays.'

He's immediately met with a volley of indignant ministers protesting: 'But prime minister, the media—'

'We need Dom to do all the policies and the planning and things,' says Blojo. 'He's staying.'

A good five ministers log off the call at this point in outrage.

We're next tasked with working out how we deal with this enormous media shitstorm.

The Big Daddy suggests we use the weekend to create a music video where, in the style of an ISIS beheading video, he kills a goat and writes 'Fuck the media' in its blood on the floor. This gets swiftly vetoed.

We make the call to label the Big Daddy's escapade 'an essential trip' and all the big names push out the 'he was just looking after his family' line on Twitter. I suppose that is one way of describing what Big Daddy Cum Cum did... That's the thing with all this stuff: it depends on how you define it. For example, with the right language you could define Harold Shipman as a man preoccupied with enforcing population control and a more generous distribution of the world's natural resources. Obviously, on another reckoning he'd be a serial killer, but Big Daddy Cum Cum definitely isn't one of those – although herd immunity probably did kill a lot more than Harold Shipman...but then surely it can't make someone deserve a public hanging to go on a walk... Is it criminal to walk? Isn't this a bit like that other bloke that Roman society hated who used to walk with the tax collectors and the sinners? Now, in the year 2020, another man associated with the modern-day tax collectors and sinners[21], the Conservative Party, takes a walk and he's publicly shamed. Surely that can't be right...

Blojo brings the meeting to a close with: 'Right, I'm not letting this take up any more of my fucking weekend. We'll reassess on Monday.'

The meeting ends.

Fucking hell.

This feels bigger than DC's pig-knob-gob fiasco.

I'm at a house party in Clapham. The weather is banging, *el vino* doth flow and *el gak* doth *disappearios* up noses.

I'm at the elite point of inebriation where I feel maximally cogent and also maximally uninhibited. I decide to use this opportunity to do a bit of polling on what everyone thinks of the now-dubbed 'Cummings-gate' in case it comes in handy over the next few days. I start a timer on my phone so I can invoice for the work.

The members of the party seem to be split 50/50 in terms of hatred vs non-hatred. Some of the girls seem to think he's 'absolutely despicable' and that the government have told us we've all got to do one thing while they're doing another, which is outrageous. I do remind these women that we're currently at a house party, which is very much not in line with the guidelines. Others think they would have done the same if they had kids and knew they'd be incapacitated within hours and needed childcare. Others still think this is a damning indictment on the state of the media (more than it is on Cummings) who are

21 I'm both lol.

generally knobheads relishing the opportunity to pile in on someone who's outsmarted them several times, which they're duplicitously characterising as a moral crusade. This is an interesting point. Surely it's not justified for the press to hound the Big Daddy like they're doing, especially when they have high-profile musicians and actors to harass! What's the point in ignoring the recommendations of the Leveson Inquiry if the media are going to fuck you when it matters most?

I decide, based on this, that we're on fairly solid ground defending the old chap.

I'm just about to embark on a gak-off with another Rafe (what are the chances this party in Clapham would have two people called Rafe?!) when my phone explodes again.

Christ alive, another article has come out about Big Daddy Cum Cum breaking lockdown. By the looks of it there's been more Cumming and going than Blojo's 'Pimlico spell' in the mid-Nineties.

I still do the gak-off but with an air of solemnity in appreciation of the situation at hand. Unsurprisingly, we all get an email calling us into work the following morning.

Sunday 24 May

Practically everyone has been called in this morning; we're all crammed into the cabinet room.

Quite a few people look like they've gone hard smelling £50 notes the night and morning before. It's an even split between people wearing suits and casual wear. I've gone for suit trousers and a shirt but without a tie and with three buttons undone, which says, 'Yes I'm in work, but I definitely haven't given up on the weekend.' Rishi is in a full cashmere tracksuit with R.S.

engraved in gold lettering across the chest.

After the new revelation about the Big Daddy, there's a lot of disquiet among the ministers about keeping him on, but Blojo remains insistent that he stays. It's absolutely fair enough that Blojo insists we keep on an unelected advisor; without him, Blojo's tennis game would suffer immeasurably and that wouldn't be fair.

Once this is established, Blojo and I get to work on this evening's conference.

We decide to go straight in with the Cummings situation.

I suggest starting with a joke to break the tension, something like: 'Who would have thought a Cumming scandal in government wouldn't have been about my willy?'

Tragically, this gets vetoed.

I do get to use my polling work from the night before however (£600.00 invoiced to the UK government; you love to see it) and we get Blojo to set out the issue plainly and simply: 'Is it one rule for the elite and another for everybody else?'

The answer, of course, is no.

While the rule was that everyone should stay at home and Dominic Cummings didn't stay at home, this doesn't count because he was in the unique situation of having to think about children.

And if you can't take that from Boris Johnson, the man with the most experience of thinking about children because he has more than anyone else, you can't take it from anyone.

We give it about ninety seconds in the speech and then do all the boring graph shite.

Thankfully, I think we've put the whole thing to bed.

Monday 25 May

Somehow Blojo's statement about how the rules apply to everyone but not Big Daddy Cum Cum, and how that's fine, hasn't calmed people down. We're getting fucked from all sides: the media hates us, the public hates us, the opposition hates us, even a sizable contingent of our own party hates us! Some Tories actually begin frothing at the mouth during the morning's GM. It's such big news, we don't even have time to formally annihilate Matt Cock-in-his-Hands. Obviously, I still fire a few spit balls at his bald spot, but there's nothing verbal at all.

Blojo's method to solve this whole fucking nightmare is his method for solving everything: just do a speech. This unsurprisingly generates mass uproar.

Nonetheless, it's agreed that Big Daddy Cum Cum will speak to the people of the UK and its journalists at 4pm.

We have a quick think about the best place to have Big Daddy Cum Cum talk on an issue a lot of people perceive to be about elites being above and better than the masses, and eventually decide on the rose garden.

A small cadre of spads made up of me, Hugo, Poppy and Felix sit with Dom in a meeting room trying to draft a statement for him to read. He's wearing a full Kappa tracksuit. I don't think he owns a suit…

The task is proving to be virtually impossible.

For some insane reason, Dom has chosen this moment not to cooperate.

Every time one of us tries to go over what actually happened and in what order, Dom will say things like: 'I reject the implicit reliance on Western linear time the question presupposes,' and then he'll just sit staring at us with his fingers interlocking, waiting for us to make the next move like some sort of chess grandmaster.

By 1.30, we all resort to drafting statements on pieces of paper, which we slide in Big Daddy Cum Cum's direction, but he rejects them one after the other.

By 3pm, Felix storms out.

By 3pm, with only one hour before he's scheduled to go out, things begin to get desperate.

'What do you want from us, Dom?' pleads Hugo.

Dom just stares, smiling at him like a crocodile.

The clock strikes four, which is the time Dom is scheduled to give his statement, but still nothing has changed.

I close my eyes and try to focus all the power of my Oxbridge brain to come up with a solution. It comes to me. I drag one of the remaining scraps of paper that hasn't been used to draft a statement and scrawl: *Surely it would be most unconventionally wise to do the conventionally wise thing but ironically?*

I push this in Dom's direction.

He looks at what I've written and unclasps his fingers: 'Of course, it would. You have passed the test, Rafe, and overcome groupthink,' and with that he picks up the first statement Felix drafted and leaves.

Some fifteen minutes later he appears in the rose garden. We all crowd around the TV in the office, watching. He seems to have rifled through the lost property bin and found a semi-formal outfit. He's wearing a yellowed shirt and some suit trousers.

Some fucking idiot is playing a screechy violin while the Big Daddy is talking, which actually works out quite well as it distracts from the conference itself. I wonder if it's Lee Cain doing it…

The bit where he's giving the statement goes very well actually but he starts getting carried away and fucking ad-libs. He talks about how he drove sixty miles to test his eyes; this is obviously ridiculous and untrue, but he'll be doing it to see if the media will widely report an absurd statement as true, to prove how much smarter he is than them. Everyone gathered in Number 10 collectively groans at Dom's riffing and looks over at me, Hugo, Poppy and Felix as if his fucking inane bollocks is our fault. He struggles greatly to withhold his scorn when answering journalist questions and keeps saying 'with respect', which he manages to deliver as if he's saying 'fuck you', which is obviously quite gangsta but really isn't helping matters.

Eventually, it's mercifully over. One of the civil servants passes round a bottle of whisky for us all to take a swig from; after a day like today we all fucking need it.

Tomorrow, and the inevitable mass briefing of ministers for the mammoth media interview spree it will undoubtedly bring, will not be enjoyable.

Tuesday 26 May

I'm on my way into work and I'm trying to think of the most plausible way to justify driving to test your eyesight. Maybe it does make sense? If you were worried you had erectile dysfunction, would you go to an orgy? Maybe? I've never had erectile dysfunction, except when the girl is butters or speaks with bad grammar, which turns me off completely.[22] Maybe testing an erection at an orgy isn't the right metaphor. After all, you can't lose control and kill someone at an orgy...unless it's

22   I was once asked, 'Does you want to cum?' by a girl I picked up in Clapham Infernos and completely lost my erection.

one of those orgies, but I'm not really into that stuff.

Fuck. What on earth are we supposed to say to the ministers? I knew this would fuck us from the moment Big Daddy Cum Cum said it.

I feel incredibly stressed and have started to develop this horrible rash up my upper back and neck.

I end up getting about ten minutes with ministers before they go out to the media and tell them to absolutely avoid answering a question on Cummings' eyesight at all costs and if you absolutely have to, say driving long distances to check your eyes is the sort of thing you do all the time.

I get back in from work, open a beer and try to switch off from the day's events.

I flick through LinkedIn and Instagram for worldies, though sadly none are forthcoming. On Twitter everyone seems to be making a lot of noise about a chap called George Floyd.

By the looks of it, he was killed by a police officer.

There appears to be an accompanying video on the whole thing, which I decide not to watch. My life is hard enough without having to actively seek out suffering and pain; just yesterday I was given a cappuccino even though I'd ordered a flat white!

Wednesday 27 May

I'm sat with Poppy over lunch in the canteen. The old girl looks terrible.

'Are you okay, Poppy? You look like you might have a touch of the 'rona,' I say.

'I'm just finding it really hard to process all the George Floyd stuff, Rafe. I didn't get any sleep last night.'

'Why on earth would someone being killed mean you couldn't sleep?' I ask, confused. 'People die all the time…'

She looks me directly in the eye and says: 'Don't you understand, Rafe? This is about racism.'

I find it very hard to hide my look of scorn at this tired woke take.

'What on earth does the death of a person who just happened to be black have to do with racism?' I intelligently riposte.

This causes Poppy to launch into an embarrassingly banal series of comments about 'racism', which is apparently 'just as bad over here'.

'Oh come on, Poppy, surely you don't think we're racist in the UK!'

'Have you not read about Stephen Lawrence, Windrush and Grenfell?!' she says, looking furious.

'Yeah, but that wasn't racism, that was just people forgetting to look after black people, which is obviously different.'

Shortly after this she picks up her tray and leaves, but not before giving me a pissed-off look.

To be honest, I don't even know if I believe any of what I've just said to Poppy. It's just entertaining to wind up woke people.

It is a bit pathetic though, the way people get totally swept up by their social group into accepting whatever completely unrefined narrative they impose on them. That's what me and the rest of the chaps at Queen's[23] think anyway.

I really don't think we're racist in the UK. I know I'm certainly not. I can't be: I literally don't know any black people!

I saw some at Oxford, and they both seemed nice enough, but given that I have no interaction with any of them it's quite literally impossible for me to be racist.

---

23 Tennis club, not the college at Oxford University, which is where I have a degree from.

I'm sat in a meeting with Hancock, Hugo and Dildo Harding in the Department of Health. They're blathering on about bringing the human contact-tracing roll-out forward, even though Hugo is nowhere near to sorting the app, in order to take the heat off Big Daddy Cum Cum. They'll talk about this for a few exchanges and then Dido will try and steer the conversation to horse racing. I'm not really listening though: I'm preoccupied with an email Poppy has sent me.

It reads:

Rafe,

After our conversation at lunch, I think a lot of what you said was really problematic and you need to check your privilege. I used to be just like this until I did the work and became a better person. I want to help you do this, Rafe. It's the least I can do as a white person. I'm going to leave my copy of *Why I'm No Longer Talking to White People About Race* on your desk for you to borrow.

Let's talk when you've read it and are in a less problematic place.

Poppy

I snort extremely loudly reading this.

It transpires that Poppy's copy of *Why I'm No Longer Talking to White People About Race* is incredibly helpful: it operates as a brilliant mat for the wine glass I'm drinking from.

Thursday 28 May

Poppy and I wander into work after a quick stop-off at Pret. I'm drinking a flat white while Poppy has a black americano, which she's pairing with 90 per cent cocoa chocolate. I get a look at her phone when she pays and see she appears to be playing the song 'Black' by a rapper called 'Dave' on repeat on Spotify. She looks extremely agitated as well. At one point we go past a black person on the street and Poppy stops them and tells them: 'I want you to know I'm one of the good ones.'

She asks whether I've read *Why I'm No Longer Talking to White People About Race* yet. I tell her I haven't yet got round to it, which causes her to launch into how important it is that I eradicate my privilege. She then tells me about how she's reached out to every black person she's ever met and has apologised, just in case she ever made any of them feel uncomfortable.

I ask Poppy what she's actually done to combat racism other than conjure up a lot of woke verbiage for her white friends. This makes her look even more conflicted and she hurries off.

I pile into work and catch Matt Cock-in-his-Hands being interviewed by Kay Burley on one of the screens in the office.

It is a new low.

Rather than looking like he's shat himself and doesn't know how to tell you, Matt has gone rogue and taken to laughing through the interview when Kay rumbles his attempt to take the heat off Big Daddy Cum Cum by announcing a roll-out of new tracers even though the contact tracing app isn't ready yet. It looks like he's arrogantly laughing in the faces of thousands of dead people and their families.

'It's absolutely priceless. Normally I'm accused of doing these things too slow,' he keeps saying.

This must never happen again. His laugh makes me feel like I want to scratch out my own eyes like a rabid cat.

I text him to expressly forbid him from EVER talking to a journalist without being briefed beforehand.

Sunday 31 May

I'm at a party of six plus VAT. Technically speaking the restrictions don't relax on this until tomorrow, but then tomorrow is a relative concept anyway: as soon as you get there it's just today again, so in philosophical terms the restrictions will never be lifted, and it's better to just lift them ourselves now.

I notice there's a black girl at the gathering who is insanely fit. She's so fit in fact that I decide for the first time in my life it's time to pretend to be woke.

'Awfully sad about that George Floyd chap. I think silence is violence,' I say, trying to regurgitate what I can half-remember Poppy burbling on about over the last few days.

'Rafe,' I say, reaching my hand out.

'Georgie,' she says, looking perturbed, but shaking my hand nonetheless.

'So listen,' I say, like a more conventionally attractive James Bond. 'I've already put down £50 for the Black Lives Matter movement this morning, but I'm not sure that's enough. Do you think I should put some more down?'

She looks a little taken aback but then says: 'Well, I think you should donate as much as you can afford.'

'Well, if I wanted to, I could afford to put at least 1.5k down,' I say, smiling seductively at her.

'Go on then,' she says, coolly.

I completely understand the subtext, which is clearly: I'll shag you if you spend £1.5K on some bullshit woke cause. This girl is definitely fit but is she £1.5K fit? After a brief consultation with my desperate venal need to put an end to my now several-month-long dry spell, I decide to part with the cashish.

'It's funny,' I say gearing myself up for the excitement to come, 'because if we go on to shag it'll be like I've paid to do it, so you'll sort of be like my prostitute.'

For some reason unbeknown to even someone of my Oxbridge intellect, this makes Georgie throw a drink on me and walk away and leave the party (which I'm sure must be assault). I spend the rest of the evening trying to get my bank and then the BLM movement to refund my money, but to no avail. I absolutely fucking hate BLM.

JUNE

Monday 1 June

Another GM this morning. This week everyone is nailing Cock-in-his-Hands for not having a successful Test and Trace app in place now that the easing of restrictions will make all the contact tracers we've rolled out about as helpful as a strap-on made of hot brie. Technically speaking, I think this is actually Dildo Harding's job but we've all tacitly made the call to blame Hancock for everything. It's just easier.

Lee Cain, rather than constructing actual sentences, just screams 'CUNT' very loudly right before Hancock is about to speak. Though Matt tries to apply the same tactic he used with Burley, laughing off the vicious attacks levelled at his character and competence, his laughter is very soon replaced by tears.

The problem here though is that everyone seemingly delights in pasting Hancock for his incompetence but no one is actually proactive enough to do anything about his failure and find a resolution. It's like they want him to fail so they can rip him.

Soon, conversation moves to Black Lives Matter, which triggers seismic jowl wobbling and uproar among senior Tories and powerful gnashing of teeth from Bully Patel. It takes several cries of 'Order' from Blojo to restore quiet.

Blojo explains to us that he's getting 'absolutely fucked' by Carrie's outlandish purchasing of tribal shields and African musical instruments in honour of the Black Lives Matter movement and, given that's the case, thinks he's done 'quite a lot more than he ought to have done'.

'My friends, we must tread the middle way. We must not be compelled to take the knee and get whipped up into some Marxist, *Game of Thrones*-esque landscape of fantasy. But equally, we should not suppress these protests…because that would be a fucking nightmare to organise. I say do nothing and it'll all go away pretty soon.'

Bully Patel, who has grown increasingly animated as Blojo was talking about not being swept up by the movement, now looks furious. She kicks the door on the way out of the meeting and her heel leaves a big dent in the wood. It's kind of hot.

I spend most of the rest of the day sifting through the emails we're being sent telling us that Big Daddy Cum Cum ought to resign then kill himself. I get forwarded one on average every ten seconds. I'm fairly sure a fair few of these are from Big Daddy Cum Cum himself, as the calls for his resignation are written in riddles and sent from rogue emails like theyretrickingyou@gmail.com and Iamtheintellectualrevolution@outlook.com.

Tuesday 2 June

I wake up to an Instagram feed full of black squares to show 'solidarity with the black community'. This makes me fucking furious. None of these self-proclaimed emotionally masturbating 'good people' will have donated even a tenth of what I've given to the Black Lives Matter movement and I don't even fucking believe in what it stands for.

After work I'm sat in the pub bored out of my mind. I text Poppy to see what she's up to. The old girl is at the fucking BLM march, for fuck's sake. I tell her to come to the pub for a break. She tells me, 'Racial injustice doesn't have a break.'

Ten minutes later I text her again and get a similar reply.

With the third text I break her spirit and she agrees to come 'for one' in Clapham.

It's an absolutely glorious day – perfect weather for *el pintos*.

Poppy arrives in a T-shirt which says 'I support black businesses'. Christ.

'The thing is, Poppy,' I say, nursing one of Clapham's finest, creamiest pints, 'is it's all very well supporting BLM in central London. But what about supporting it in Clapham? I don't see anyone fighting the good fight here.'

'Do you think?' Poppy says, looking nervously attentive.

'I definitely think. Honestly, I'd say the best thing you can do for the BLM movement is to stay in the pub in Clapham with me.'

'And it is really hot outside and I do feel really exhausted,' Poppy says.

'Exactly, and I've actually read that being tired and supporting equality actually creates more racism.'

'Who wrote that?' Poppy asks, failing to conceal her eagerness for me to give her a legitimate excuse to sack off BLM.

'Oh, someone from Oxford.'

'Someone from Oxford?' she presses.

'Yeah, someone from Oxford.'

'Oh well, if it's someone from Oxford they must know what they're talking about and I should probably just stay here. The thing is, I definitely think BLM is really important. It's just sometimes you just need to be in the pub, don't you?' Poppy says, relief spreading across her face.

After about fifteen minutes she puts a jacket on over her 'I support black businesses' top and we have an entire conversation without mentioning injustice. It is truly wonderful.

Not only has Rafe Hubris got his friend back, he's converted someone from the hard Left back to the right side (and wing) and stuck it to the duplicitous thieving Black Lives Matter movement in the process. Step aside Laurence Fox. Rafe Hubris is the true anti-woke hero of our times.

Thursday 4 June

Cock-in-his-Hands runs to my desk in the morning, sweaty-faced and panting, to announce that it turns out masks are a good idea for protecting people from a respiratory virus. We pull another Dua Lipa (sadly, not me in the sexual sense actually pulling Dua Lipa, which I would literally break my legs to do).

'It's not the end of the world, though, I guess,' says Cock-in-his-Hands, trying to reassure himself.

I mean it quite literally was the end of the world for many people who will have caught and died from Covid because the government, specifically Matt Cock-in-his-Hands, didn't insist on the use of masks…

This is quite an unpleasant thought though, so I decide to just not focus on it, a bit like with the vast sum of money that was stolen from me by the BLM movement. I've found the best way to deal with it is just not to mentally go there at all. Also, it's really not worth worrying because it's not me who's going to be absolutely pasted in an inquiry over this; it's stupid, feckless, awkward, sweaty, balding, led-by-the-science-but-not-really Matt Cock-in-his-Hands, so it's fine.

I wonder if he'll shit himself in the inquiry…

I have a very entertaining mental image of him insisting he was 'led totally by the science' while realising he's shat his pants.

I suppose he has been led by the science, to be fair to him – just not the science of science but rather the science of haphazardly flapping from one disaster to the next in the hope that the next one won't be as viscerally embarrassing as the one that preceded it.

Learning from prior mistakes, we workshop his speech to within an inch of its life.[24]

Moments before he goes out to address the nation, Hancock looks me square in the face and says:

'I think we're doing really well.'

Monday 8 June

Given that everything is pretty chill now, we've sacked off Monday GMs. I take the opportunity to run a 5k and start the week off vary wall. I charge round Battersea Park and complete the distance in just under twenty minutes (22:30 but I was running into a headwind so my real time is sub-twenty).

I roll into work around 10.30.

The atmosphere in Number 10 is like one of form-time at the end of term, where you could just sit and eat chocolate and watch films and discuss where you'd be skiing that vac. Hardly anyone is in and the people who are just seem to be watching YouTube videos.

---

24 We have termed the directive to have him heavily workshopped before he goes out to the public 'Operation Supervision Cock'.

After work I slide into what I have termed 'post-apocalypse drinks' (classic).

Hancock is stood at the bar with his tie around his head, drinking an IPA, occasionally saying 'woohoo' into the ether (because no one is talking to him) and ogling some of the female spads. He keeps hovering at the edge of conversations hoping someone will invite him in, but no one does.

Everyone looks ecstatic – except Poppy, who appears to be crying. All the 'Parli girls' (Emily, Liv, Carrie, etc.) are gathered round her, cooing. I decide not to get involved. I don't want a flare-up of the Emily stuff again and if me being even remotely close to her gets photographed I'd be fucked. Poppy's probably just rewatched *The Notebook* or something. It won't be a biggie. Also, after my sub-twenty 5K I'm not sure I have the energy to have to hear women talk about things, which I do find can be quite taxing if they're not about to have sex with me.

I sink back into conversation with Hugo, who tells me that apparently a load of protestors have pulled down the statue of Edward Colston, a slave trader in Bristol, and chucked him in the water at Bristol docks. I've never been to Bristol, although if by some tragic accident I'd been born mentally deficient, I could have ended up at uni there. Hugo says he's spent the whole day trying to curtail Bully Patel's rage. Apparently, the old girl had to be talked down from finding all the protestors and drowning them in the docks as punishment.

We exchange a knowing glance which says: *Though this is obviously bad, unfortunately, once again, it is quite hot, which kind of makes it fine…*

Tuesday 9 June

It turns out Poppy has broken up with her boyfriend.

She starts crying while telling me over a coffee. Apparently, Alex, her ex, went off with some other girl from his office at KPMG. I find her tears incredibly difficult to deal with. It's such an uncomfortable and alien thing for me to witness because I never cry; not the first night I boarded at Dragon[25] when I was four, not when someone wrote a sign with the words 'Rafe MANBOOBris' above my bed at Eton, not when I didn't make the Blues side for golf Varsity at Oxford. It's literally never happened.

I really don't like seeing Poppy upset, though, so I try to say encouraging stuff like: 'None of us ever liked him,' and, 'You'll find someone new.'

But this just seems to make her cry more.

Luckily, a female spad comes along and says encouraging things so I get to nod reassuringly while she says stuff until Poppy looks a bit less sad.

Thursday 11 June

All the spads have been called into a Big Daddy Cum Cum illumination session, which for some reason he's chosen to host at the Ministry of Defence rather than Number 10.

Big Daddy Cum Cum has started giving us 'cognitive homework' now all this Covid stuff is over.

He's told us to watch *The Truman Show* while listening to 'Saint Pablo' by Kanye West and we all have to explain what

---

25   For non-Oxbridge readers, this is the one true prep school which is a feeder to Eton College.

both works are saying through the Spiderman meme format. He leaves in a puff of smoke, to be replaced by Dildo Harding, who is trying to give us a speech about technology in the workplace but she doesn't seem able to work the projector in the meeting room.

Poppy has got up to help her and bends over the projector, trying to show her how to work it. As Poppy is doing this, Hugo gestures to some of the other male spads to get a load of her arse.

He then gets up and pretends to hump her behind her back!

Normally, this would be classic, but Poppy has been through a lot recently. I can't believe he'd do this.

I see him mouth at Felix: 'Mate, I am definitely going to have a go on that now she's back on the market.'

'Mate what the fuck was that in the meeting?' I say, accosting him outside.

'What are you talking about, mate?' says Hugo indignantly, trying to square all five foot eight of his inches up to me.

'You know Poppy feels like shit, having been broken up with, and you're just treating her like a piece of meat.'

'Mate, that is genuinely the gayest thing I've ever heard you say. If I want to crack on with Poppy, I'm going to crack on with her and I don't need your permission, you fucking chopper.'

He walks past me, hair flopping slightly as he does.

The stupid minor-public-school prick.

Friday 12 June

I'm doing some essential work with Blojo over lunch. I say 'essential work'; we're playing tennis at the Hurlingham Club, but occasionally we do refer to the office, so we are working… essentially. Carrie is there with Blojo's baby Wilfred, who is unmistakably Blojo's son – the flaxen hair, the full cheeks; his cry also sounds plummier than that of other babies.

Carrie tells me they've already sorted Wilfred's place at Eton, along with membership of Queen's and the Hurlingham (the Holy Trinity as it's known), which is smashing news.

I'm hitting the ball vary, vary wall, as ever. Blojo, by contrast, is still struggling with his breath and every time Carrie's sausage dog, Winston, charges onto the court, he doubles over panting. We cut the session short after forty minutes and tuck into some 'emergency champagne' Carrie has produced from a Fortnum and Mason hamper she's brought with her.

'I'm really sorry it's Moët,' says Carrie, as I'm tucking into a lobster roll. 'We've run out of Cristal. I laterally feel like such a chav offering this to you.'

Blojo spits the champagne out, shouting, 'Ugh, Moët. Disgusting!' to wind Carrie up.

I notice his phone is exploding next to him.

'Don't worry about that, old chap,' he says, noticing my eyes wander. 'It's just Dom Cummings.'

'We won't be letting *him* ruin the vibe,' says Carrie, taking Blojo's phone and throwing it away into the grass.

Carrie asks me how Poppy is doing after the incident earlier in the week.

I explain how she's still feeling pretty shit and tell her about the Hugo situation and how I told him to stop being a prick.

'Cockblocking 101. Poor form,' says Blojo, making faces at baby Wilfred.

'It's not like that,' I say. 'Hugo's a shit bloke who just wants to use her for a quick fuck. Poppy's vulnerable. She needs to be around people who have her best interests at heart.'

'It sounds an awful lot like you want to shag her, old boy,' says Blojo.

'Stop it,' says Carrie, her hand on Blojo's forearm. 'I think you're being so sweet, Rafe. Not every male-female friendship has to involve sex, Boris.'

He audibly scoffs.

Saturday 13 June

'You're not going to have sex with Hugo are you?' I ask Poppy at the Pear Tree Café in Battersea Park.

She pauses, looking slightly taken aback.

'Hugo? I wasn't planning on it. He looks like Lord Farquaad from *Shrek*...' she says, a look of half-mirth, half-disgust on her face.

As soon as she says this I feel all this tightness I hadn't even realised I'd been carrying in my back loosen.

'What would give you the idea I'd want to sleep with him?' Poppy asks.

'It's just he's been saying all this stuff about cracking on with you and was pretending to hump you in the meeting and stuff and I thought maybe he might have tried t—'

'He was pretending to hump me?' Poppy interrupts.

'Yeah, when you were helping Dildo Harding with that presentation.'

'Why the fuck would someone do that? That's so fucking disrespectful,' she says, a look of real anger spreading across her face.

'I told him he was being a fucking prick. I told him you were going through a really tough time at the moment and that he should back off.'

Fuck you, Hugo. Fuck you and your stupid fucking hair.

'You know, you've really been an amazing friend to me during all this, Rafe,' Poppy says and squeezes my hand.

It feels warm.

Monday 15 June

I'm sat at my desk scrolling through Twitter and keep seeing people tweet about this Marcus Rashford guy. I've never heard of the chap but log onto his profile and see he's a footballer – and a successful one at that (that's if you think being a footballer is 'success'; I've always found the whole endeavour to be a bit working class if I'm honest).

At the top of his profile, he's penned a letter to 'All the MPs in Parliament'. On seeing this I let out a loud groan. It's one of these fucking letters. Predictably, it contains all the usual kind of preachy virtue-signalling wank you tend to see when celebrities get involved in public issues.

Marcus this, Marcus that.

Look at me, I'm black. I play football.

Feed the children.

I get up to the bit about his mum being on minimum wage and not being able to afford food (couldn't she have just got another job? Surely there wasn't anything stopping her doing that other than laziness?) before I stop reading. I don't really agree with anything this chap has said: we've literally created the very fair and dignified system of food banks to deal with this exact issue. This said, I notice that the tweet has a shit-tonne of favourites and could really fuck us if it blows up.

I take it to Blojo. His office has a 'Do not disturb' sign on the outside. I barge in to see him playing solitaire on his laptop.

I explain the situation and he comes back with a flat 'no' straight away.

'Why on earth would we heed the advice of some footballer? We're not LBC, Rafe. We don't champion the voices of idiots. It's an open letter. It'll go away in a couple of days,' he says, flapping his hands around as he does in dismissal of the whole thing.

'But mate, our approval ratings are so low after the Cum-scandal. People don't really like how we dealt with BLM. If we can ally ourselves to a black footballer it might make it look like we care about that, which will give us more approval again.'

'Rafe, I've got senior Tories in one ear lobbying to replace state schools with workhouses, and Carrie in the other ear lobbying me to buy some Venetian blinds made of gold costing 50k for the flat. Beautiful women are like Ferraris: they cost a lot in maintenance. How the fuck would a decision like this not fuck me royally in the arse? The backlash would be horrendous and we don't have the fucking money to begin with. I'd love to help the starving children but they're just going to have to get jobs or something.'

At this point Blojo's Deliveroo arrives and he ushers me out.

Over lunch I check Twitter again.

This thing isn't going away. It's snowballing. We can't just leave it.

I barge back into Blojo's office and show him the tweet numbers, which are rocketing.

His eyes widen; he absolutely hates not being popular.

'We need to nip this in the bud now, mate. Think of it as like taking a tactical chunder at the Number 10 Garden Party: unfortunate but necessary,' I say.

He sighs, looking very middle-aged, running his hands

through his hair repeatedly, like a man waiting outside a prostate consultant's office.

Finally he says: 'Fine. Give him some money. But not too much. Carrie wants to have a Cristal fountain in our living room… You have no idea how many fucking peerages I've had to give out to fund it,' he says.

'Four hundred mill should do it,' I say.

'Done,' replies Blojo.

The good thing about this choice of action is that it's classic Blojo and therefore vary easy to spin. What Blojo likes to do is wait right until the final hour before he acts on something in the hope that things will have got so bad there's only one option to take. What we as the government do when this happens is argue that 'this was the only option we could have taken', which of course is true but doesn't acknowledge the fact that in reality many other courses of action could have been taken if Boris hadn't spent most of the time watching soft porn on his laptop and chomping through Deliveroo. The public doesn't need to know that though…;) This, my friends, is the art of spin. RAFEal Nadal is back.

Another triumph for the government.

Tuesday 16 June

I'm briefing the master in PR disaster, Matt Cock-in-his-Hands, ahead of media appearances where he will undoubtedly be cross-examined about the Marcus Rashford situation. He's bought me a cappuccino with 'My best buddy' written on it in Sharpie; I don't drink it. I don't drink cappuccinos (to maintain my excellent rig) and, rather like a girl accepting a drink in a bar, I don't want to accept his gift and then owe him whatever

189

the friendship equivalent of a hand job is.

I'm explaining to Cock-in-his-Hands how he categorically cannot fuck up the interview with Kay Burley this morning after fucking up so many interviews so often. The line this morning is just to go in and praise Marcus Rashford for his activism because it simply hadn't occurred to us that we ought to feed the starving kids.

Just as I'm getting Cock-in-his-Hands to repeat 'Marcus Rashford' with me, Daniel, the new intern, brings me a flat white and takes away the cappuccino. I thank him.

'Do not fuck this up,' I say to Cock-in-his-Hands.

He smiles idiotically back at me and raises his hand to offer me a high five, which I air and leave the room.

Metaphors about someone's gran and missing an open goal cannot describe how spectacularly Matt Cock-in-his-Hands bombs his interview with Kay Burley. Not since Theresa May and the fields of wheat incident has someone fucked something quite like this.

He calls the footballer Daniel Rashford. Daniel. Fucking Daniel. Daniel Rashford. For fucking fuck's sake.

I phone him immediately.

'What the fuck was that?' I ask.

'I know,' he says. 'I'm feeling so rad right now. It went so well, let's go for an IPA to celebrate.'

'It would have gone well, Hancock, if you hadn't called the man fucking Daniel, but you did, you called him Daniel Rashford not Marcus Rashford, you jizz sock. As a party that really struggles not to look like it's mocking the working class, how do you think getting a former inner-city kid's name wrong on live TV looks?!'

He leaves a long pause and then tries to lie saying: 'Rafe, I didn't say Daniel, I said Marcus.'

'Don't fucking lie to me, Hancock. I just watched you on fucking television.'

'Okay I did call him Daniel, but I'm sure no one will notice… We're still best buds, right, Rafe?'

I put the phone down. The man is a fucking embarrassment. We're going to have to ban him from interviews.

Wednesday 17 June

I spot Lettie in the canteen, sat next to Poppy and some of the other female spads.

'I had no idea you were back!' I say, sliding into the conversation.

'I've only been back since this morning,' she says matter-of-factly. 'I've actually been working on revamping Boris's plane.'

'Boris's plane?!' I ask, perplexed. 'Is it broken? Surely he doesn't need to be jetting all over the place now?'

'No it's not broken,' she says. 'Carrie just wanted a refurb and I've managed to do it for, like, only nine hundred.'

'How on earth have you managed to refurbish a plane for nine hundred pounds?' Poppy asks.

'No, nine hundred grand. You're so funny, Poppy. You wouldn't even get a square centimetre of the rug made out of mink Carrie needs for that money. I'm actually so proud of myself, though. I'm like so good at budgeting.'

I let out a squawk.

'We've missed you, Lettie.'

As I return from lunch I see Lettie has been re-furloughed.

After work I sit with Poppy, drinking on her terrace.

She seems much happier than she was after the break-up. It's like she's risen up and back into herself.

She's also wearing her hair differently; it falls around her face, framing it like a heart.

We drink into the evening and at about ten I go to leave.

As we hug to say goodbye I feel the curve of her hip against my hand; we pull away and look at each other for a couple of seconds, then I smile and tell her I'll see her tomorrow.

Thursday 18 June

I meet Poppy for a coffee before work. She's on cracking form.

She's definitely become more classic since she's become single.

She really is a vary good girl.

She has her hair up today, which makes her eyes large and round. They're brown, her eyes. Light brown. Kind of like the colour of the coffee I've just bought her.

Number 10 is particularly lively today. Hugo appears to be sounding off about some gaffe Dominic Raab has made about taking the knee and *Game of Thrones*, and Bully Patel, having heard news of Daniel the new spad, has come over to Number 10 to butcher him, just as she did with Hugo at the start of the year.

I'm on Tinder. I'm not really into it for some reason, though. The girls all just seem a bit vulgar. I've matched with plenty of worldies and yet I don't really want to message any of them.

I have a brief moment of existential crisis, worrying this might mean I've turned gay. I'm nearly certain I'm not gay but if I wasn't, why would I be off Tinder? I decide to just stop thinking about this and focus instead on Bully Patel's savagery of Daniel. Today's pasting is particularly remorseless and involves a black bin bag...

Saturday 20 June

I've been invited to a party this evening by Spencer (one of the older spads), Radley, Pembroke, in a suitably South West London location.

I'm meeting Poppy beforehand for a drink and then we're heading over.

I spend a good fifteen minutes considering what to wear, which is very unlike me. Normally my instincts are *très* strong, but today I seem to keep second-guessing them.

Do I wear a pink shirt with my Oxford golf tie? Will a tie make my neck look long like a giraffe's neck? Do I wear no tie at all? Will that make my neck look even longer?

Eventually I decide on the tie.

'You look nice,' says Poppy as she opens the door and hands me a glass of rosé. 'Though you still can't tie a tie apparently,' she adds, undoing mine and redoing it, an eyebrow raised in mock scorn.

She's wearing a red dress and the top of her head comes up to just under my chin with the extra height from the heels she's wearing.

I'd never noticed before but as she's sorting my tie I see she has a scattering of freckles across her nose and cheeks.

We spend most of the party in each other's company.

Normally, I'd spend the evening crawling around looking for a line of gak or crushing the San Miguels with the chaps, but tonight I don't really want to do that.

On the way home, Poppy keeps pretending she and I are a married couple and that we need to be home in time for the children; it's hilarious.

Just as we pass Clapham Junction station I feel something warm and delicate glide between my fingers and squeeze, and with it a jittery, giddy warmth shoots through my body.

In that moment, everything begins to make sense: why I'm off Tinder, why I'm nervous, why I felt so furious with Hugo in the meeting. It's not because I'm gay. It's because of Poppy.

I squeeze her hand back and in that moment feel more alive than I've ever done.

'It's just here on the left,' Poppy says to the driver.

We both get out, still holding hands.

She leads me to her door and when we get there she turns round and kisses me.

It feels like someone has popped a jeroboam of Taittinger in my chest.

'Poppy, before we do this, I just really don't want to be someone who's preying on someone who's just gone through a break-up, because I really care about you and I feel really guilty because we're friends and it's like I've abused your trust and that feels wrong but I—'

'Shut up, Rafe,' she says and kisses me again and pulls me inside.

Afterwards, I force myself to stay awake holding Poppy for as long as I can because I don't want the feeling to end.

Sunday 21 June

I wake up in the late morning and go out to get us both a Pret breakfast and bring it to Poppy in bed.

Normally with girls I feel this enormous urge to put myself on the exact opposite side of the world to them after we've had sex. In fact I actually once looked up international flights so I'd have an excuse to get a girl out of my bed. But with Poppy I feel the total opposite. I need to be as close as possible to her.

We spend the whole day together and as it gets to eight o'clock Poppy tells me: 'You can stay if you like.'

I can think of nothing I'd like to do more.

Monday 22 June

I'm sat in a meeting with Blojo and some of the scientific advisors at the Department of Health. Van-Tam, Wetty and the nurse woman are all there. They're stressing that just because cases are nice and low and the sun is out, there is still likely to be a second even more deadly wave that we need to cautiously prepare for.

Boris is having none of it though. He wants to downgrade the threat level to Level 1 so we can 'reclaim our summer'.

I'm supposed to be minuting the meeting but instead I'm drawing a picture of Poppy's incredibly lovely and beautiful face. God, she is so amazing. I wish she was in the meeting just so I could look at her, but alas she's doing something for Govey. Oh Poppy, shall I compare thee to a night in Clapham Infernos?

I'm brought out of mental images of Poppy and me striding through great Mediterranean fields wearing white linen by

Chris Wetty saying angrily: 'We cannot rush into unlocking, Prime Minister, or we'll end up right back where we started.'

Blojo lets out an odd murmuring sound, as if to imply Chris Wetty is being excessively cautious.

'My friends, he who agonises over tomorrow has missed the joy of today. I refuse to let the people of the UK be ruled by Kung Flu. I say "Kung Flu, no thank you." My friends, we must unlock.'

He then leads us in a chant of 'UN-LOCK' like we're back in the canteen at Eton. It's amazing.

Thursday 25 June

Poppy and I have spent every night at each other's this week. I feel like I know her so much better now than even twenty-four hours ago. I have embarked on learning this girl with a rigour the likes of which I didn't even exhibit as a finalist at Oxford University when I was studying to get my degree from Oxford (I have a degree from Oxford). I know everything about her, from her favourite type of rosé (AIX) to her Pret order (falafel and halloumi wrap with dark chocolate rice cakes and a 750ml bottle of still water).

Even though I'm with her pretty much all the time, I miss her so much when she's gone. I miss her when she goes to the loo, when she goes to the bathroom, when she falls asleep before me. In fact I always try to fall asleep first so I don't have to be without her.

Everything is going amazingly. At work we've halved the two-metre rule, Covid is over and I'm in love. I'm in love with Poppy.

I've even drafted a poem to deliver to her:

Poppy Poppy Poppy,
No other girl could copy copy copy,
You make my legs go floppy floppy floppy,
When I can't see you I feel stroppy stroppy stroppy

I haven't thought of how to end it yet, but it definitely shows promise.

I decide the time has come for Poppy to be my girlfriend.

I ask her in the most romantic way I can think of: in the three minutes she spends in the loo, I retrieve several small sachets of Pret seeds from my back pocket and set about writing 'Girlfriend?' on the carpet.

Unfortunately, by the time Poppy gets back I've only written 'Gir'.

It doesn't matter though; I just ask her with my mouth.

She says yes immediately and jumps into my arms.

'I love you,' she says.

'I love you too,' I reply.

It feels like my life has begun again in that moment and we urgently make love on the seeds all over her carpet.

As I hoover up the seeds while Poppy fetches us some AIX rosé from the kitchen, I reflect on how I would even do a job like this to be with her if it came to it. Obviously, I wouldn't ever find myself in a situation like that, but if becoming a cleaner was the only way to be with Poppy, I'd endure it.

'Darling,' I say to Poppy, who is lying next to me in bed.

'Yes darling,' she replies.

'It's my birthday next week and I was going to take the week off; say you'll come with me. I want to be with you and just be in love,' I say.

'Of course I'll come with you,' she says.

I look into her eyes and kiss her out of love.

I am extremely in love.

Friday 26 June

Big Daddy Cum Cum has organised a 'future prediction weekend' the weekend after this coming one for the 'spads of tomorrow' (fifteen of the most promising spads, of which Poppy and I are obviously members).

Today, the Big Daddy is wearing a mask of his own face and has 'The Real Slim Shady' playing out of a tinny phone speaker that Lee Cain is holding in the background. It's just loud enough so that we can hear 'Won't the real Slim Shady please stand up?' when the chorus comes around.

As a boyfriend of a girlfriend, I don't totally approve of Eminem's lyrics because they can be quite misogynistic, and as someone who prides himself on looking after his girlfriend, I think he should really try and do a little better.

The Big Daddy is handing out copies of the book *How Only the Paranoid Survive*, which we're supposed to read before the weekend to be tested on. I have absolutely no intention of reading the book; I've never read an entire book in my life and I'll be too busy romantically with my love to focus on this. I'll just get a synopsis from Sparknotes and wing it.

Poppy and I are piling into a curry back at ours. Poppy hasn't seen *The Wolf of Wall Street*, so I'm taking great pleasure in showing her what is surely the finest piece of cinema in the twenty-first century.

'This is so hot,' says Poppy, struggling through a vindaloo. 'I'm not sure I can finish it.'

'Don't be such a wetty,' I say. 'It's literally so mild I can hardly taste it.'

We get to the classic bit where Jonah Hill's character starts masturbating at Margot Robbie's character (which I actually think is a bit inappropriate given that at this point in the film Margot Robbie's character has a boyfriend…) and I notice Poppy has fallen asleep.

You hate to see that.

I start to feel incredibly hot.

I open the window, but I'm still hot.

I decide to untangle myself from the covers and eventually drift off into sleep.

Saturday 27 June

I wake up and I'm still hot.

I also keep coughing, but it's dry; I can't get hold of anything.

'You're boiling,' Poppy says, checking my forehead.

I keep trying to breathe in but I can't: it's like someone's put a steel band round my chest.

I start panicking. I feel like I'm drowning. I feel like I'm sinking.

'What if it's Covid?!' I say, looking at Poppy then frantically round the room. 'The cases are so low, surely it can't be that?' I stammer, looking at her left eye and then the right, as if to catch the other one out.

I can't have Covid. I'm too high-end. This sort of thing shouldn't happen to people like me. I'm too important. I'm with Bupa. There are no cases in London now. How could I have caught it when there are like no fucking cases?!

I spend the next half-hour pretending I can breathe unimpeded and am totally fine but by the evening I'm feeling terrible and Poppy confines me to bed.

I'm drifting in and out of consciousness and seem to be in some sort of cruel purgatory, some liminal state between death and life.

Poppy occasionally appears to check on me and produces a Covid test for me to do.

The process of doing one is horrendous. Not even in my wildest nights has anything gone that far up my nose.

As soon as I've done the test I drift back into my barely conscious state.

Sunday 28 June

I wake up to Poppy stroking my forehead and the words: 'It is Covid, Rafe. I think I have it asymptomatically. I'm here to look after you, okay?' she says, looking deep into my eyes. I don't think I've ever loved anyone more than I love ~~Mummy~~ Poppy.

Though the end may be very near I think I could be okay with dying if Poppy were to be by my side for it.

She looks after me like a beautiful matron, a sexy nanny, there for my every need in the moments that I'm awake, a companion to watch films with who'll occasionally pull me off into a flannel.[26]

My symptoms are wide-ranging; tiredness, a cough, a temperature, but perhaps the cruellest is my loss of taste.

I can no longer taste the zing of a Pret mango smoothie.

No longer can my taste buds appreciate the bitterness and

---

26 No, Nanny never did this for me, I should clarify!

sweetness of a rice cake dipped in dark chocolate purchased from a white person with dreadlocks and a lip disc.

That, my friends, is a terrible thing.

I spend a lot of my time thinking about death.

What is it?

Is there an afterlife?

What does the afterlife even look like?

Is there a VIP room?

If there is a VIP room, would I be in it? Surely the answer to that is yes. God is definitely a member of the Conservative Party; look at how long he lets us all live! Would a left-wing God allow that? I think not. If God was left wing he definitely wouldn't have put Eton and Slough right next to each other – a constant reminder of the rightful inequality in society.

But what if there isn't a God?

What if being dead is just nothing?

How would I cope with that? What would that even mean?

I've never done nothing. I've always been productive.

Monday 29 June

I think I may have turned a corner. My cough feels like it's clearing up.

I might be throwing this off.

I'm sitting up in bed today and I feel like I can taste some of the saltiness of the pastrami in the Pret baguette Poppy has brought me this morning.

She brings me a card with 'Get Well Soon' on it sent from Mummy and my father with 'Best wishes and also Happy Birthday for tomorrow, Mummy' written inside.

Maybe I'm not going to die.

Maybe I'm going to live and marry Poppy at Exeter College, Oxford[27] chapel.

Tuesday 30 June

Today is my birthday.

I am twenty-five years old and, in some cruel and vicious practical joke, I feel the worst I've ever felt in my entire life on this, the day that is all about me. Perhaps God isn't a Conservative after all. Perhaps God is ushering me towards death on a day where I celebrate – all things being equal – a fifth of my life having elapsed. Surely only a sadistic, cruel God would infect me with Covid on one of my precious weeks of annual leave…?

I spend nearly the whole day asleep and get roused at points by Poppy, who has made me a cake which I can't taste.

None of the chaps have wished me a happy birthday, but Carrie has sent over some pieces from Reiss on the government account, which is kind.

Poppy spends most of the day sitting by my bedside and making notes on *How Only the Paranoid Survive* ahead of the future prediction weekend.

Her hair falls in front of her face as she's studying; it's beautiful.

I try to start writing a will but I keep falling asleep on it.

I get Poppy to promise that if I do die she won't run off with Hugo.

'You're not going to die, Rafe,' she says, her hand on my forehead. 'By all accounts you've got a pretty mild case. You'll be fine in a couple of days.'

She doesn't know I'm not going to die.

27 This is where I studied at university.

JULY

Wednesday 1 July

I wake up to discover that, incredibly, I haven't died of Covid in my sleep.

I actually feel a little better this morning. My breathing is easier. I'm still coughing but much less aggressively than before.

'You've got much more colour in your face,' says Poppy, pulling the curtains open and letting in some gentle mid-morning sunlight.

I think I might be cured. I think I might have thrown off Covid-19. I knew I didn't need to worry about getting it. My immune system, like my intellect, is elite. Just like David Cameron and the social welfare system, I've fucked it! Fuck you, Kung Flu!

'I still don't think you should go on this weekend with Big Daddy Cum Cum though, Rafe. You want to ease yourself back into work gradually. This weekend will be intense. I'd spend the next few days in bed,' says Poppy.

I think for a moment.

If I don't pitch up for this, I'll lose my place as one of the spads of tomorrow. If I'm not a spad of tomorrow, I'm not achieving. If I'm not achieving, I'm nothing. If I'm nothing,

I might as well have been struck down by Covid. For what is a man if not the sum of his achievements? What else would there be to distinguish me from the rest of my year at Oxford and Eton?

'I'll make a call about it on Friday,' I say.

I'm definitely going to go.

Friday 3 July

I'm feeling much more myself today.

I've tentatively gone out to Pret twice over the last couple of days. My temperature is totally gone, and my cough is only very mild now.

'I'm going,' I say to Poppy on Friday afternoon.

I've definitely fucking got this.

Saturday 4 July

As we all assemble outside Number 10 in the morning light, I feel dizzy but otherwise I'm fine.

Everyone is there by 5.30am: me, Poppy, Charlotte, Hugo (the prick), Jamie, Felix, Tabby, Abby, Henry, Alexander, Max, Ben, Liv, Emily and Cecilia.

Then, seemingly without arriving, or being noticed by any of us, Big Daddy Cum Cum appears from the crowd.

He's wearing a T-shirt which says 'Amazon' on it (a nod to Bezos?!), is carrying a large stick and appears to be wearing some patterned, floaty trousers, like a girl who has travelled to Bali might wear.

'Welcome bees,' he says gleefully. 'You must all put all your possessions and clothes into the bucket to my right. Your new clothes are in the bucket to my left. Fifteen of the most promising spads come into this weekend – let's see how many of you deliver on your promise. From now on you do not have names –only numbers. In this bucket you will find yours.'

The 'clothes' Big Daddy Cum Cum has promised are just human-sized bin bags.

Hugo gets to the bucket before me and claims number 1. I'm left with 13.

Lee Cain then blindfolds and forces us on to a great big school bus (?!) that Big Daddy Cum Cum has somehow commandeered. The Big Daddy drives like a lunatic, speeding round corners and blaring 'Anarchy in the UK' by the Sex Pistols on repeat at the highest volume.

After about thirty minutes of this, Big Daddy Cum Cum pulls up and we all pile out of the school bus.

Lee Cain removes our blindfolds for about ten seconds, and we all see we're back at Number 10. I look out for Poppy who seems a bit shaken but okay.

'Look, we're right back where we started, you idiots. Reality doesn't mean anything any more,' says Dom.

Lee Cain then puts our blindfolds back on and forces us back onto the bus.

The music begins again and this time the journey is longer: it lasts at least three hours. The driving is still phenomenally fast, but the roads are straighter. By the end of the trip, I can't tell if he's stopped playing 'Anarchy in the UK', It's ringing in my brain, and I can't make it stop. I've also got a splitting headache.

We're outside and Lee Cain rips off our blindfolds and I see we're all assembled in a circle with Lee Cain and Big Daddy

Cum Cum in the middle. In the background is some kind of castle.

'Bees, what the hell are you doing? Hunt for the runes! I am your Queen, and you will bring me my runes!' Big Daddy Cum Cum shrieks at us all.

'Get on your knees and hunt for the runes!' screams Lee Cain right in Emily's face.

None of us have any idea what we're doing but we all crawl around trying to make it look like we do.

Lee Cain has a cigarette lighter he keeps using to burn people who look like they're slacking.

'You can always give us your number,' Lee Cain keeps shouting as some of the girls start crying.

We all crawl around for about an hour before Big Daddy Cum Cum says gleefully: 'You fools, there were no runes after all.'

We then all sit around a fire and one by one get pulled off for interrogation.

Hugo goes, then Poppy goes, then Emily.

When Poppy returns she looks shaken but okay. I try to meet her eye, but she seems too afraid to look up.

Finally, a hood gets put over my head and when it's pulled off, I'm in front of Lee Cain by himself.

My heart is beating very fast. I haven't had a drink of water in hours, and I feel terrible. I shouldn't have come on this weekend.

I'm expecting Cain to scream but he's so gentle with me – in a way I didn't think he was capable of.

'Are you okay, Rafe?' he asks.

I pause for a moment then, voice shaking, say softly, 'I don't feel amazing to be honest. I don't think I've fully recovered from Covid. I feel weak and dizzy.'

'Did you get round to having a read of that book?' he says maternally.

'No,' I say, and close my eyes as I do, hoping this will all be over.

When I reopen my eyes, I'm sat across from Big Daddy Cum Cum who's screaming at me: 'Number 13! You chatty rat! It was me all along, you fool. You've just admitted you haven't done the reading! You haven't read *How Only the Paranoid Survive* have you?! Admit it!!'

'I have, Dom, I promise,' I lie.

'What's the first chapter called then?'

I pause.

'I don't know,' I say.

'Traitor!' he screams. 'Take him away!'

Then I'm sat at the fire again.

Sunday 5 July

I wake up in my bed in Clapham, but something doesn't feel right.

Though I can see my room before me, it's so cold and I can feel the wind.

I realise Big Daddy Cum Cum has put a VR headset on me in my sleep! I'm still on the future prediction weekend! I rip off the headset and see the same frightening, anxiety-inducing setting from the day before, and the castle in the background, which I now recognise to be Barnard Castle. Of course.

Today's assault is more mental than physical; there is no crawling. Instead, Big Daddy Cum Cum will read out a quote from his blog and we all have to compete to tell him which blog on which date it's from.

I get none of the references – unlike fucking Hugo, who offers correct answer after correct answer like a virgin in a quiz. I feel slow, and mental concentration feels almost intolerably effortful (is this how non-Oxbridge people feel all the time?).

At around lunchtime we all pile back into Big Daddy Cum Cum's school bus and Poppy and I are back in Clapham by the early evening. Poppy is very emotional after the whole thing. She spends about an hour showering and I think I hear her crying.

I'm actually dealing with getting Covid and the mass psychological hazing I've experienced over the last week vary wall.

I order a large Domino's pizza and work my way through it. Normally I wouldn't eat something this working class but today I just really feel like it for some reason.

Poppy comes and cries on me for a bit, I hug her while I'm eating and when she heads off to bed, I order some fried chicken on Deliveroo; it's so delicious I order some more. I just really feel like eating.

Monday 6 July

I wake up feeling totally recovered from Covid and the weekend, but as I come out of the shower I see an Apple News alert informing me that Ghislaine Maxwell has been arrested, which is really crushing news. I don't know Ghislaine but she's exactly the type of high-functioning, networking girl putting Oxford on the map, and you hate to see someone like that get taken down for stuff that could really be taken both ways.

Poppy is still bad this morning. She keeps crying and tells me she's going to take the day off. I think the old girl has taken the whole future prediction weekend quite badly. That's the thing about women: they do struggle to manage their emotions.

She asks me if I want to talk about what happened over the weekend, but luckily I'm fine so tell her I don't need to, with a smile.

I stop by Pret in the morning and grab an egg and bacon baguette; classic.

I wander to my desk and see, bizarrely, that Hugo is sat there…

'I know you only studied at Regent's, Hugo, but surely even you are clever enough to know this isn't your desk,' I say acerbically.

'I sit here now, mate,' he says without looking up from his laptop. 'I don't think Big Daddy Cum Cum was very impressed with your performance over the weekend. Enjoy working on Test and Trace – there's lots to be done.'

I can't believe this.

Hugo, the Harrovian chopper, has taken my place.

The Harrovian chopper from Regent's Park has usurped future Prime Minister Rafe Hubris.

I stride, furiously, to Hugo's desk, which has on it some tablets, an enormous folder and on that a piece of paper which reads:

Drone Bee, Hubris R,

Your performance over the weekend was decidedly sub-intellect.

To regain the status of worker bee you must embark on this course of mental enhancement medication and will be redirected to Test and Trace.

Read all the essays of Warren Buffett before I next see you.

Osama

I'm so angry I throw my Pret egg and bacon baguette across the Number 10 office with all the power of my 130mph serve.

I instantly regret this and, as it hurtles through the air, I pray it doesn't hit anyone important.

Fortuitously, it hits the new spad, Daniel, who, despite my demotion, is still very much beneath me.

Unfortunately, my blind rage drowns any relief I might otherwise have felt.

I briefly consider killing myself but stop myself acting on it because I have Poppy to live for; I also have money to collect from my tenants and if I'm dead that won't be possible.

When I get home Poppy seems much better. She's had a conversation with her mum, and she looks happier and calmer.

'Are you okay?' she asks, stroking my hair.

I tell her about Hugo. I tell her that she and the knowledge that I will emerge from this as prime minister are about the only things keeping me alive.

We make emotional and deeply meaningful love and as I ejaculate, I think about Hugo being handed a P45 form.

The stupid, slimy Harrovian prick.

Wednesday 8 July

My fury has been replaced by depression.

This depression also isn't helped by the fact I've had a proper look at what Hugo's been doing on Test and Trace for the last three months and it's basically fucking nothing.

He went to Apple and Google in April and asked them to sort an app for us,. He then fell out with Apple and Google and arrogantly decided to create the app himself, which he completely fucked. By the looks of it he then gave up on the whole thing in mid-June.

In essence then, we're no closer to sorting a Test and Trace system than we were in April and my only option is to send a long grovelling email to Apple and Google asking if they can help us wipe our own shit off ourselves. I simply don't know if I can do this. I'm depressed and it's incredibly common to grovel.

I decide in the meantime to focus instead on the Texas BBQ chicken pizza from Domino's that's just arrived. As I'm about halfway through the pizza (but totally out of garlic and herb dip – you hate to see it) I get an email from osamabinladen@gov.uk which says:

Bees!

Rishi has come up with an unconventionally wise plan to help kickstart the economy and get the herd eating again. We need something to advertise it; the spad that can come up with the best wording in the next fifteen minutes will be promoted.

Email me with your submissions.

Osama Bin Laden/ Classic Dom

My heart flutters. This could be it. This could be my way out of this horrible dark hole I currently find myself in.

I apply all the focus, energy and concentration of my

Oxbridge brain to come up with three of the pithiest zingers I can think of.

I go over to Poppy's desk, refusing to even look at Hugo sat next to her (the prick) and ask which is the strongest out of:

Masticate to stimulate
Eat out to help out, and
Go out for dinner to stop the economy getting thinner.

'Definitely *Eat out to help out*, Rafe,' she says clearly and confidently.

I rush to my desk and email Dom.

I throw the pizza in the bin.

I don't need pizza where I'm going.

Fifteen minutes later, Dom appears in the Number 10 office.

I start packing up my stuff to move back to Hugo's desk.

'Thanks for your submissions, guys,' says Dom. 'Some really inventive ones.'

Yes.

'The clear winner though is…'

Yes.

'Eat out to help out.'

YES. FUCK YOU, HUGO, IN YOUR STUPID SMUG FACE.

'By Hugo.'

What the fuck?

'Well done, Hugo,' says Dom, and with that he leaves.

He's stolen it from me. He's stolen my fucking zinger.

'Mate, do you want to tell me why you stole my fucking zinger?' I ask him.

'I didn't steal anyone's zinger, I thought of that myself,' he says, looking me square in the eye as he does.

The man is an audacious cunt. Obviously I did the exact same thing to him with *Bung a Bob for Brexit Bongs*, but that was totally different because it benefitted me; this completely screws me over, which is completely fucking out of order.

I return to the bin and retrieve the Domino's pizza and carry on eating.

Friday 10 July

'Rafe darling, you're eating an awful lot at the moment, do you not think maybe you should slow down?' says Poppy, as the pair of us are eating a carbonara.

I've already had a pizza for dinner but this is my second dinner.

I'm also on my second bottle of Sauvignon blanc.

'I'm eating because I'm hungry,' I snap at her. 'I've spent all day busting my balls at work and that makes me incredibly hungry. You know that, Poppy.'

'Yes, but do you not think maybe you've had a bit too much high-calorie food this week?' she says. 'How many Dominos have you had since Monday?'

She makes me check my email receipts. It's seven. But they were seven necessary Dominos. I needed them to keep my blood sugars up.

'Are you saying I'm fat, Poppy, and you don't want to have sex with me any more?'

'I'm not saying that,' says Poppy.

'Well it feels an awful like that is what you're saying,' I say, taking an enormous mouthful of carbonara.

'I just think, Rafe, you're upset about what's going on at

213

work, and probably also processing the anxiety of getting Covid and the future prediction weekend, and instead of dealing with it, you're using food to compensate. I think we should talk about why you're feeling like you're feeling.'

'There's nothing to talk about! I'm fucking going to bed,' I say.

I take with me the cheesecake I'd ordered for pudding.

The front door slams as she leaves.

Why do women constantly want to talk about feelings? I'm fucking fine. I'm obviously fine. If Poppy wants to be a wetty and cry all the time that's her own fucking lookout but I'm not going to be dragged into it. I'm a man; we don't really experience negative emotions,. We're more evolutionarily adapted in that way.

About half an hour later I miss Poppy terribly and regret shouting at her. I call her several times, but it goes through to voicemail. She's either gone to bed and put her phone on aeroplane mode or…she's fucking Hugo and keeps pressing the call decline button as soon as I ring, every single time.

I can't stop thinking about this dystopian nightmare; first Hugo takes my job, then my woman.

I do not sleep very well.

Saturday 11 July

It transpires Poppy had gone to bed and wasn't fucking Hugo.

I spend the morning workshopping the poem I'd written for her and deliver it to her along with coffee and flowers.

While we make forgiveness love I notice I'm breathing a little more heavily during sex than I normally do and I struggle with a few more of the athletic positions this time. I sweat quite a lot too and at one point a drop from my forehead falls into Poppy's eye.

'This evening I've got some of the girls from work coming over,' Poppy says.

'Do you need me to get some wine for us?' I ask.

'Actually, Rafe, I was thinking it was going to be more of just a girls' night. We've been spending so much time together it might be good to have a night off.'

'Sure,' I say, struggling to hide how hurt I feel as I digest the news. 'Would you mind leaving your phone on tonight? It's just I tried to call you last night and I thought you were fucking Hugo behind my back.'

'Rafe.'

'You weren't, were you?'

'Of course not. I don't know where this has come from, Rafe,. We had an argument – that's normal in a relationship. It doesn't mean I'm going to go and have sex with someone I don't even fancy behind your back!'

'So you'll check your phone?' I press. 'It's just you're the best thing in my life, Poppy. I don't know what I'd do without you. I love you,' I say.

'You know I love you too,' she says,. 'I'll have my phone on, but my attention is going to be with the girls. I'll phone you before bed though, okay?'

I check my phone at ten-minute intervals throughout the night and fixate on Poppy's WhatsApp to see whether or not she's 'typing…' and if so, to who.

I get a horrible feeling that Poppy has created the idea of a girls' night as a ruse to get Hugo round and have sex with him behind my back.

I start drinking because it helps me worry a little bit less about the image of Hugo's massive Farquaad-esque chin jutting into the ether as he rails Poppy in various positions. He is such a prick.

It gets to eleven (surely a reasonable time to go sleep?!) and no call from Poppy. Midnight: no call. At about half past midnight I text Poppy telling her I'll be going to sleep and that I thought she was going to call?

I pretend my phone is about to be put on aeroplane mode to get her to text back quicker but she doesn't.

She's definitely fucking someone else. I can't believe she would fucking do that to me.

I sit awake on a website called 4chan reading an entry by someone called 'incelebration' called 'Females: their duplicity explained'.

At 3:10 Poppy texts:

Hey babe,

Sorry I missed you, was having so much fun with the girls.

Going to bed now. Night night, love you and see you tomorrow.

She wasn't fucking someone else and she wants to see me tomorrow! I feel such relief. God she's lovely. I am so in love with her.

Monday 13 July

At eleven, I get a tap on the shoulder at my desk.

It's Dildo Harding.

'Rafe!' she says, glasses askew, a scarf messily thrown over her torso. 'I've been emailing your website non-stop, but I haven't had any texts back!' she says.

After some back and forth, I ascertain that by 'emailing my website' she means she's written 'Rafe, let's meet for a coffee' several times in a Word document because she hasn't worked out how to use the internet.

It becomes abundantly clear that getting into a conversation that's even mildly technical with Dildo Harding is going to be a dead end. I tell her the best thing for us both to do is go back and email each other's websites for the rest of the day so she'll leave me alone.

I haven't emailed Apple and Google yet. I just don't know if someone of my position in society ought to have to apologise to someone.

At lunch I go to sit next to Poppy, who's sat with some of the other girls from the office. She's laughing and joking with them all and it makes me feel incredibly fucked off that she's not laughing and joking with me. I decide to text her while we're at the table:

'Let's go and sit somewhere else. I want it to be just us.'

She sees the text flash up on her phone and turns her phone over.

Wednesday 15 July

Given the predilection of senior Tory MPs for committing racial gaffes it's been decided that MPs need to be put through unconscious bias training. Unconscious bias, as I understand it, is where someone unconsciously discriminates against a particular group because of a set of preconceived, unconsciously held notions about said group. For example, someone might look at the group of conventionally attractive white men, of which I'm obviously a member, and think we'd have boring and samey chat because we haven't had to develop interesting personalities because our good looks have carried us through. This is patently false in my case, as this memoir will attest. My chat is as varied as it is high-end.

Rather than educating ministers about unconscious bias against chaps, though, I've been given the thankless task of educating ministers about subconscious bias around race.

The meeting is difficult.

In the first five minutes one of the senior Tory MPs barges into the room shouting 'Thought Police!' and brandishing a copy of George Orwell's *1984*. After twenty minutes I haven't even got beyond the first slide of the presentation I've put together.

What happens is, I advance a premise and immediately one of the Tory MPs will pipe up and challenge it, for example:

> *Rafe:* We can all agree that racism is bad.
> *Tory MP:* Well, hang on. What's the context? Surely, you're not suggesting racism is always bad!? What if it's towards the French?!

This will attract murmurs of approval and send us down the path of painful ethical debate.

Many of the ministers look bored. Some of them are on their BlackBerries, others talking among themselves.

That is until I receive a notification that makes the whole room go silent.

All the colour drains from my face and I drop my phone.

'What on earth is the matter, boy?' asks one of the MPs.

'It's Pret,' I say, voice shaking. 'Pret is struggling as a result of the pandemic. It might have to close down.'

In unison, all BlackBerries are dropped and all conversation stops. It's as if time has stood still.

'There must be something…anything we can do,' says one of the MPs.

'We cannot just sit idly by and let this happen,' says another.

'This is the greatest injustice Britain faces today,' says a third.

We scrap the racism stuff there and then; it can wait.

We rename the meeting 'Pret a Récupérer', which is my wordplay and would be funny if this all wasn't so serious.

We sit feverishly brainstorming what we can do, and how much money we can throw at it to help.

'I'll take some out of my children's education fund,' says one.

'I'll give some of the money I'm paid to consult with big banks on the side,' one more says.

By the end of the meeting, we have a semblance of a plan and agree to meet every Wednesday to monitor Pret and reassess what we do relative to its financial status.

Friday 17 July

Poppy hasn't been replying to my texts recently, which is really odd.

I wonder if she's slumped into a depression at the news of Pret…

I text her lots so that she feels valued. Less emotionally aware chaps might not do something like this because they don't really understand how women work. Luckily I do; it's what makes me such a good boyfriend.

Eventually, I get a text from her telling me that we need

to talk. I knew that was the right tactic: message her enough that she feels comfortable to talk about her Pret grief. Elite boyfriending.

This evening I go all out on the food and drink front.

I buy three bottles of AIX rosé, a charcuterie board, some lamb with dauphinoise potatoes for the main course and a chocolate tart for pudding.

Poppy arrives at seven.

She looks conflicted – guilty even, which is a classic sign of depression.

I offer her a glass of wine but she says she won't be drinking.

'Rafe…I don't think I can do this.'

'If you're not hungry you could just have one course,' I say understandingly.

'Not the food, Rafe; me and you,' she starts to tear up. 'I love you, but I just don't feel like this is right. We're not working together. We're arguing. I want for you to be with someone who makes you happy, not someone you're snapping at all the time. I need someone who wants to talk about emotions and stuff and every time I do that, it feels like you resist. I was so heartbroken after Alex ran off with that fucking bitch at KPMG and I feel like I rushed into this too quick, and you were lovely, but I don't think this is right… I love you, but I think we need to be apart.'

She wipes the tears from her eyes and leaves.

As the door closes, this incredibly weird thing happens.

Water starts falling from my eyes and I start breathing in and out really fast. It's definitely not crying. I'm fine – it's just water falling from my eyes.

Saturday 18 July

I wake up and I'm absolutely fine although I do feel like an enormous hand is pushing me down into the floor and like I'll never know anyone ever again and that no one cares about me.

I invite Matt Cock-in-his-Hands over for brunch.

Normally I'd find his weird cloying attentiveness too much but for some reason today it makes me feel a bit less shit. Even though deep down I'm fine, obviously.

I tell him both me and Poppy agreed that we shouldn't be together any more and that I suggested it and though she found it hard to take, she accepted it.

He flicks on a playlist that he says 'really helped him with some break-ups with the *chicas*' (mostly the music of Travis and Keane) and sits with his collar popped and sleeves rolled up like some sort of diabolical Soho creative.

'Listen buddy, if there's one thing I know about the ladies it's that they love a boy who don't play by no rules. I've actually been doing the bad thing with one of the girls in the office; why does she want my hot love? Because I'm a bad boy, Rafe.'

Though the image is obviously absolutely atrocious, there's something kind about this. Matt Hancock cares about me so much he'd make up that he's having an affair to make it seem like anyone can get a woman to have sex with them. This actually might be the nicest thing anyone has ever done for me.

We sit drinking for most of the day in my lounge. I'm still wearing the same clothes as the night before.

Sunday 19 July

I'm making the journey to Virginia Water to celebrate my father's seventieth and Will being made partner at Slaughter and May.

I'm still wearing the same clothes as Friday and spend the entire journey listening to the song 'Bedshaped' by Keane on repeat.

I arrive and stand at the back and let all the speeches wash over me. When they finish I don't really want to talk to anyone so just pile into the buffet. I load my plate up with everything I see that looks good – mostly baguette, profiteroles and smoked salmon. Just as I'm about to go back for more baguette I hear a voice say: 'Fucking hell, Rafe,. Leave some for the rest of us!'

It's Will.

'Jesus Christ, Rafe,' he says. 'I've never seen you so fat.' He then goes to grab my stomach, which isn't even that big. 'Where's this new girl then? Is she hiding behind your massive girth?' he says, laughing.

I refuse to look him in the eye and instead pin my gaze somewhere in the area just above his left shoulder and say: 'We're not together any more.'

'Oh mate, that's heavy. I had a quick stalk of her on LinkedIn though, and she really wasn't very fit – so no big loss.' He pats me on the shoulder and walks off.

In this moment I want to pull him to the floor and shove the vast quantities of baguette on my plate down his throat so hard that he chokes to death and then I want to jump up and down on his stupid face.

I breathe in and let it pass and redirect my anger into absolutely annihilating the buffet.

I get a text from my mother that evening telling me it's a shame I didn't make time to come and find her and that Will says I've put on lots of weight.

I don't reply.

Monday 20 July

I'm totally fine but I'm also kind of dreading the prospect of going into work, but Matt has told me we can just play Grand Theft Auto with Gavin Williamson to get away from everything.

Matt takes me into a side room in the department for Digital, Media, Culture and Sport (a department so unimportant no one will ever look for us there) and hands me a PSP.

I get stuck into gameplay and drive around beating up prostitutes and running away from the police, which is incredibly cathartic.

I play up until about lunch, when I get called into Big Daddy Cum Cum's office back at Number 10.

'Ah yes, Rafe. I thought you might come here,' he says, stroking a large crystal ball in the centre of a desk.

'You invited me here,' I say blankly.

'Tell me, Rafe,' the Big Daddy says, stroking the ball between us. 'Notice anything different about the air?'

I breathe in and smell the slightly synthetic smell of carpet and the waft of coffee.

'Not really,' I say.

'I've been sucking the CO_2 out of it, Rafe. It's got less CO_2 in it. I got funding for it to fuck the elites, Rafe. I'm creating a revolution of the air,' he says, like a child wild on E-numbers.

'Is that why you called me here?' I ask.

'In an unconventionally related way, yes Rafe, yes it is. I've called you here because I need someone to accompany the prime minister to Scotland on Thursday to save the union. We need them so we can continue to suck out CO_2 from the Scottish atmosphere to fuck the elites even further.'

I agree to this and leave.

I'm sat in my lounge listening to Hancock's playlist.

I sit trying to remember the feeling of Poppy running her hands through my hair but it's like trying to grasp air.

I've never felt so alone.

Luckily I'm obviously fine with that.

Tuesday 21 July

I'm sat with Matt and Gavin Williamson in the canteen.

I see Poppy enter and sit down a good five or six tables away from me; my stomach plummets.

She sits next to Hugo and I can't look. I take my tray and leave the canteen just as she's laughing at one of his stupid-prick jokes. The bitch. I knew they were fucking behind my back. Women lure you in with their big eyes and tying your tie and then they're gone. Women are evil.

I explain the whole situation to Dildo Harding after lunch and she takes me to one side and says: 'Listen love, I know it can be hard, but things really do get better, I promise. Hard times go; they pass,' she says.

'How though?' I say.

She smells of nice mumsy perfume.

'When I used to work at TalkTalk, I lost my job because we got hit by a cyberattack. I was sad – of course I was – but soon

I got a job working in tech at the government,' she says.

'You got sacked for being bad at tech and then went on to get another job in tech given to you by the government?'

'Exactly. So however you're feeling it *does* get better,' she says, returning to her Word document.

This is incredibly heartening actually.

Thursday 23 July

Blojo and I are sat on a private plane on the way to Scotland.

He tells me the ingenious plan he's concocted whereby we fly right to the north of Scotland, do a couple of press videos about how important the union is, then fly back by the end of the day.

'The beauty is, we get to maintain the economically useful partnership without having to run into any of the fucking Scots or the fucking Scotch Egg,' (his name for Nicola Sturgeon).

Blojo then embarks on his impression of Nicola Sturgeon, which makes me laugh.

I still can't totally rid my mind of images of Hugo fucking Poppy – in the store cupboard, in the canteen, outside Embargo's – but this is a good distraction.

Blojo and I mess around in front of planes and other nondescript rural Scottish locations and, as promised, don't run into a single Scot. It's bliss.

'You seem a little subdued, old boy,' Blojo says on the plane back.

I tell him about Poppy and the whole situation.

'Ah,' he says. He finishes his whisky and looks right at me.

'A little advice on women, old boy... Women are like cars.

When you've got one, at first, it's incredibly exciting. It looks amazing, it smells great, you'd do anything to have a go in it. But just like cars, women break down a lot. When one of them breaks down, the answer isn't to try and fix her, it's to go and get another car that makes the previous one look like shit. Then you realise the previous car wasn't as great as you thought it was.'

This is the best thing anyone has said to me during this whole thing.

I feel lighter.

I can go and bang someone fitter than Poppy.

I don't need her and her large eyes and her caring hands. I need a fucking worldie.

I sit with Blojo on the plane's WiFi, resurrecting my Tinder.

Rafe is back.

RAFE IS BACK AND VARY, VARY WALL.

Friday 24 July

I wake up to two Tinder matches and feel completely fine again.

Not that I ever felt bad about the Poppy stuff.

With a bit of reflection, I've realised we weren't gelling because she was holding me down when I needed to spread my wings and fly like a bluebird to places like Bluebird to encounter blue-blooded birds. My job has always effectively been my girlfriend anyway, and sadly I don't think Poppy could deal with that. I might meet someone in due course who makes me reconsider everything, but in the meantime this rogue won't be tamed.

Plenty has changed since Poppy and I were together: I've

traded in most of my Ralph Lauren for GANT, I've also changed my fragrance from Chanel Égoïste to Chanel Bleu; I'm basically a different man. From the ashes has risen a better-dressed, better-smelling Rafe.

I'm decisive at work today; focused, sharp.

I bite the bullet and finally email Apple and Google about the Test and Trace app. I manage to avoid grovelling by ending the email with the words:

I look forward to seeing what you can do for me.

I excitedly tell Dildo Harding about my really excellent work here, but I soon realise it's a waste of time trying to explain things to her. She keeps asking whether I mean Braeburn or Pink Lady when I'm talking about Apple, but not as a joke... it's actually quite concerning...

Saturday 25 July

At 11.30 I get a text from Poppy:

Hey Rafe,

How are you doing? I've found this really hard but know it's the right decision. Do you want to have a chat over a coffee or something? We could just talk. No pressure though. I really wouldn't want any of this to stand in the way of work, which I know is really important to us both.

P xx

I can't believe Poppy would fucking do this. How dare she ask how I am? The insensitive prick. I'm obviously fine. She's so fucking toxic.

I phone up Mummy and I tell her about the whole situation but when I ask her for advice all she tells me is to 'keep my chin up'.

I end up inviting Hancock over for a barbecue. We find a way of hooking Grand Theft Auto up to my TV and play together.

'You know Poppy sounds like a real bitch, Rafe,' says Hancock, rubbing some relish he's smeared across his cheek off with the back of his hand, 'and ain't no bitch gonna treat my main homie like that… I've been listening to Stormzy,' he says, eyes wide, grinning ecstatically.

'Thanks mate,' I say, passing Hancock a San Miguel.

Normally I meet Hancock's eye for about 5 per cent of the time as he stares adoringly at me. Today I'm up to at least 70 per cent; he doesn't seem weird any more, he just seems like a friend. I say that… Obviously he's still a bit creepy but it's barely noticeable.

We drink for hours.

'Haven't you got some work to be doing?' I ask.

'I'm not letting anything get in the way of hanging out with my best buddy,' Matt says.

Monday 27 July

At work all I hear is Poppy and Hugo endlessly talking. They won't stop fucking talking to each other. It's intolerable.

I'm sure he's been having sex with her. I can just sense it.

I'm so overcome with fury that I can't take it any more.

I create a fake email account and construct an email to osamabinladen@gov.uk:

Dear Osama,

It has come to my attention that two of your spads, a Mr Hugo Gill and a Ms Poppy Anderson, were copulating in the store cupboard rather than reading *The Myth of Secularism* by Phillip L Troyer as you'd instructed your spads to do.

Do with them what you will.

Yours,
Anonymous

It takes about 25 seconds before Big Daddy Cum Cum has emerged from his office and is interrogating the pair of them.

'You've been copulating haven't you?!' he screams.

'Dom, what are you talking about?' says Hugo.

'You've been copulating in the store cupboard when you should have been reading!' he cries.

'No we haven't,' says Poppy indignantly.

'That's exactly what a guilty person would say. Demoted!' he shouts. 'You are no longer worker bees, you are hereby demoted to drone bees. To the department of Digital, Media, Culture and Sport with you!!'

As the pair of them clear their desks, looking bewildered and angry, I get an enormous rush of serotonin. It's like someone has changed the world from being in black and white to being in colour.

I return after lunch to see a note from the Big Daddy which reads:

Hubris, R,

I know it was you. I know everything. As a reward for your loyalty you have been upgraded to 'worker bee'.

Conventional wisdom is for cunts,

Osama Bin Laden

I also get an email from some techie at Google or Apple. I don't really care. Within twenty minutes, I've got them to agree to start developing an app for us.

I have absolutely fucking crushed work today and you absolutely love to see it.

Tuesday 28 July

I wake up to a text from Poppy: 'I know it was you that made up that false rumour about me and Hugo. I can't believe you would do that, you fucking prick. It doesn't matter how badly you're taking a break-up, you can't just go around destroying people's careers.'

I reply, telling her I'm sorry if she feels I made up a false rumour and then swiftly block her number and all her social media.

It's the only way to deal with psycho women.

I can't believe I haven't done this sooner. It feels amazing.

Friday 31 July

I stride into Number 10 and see a note on my desk telling me I've been moved to the Department of Education to assist Gavin Williamson. I'm definitely slightly fucked off to have been moved from my rightful place in Number 10 but then I remember Poppy will be working in the department of Digital, Media, Culture and Sport and Hugo will be back on Test and Trace with Dildo Harding, which makes me feel better about the situation.

I find Gavin predictably playing Grand Theft Auto with Matt Cock-in-his-Hands, this time in the Department of Education.

'Hey, Rafe, we've missed you at Grand Theft Auto Club,' says Matt, springing out of his chair and clapping me on the shoulder.

'Can you not touch me please, Matt Cock-in-his-Hands? It's fucking weird,' I say in disgust.

He looks crestfallen and slowly gathers his things and leaves.

'Gav, shall we chat plans for mid-August?' I ask.

'Don't worry, Rafe. That's all sorted,' he says. 'Why don't we just pick it up on Monday?'

He gives me a fist bump and returns to his game.

Thank Christ for that. I was really worried he might just have been playing Grand Theft Auto the whole time and not done anything on it.

AUGUST

Monday 3 August

August is in full flow and I'm eating out with Gavin Williamson.
I should clarify this: I mean I'm eating out in a Pizza Express
with Gavin Williamson to help out the economy (under Rishi's
new economic scheme). I'm not eating out a girl, assisted by
Gavin Williamson. I've actually never eaten out a girl... I just
don't think it's vary important...

I ask the Pizza Express waitress for 'the Prince Andrew
special minus the underage girl'. She doesn't get the reference
so I have to painstakingly explain I want an American Hot.

'So Gav, let's talk exams. What plan have you put in place for
grades, et cetera?' (lovely use of Latin) I say, with the business-
mindedness of a conventionally attractive Jeff Bezos.

'Yeah, there's loads of stuff. I've definitely done lots,' he says.

'Great, so what have you done?' I ask.

'Well, I guess the real question is what haven't I done?' he
replies.

'Well, maybe we should start with what you have done first.
Have you got a folder on this?' I ask.

'I definitely have,' he says and looks lost before seemingly
remembering the words, 'but I've misplaced it, unfortunately.'

He seems to remember to look mournful halfway through delivering this.

'Okay. Fine. Let's just talk about the plan,' I say.

He sits for quite some time fiddling with the side of the menu.

I eventually break the silence: 'Gav, you have done work on this, haven't you?' I say, an enormous feeling of dread gripping my stomach. 'Because if you haven't, that would be an enormous fucking problem.'

Gavin then looks at his phone, which is face down, and says: 'Oh is that the time? Sorry, Rafe, I've got to get back, but why don't you get stuck into this for me?'

He then runs out.

He fucking runs out of Pizza Express.

Rafe Hubris has been both metaphorically and literally abandoned, just like his first day at Dragon all over again – except this time it's actually going to affect him in later life.

I sit colouring in the paper chef's hats they give to children in Eton colours while I consider how the fuck I'm going to sort out the entire nation's results in precisely ten days because the minister who was supposed to be doing it has spent the last five months playing on a PSP, drinking strawberry milk and napping in the fucking canteen.

Fuck.

Fuck.

Tuesday 4 August

I'm eating out to help out in Coppa Club today. The whole feel of the establishment is a little middle-middle-class trying to pretend it's upper-middle, which, for me, is a little try-hard.

Nonetheless, I'll continue to do my bit for the economy and conduct practically all my work eating out to help out. I've got this wonderful system in place where I charge the government back for the money I spend on meals, so, really, everybody wins, except I suppose the taxpayer, but then they'll never know so it's fine.

I'm also eating out to help out to assuage some of the immense stress I feel at being completely fucked by Gavin Williamson. I've sent him precisely forty-six emails and have had no replies. I've also scurried round the Department of Education, Health, and Digital, Media, Culture and Sport, but neither he nor his PSP are anywhere to be seen.

I'm meeting Lee Cain to see how we might resolve this tsunami of shit. He arrives looking like he hasn't slept in the last three days. His eyes are bloodshot and he stinks of cigarettes.

He declines when I ask him if he wants food and instead orders two pints…at 11am.

I try to get into explaining the whole exam situation to him but he becomes very agitated by a waitress who comes over and asks us if we're enjoying everything.

'Don't you pretend to fucking care about me,' he says, slurring slightly, "cos you don't – not really. Not when it matters; you'll tell me you want to know how my order is but where are you when I need ya? Fucking nowhere!' he screams, looking like he might be on the verge of tears.

He downs both pints and storms out of the Coppa Club, smashing the door against the wall as he does.

I think the man might have some stuff he needs to work through.

The ominous tunnel of catastrophe continues to loom.

Thursday 6 August

I'm still no further with education. The stress rash I had on my back in May has returned and my upper back now looks a bit like it's made up of pink, fleshy puff pastry. I know I absolutely cannot fail here; it would be wrong ~~for schoolkids not to get the right grades~~ for kids from the right schools not to get the right grades. I recognise this to be my greatest mission thus far in politics; they make you say *Floreat Etona* (May Eton flourish) when you leave school and now is my chance to enact it. Now is my chance to ensure that the bankers, judges and consultants of tomorrow get the places at Oxbridge they deserve. Dare I say it? There is no nobler pursuit.

Given that Lee Cain was about as helpful as Matt Cock-in-his-Hands giving a best man's speech, I've enlisted the help of perhaps the biggest gun there is: Big Daddy Cum Cum. Despite the urgency of the issue at hand I haven't let this stand in the way of my ongoing support of my commitment to Rishi's 'eat out to help out' scheme. It's funny because you'd think chucking us all into restaurants would spread Covid more freely…but then it's government policy, so that can't be right.

I'm sat in Locale, Waterloo, enjoying some gnocchi, when Big Daddy enters. Today he's wearing a Yankees cap, blackout sunglasses, some tight cycling shorts and an oversize jumper. I feel like this is some sort of reference to Princess Diana and may be the old chap leaning into his new-found status as the subject of paparazzi hounding.

He refuses to eat anything from the menu, although he does periodically pour sachets of seeds into his mouth from what look like test tubes he produces from his rucksack.

I explain the situation with exams, my concerns about how to ensure that Eton flourishes and Gavin Williamson's incompetence. Dom sits in silence for about twenty seconds then pushes something towards me. I think it's supposed to be a book but looks more like a sort of folder; it certainly hasn't been properly published. On the front I read: 'Algorithms for the Intellectually Unenlightened, written by Dominic Cummings.' I briefly thumb through; there's about twenty pages of various memes with analysis, some graphs, a transcript of one of Dom's finals papers from Oxford and a picture of Mark Sedwill (the former head honcho of the civil service) with the word 'CUNT' written above it in red letters.

'You think the cure is in some sort of algorithm?' I ask.

But he's already gone.

I guess an algorithm does make sense. I mean, I suppose we could listen to the teachers about where they think their pupils are at, and base grades on that, but then we might get grade inflation from the shit schools, which would devalue the grades of people from high-tier public schools, which just wouldn't be fair...

An algorithm it is.

Hubris triumphs again.

I text Matt Cock-in-his-Hands, asking him to join me in Locale.

When he arrives I leave immediately so he has to pick up the tab. I could have just paid for this on the government account of course, but there's nothing quite like seeing Hancock angry and confused. Moves like this also remind him who's boss, which is essential for Cock-in-his-Hands; he needs reminding. He's like a dog in that way.

Friday 7 August

Today I'm eating out to help out in Pizza Hut, which is really quite fascinating. The owners have clearly made the restaurant into a sort of ironic take on a food bank where all the food and decor is deliberately shit and low-end. From the disinterested staff to the loud and crass supporting cast of 'diners', not a detail has been missed. It's like something at the Edinburgh Fringe, it's so immersive.

I debate starting work on the algorithm before the weekend as I'm watching a particularly promising child actor fist the coleslaw in the salad bar (this is perhaps the one detail they've got wrong as it's a well-known fact that poor people don't eat salad). After some reflection I decide there's no point starting the algorithm this close to the weekend. Given that it's already eleven o'clock, if I start now it'll be time for the weekend just as I'm getting into it, which means I might as well just start on Monday. The thing is, the hard part is working out what we're going to do, which I've already done. Actually doing it is a fucking breeze.

I close my work laptop and ask the waitress for a copy of the *Telegraph* but she refuses to break character, which I greatly respect, and looks at me with a mixture of irritation and disgust before walking off. Instead, I sit scrolling through the nation's finest paper's articles on my phone. I read an article about how apparently we've slapped the north under lockdown to curb a rise in cases. This is so clever that I'm not entirely convinced I wasn't the one who put it in place… This has Hubris written all over it. It makes perfect sense: close down the main club so VIP (the south) can stay open. Genius.

I ask on the WhatsApp chat who was behind the initiative to make the north static to keep the south classic.

This evening I'm told Hugo was behind the northern move which, let's face it, isn't actually that impressive. Anyone could have thought of it. It's also a bit obvious and isn't the sort of more advanced thing Hubris would have done in that position. What Hubris would have done would be to put steps in place to launch northern independence so we don't have to fucking deal with them at all any more. Make Marcus Rashford the prime minister and Gary Lineker the deputy and fuck off and leave us alone. Like all Harrovians, Hugo has fallen short once again, it would seem. He's also a short man so he's fallen short in the physical sense as well.

Sunday 9 August

I read that Pret is asking its workers to reduce their hours as it continues to struggle financially. This really affects me. I make sure I whack out an email to everyone in my contacts:

> Chaps,
>
> I write to you on a matter of grave urgency.
>
> This is an appeal to something close to all of our hearts: Pret.
>
> Pret continues to flounder in the liminal space between financial ruin and prosperity. We must not let it fade away.
>
> Please take this opportunity to buy exclusively from Pret. I reckon we can keep it afloat if we do.

Yours turbulently,

Rafe Hubris
BA (Oxon (2:1 (could have been a first if I'd stopped going out in finals term)))

Monday 10 August

Having fulfilled my moral duty to Pret first thing this morning, I'm eating lunch to help out in perhaps the most classic Rafe place of them all: the Ivy, Chelsea. Dining here is such a Rafe thing to do and you love to see it.

Unfortunately, however, the normally sublime culinary experience I enjoy here is somewhat marred by the fact that I'm yet to hear back from my tech drone at Google or Apple or whichever fucking one it is about sorting this education algorithm. I sent him an email this morning pre-French press coffee and he still hasn't got back to me by lunch! Who the fuck does this prick think he is?

I told him expressly to ditch the app and create me an algorithm to get out of all this fucking mess ASAP Rocky, and he hasn't fucking replied, as if he doesn't work for me?!?

Several hours and a lobster linguine and crème brûlée later, I finally get a reply from him. It reads:

Hi Rafe,

Thanks for this.

I'm going to struggle to get this done by Wednesday night to be honest. Surely you guys have something in place...?

Sorry I can't be of more help,

Alex

Obviously we don't have anything in place, Alex, you fucking BTEC bandit – that's why I'm emailing you, you fuck.

This is not good.

This is really not good.

Fuck.

I send Gavin Williamson a long email pleading with him for help but I know it's a waste of time. I know he'll be playing Grand Theft Auto. I know he probably hasn't ever even logged into his email during his tenure as Education Secretary.

I'm so desperate I thumb through Big Daddy Cum Cum's algorithm book/dossier back at my flat. This is also useless; it's just full of riddles and memes that don't really mean anything.

I pace frantically around my flat, engaging every fibre of my superior Oxbridge brain looking for a solution. Unsurprisingly, it comes to me immediately.

The solution is intimidation.

I must embody Big Daddy Cum Cum when he tried to push that businessman down the stairs after their debate about the euro on BBC radio.

I sit and phone Blojo on WhatsApp audio.

Incredibly, he answers.

'What is it, Rafe?'

'Boris, I need your help, old boy. I need an address. My tech drone from Apple is refusing to do an algorithm for the exams and I need to go round there and intimidate him, ruff him up a bit.'

'How badly are you gonna hurt this guy?'

'Not badly at all.'

240

'If this guy sues me I will be fucking furious.'

'I guarantee you he will not be seriously hurt.'

'How badly hurt will he be?'

'The worst he'll get is a cracked rib. Nothing you didn't suffer at rugby,' I assure him.

He tells me he'll look into it and puts the phone down.

This had better come through or I'm absolutely fucked.

Tuesday 11 August

I wake up to nothing from Blojo.

I'm checking my phone every ten minutes, desperate for him to text back. For the first time in my life I know what it feels like to be one of his spurned mistresses.

It gets to midday and nothing.

One o'clock and still nothing.

I'm starting to assess my options now: I could just resign, sack it off and get a job in consulting or journalism and become prime minister that way. 'Rafe Hubris, BCG, associate' does have a nice ring to it, it has to be said. I could also probably start as an associate, given my masses of experience in government.

I go to the pub and sit watching Sky News on the big screen. They're showing migrants crossing the channel. Families of refugees fleeing France and seeking refuge in the UK. They look scared and distressed and anxious; if only they knew what I'm going through.

Eventually, I bite the bullet and phone Blojo.

'Blojo, have you got this address for me?' I ask, pleadingly.

'Yes, yes,' he says and gives it to me.

'You're truly brilliant, Blojo,' I say, warm relief spreading

241

across my chest.

'Do not fuck this up, Rafe, It's my fucking bollocks on the line,' he says and puts the phone down.

By the evening I'm stood outside techie drone Alex's flat. I'm wearing a balaclava and I'm armed with a crème brûlée torch. I didn't want to go for a big knife: I'm not a thug, but I did want to make him feel somewhat intimidated, so the crème brûlée torch seemed like a nice compromise.

He answers in a dressing gown.

'Mate, I need that algorithm for the exams done or I'm afraid you're going to get brûléed,' I say, calmly pacing into his flat.

'Rafe, what are you doing?' says Alex, bemused.

How the fuck did he work out it was me? It must have been my clipped RP drawl. I knew I should have workshopped a different accent. This literally has to be the only context in life where speaking with RP puts you at a disadvantage.

'How did you know it was me?' I ask.

'How many other people do you think have emailed me about doing an algorithm for the government?' he says, bemused.

Fuck. That's a good point, actually. I don't think I'm cut out for all this violence and intimidation. My excellent teeth, chat and charm mean I'm much more of a networker than an intimidator...

'Look, I can do something for you tonight, if you leave me alone afterwards,' he says, opening the door further to welcome me in.

His flat is *très, très* strong; spacious, lovely city views. Sure it's not Clapham, but it's still vary strong. I take off the balaclava and sit down while Alex hunches over a laptop in a desk in the middle of the room.

'So obviously there's not time to do a detailed algorithm, which would create the fairest option,' he says matter-of-factly.

'That's fine, mate. To be honest, as long as some of the staties have blaps so we can look after the chaps, I really don't mind.'

He gets the algorithm done in ten minutes.

This has to be the finest day of my career.

From the jaws of defeat, Rafe Hubris triumphs. *Floreat Etona! Dulce et decorum est.*

Wednesday 12 August

Gavin Williamson finally replies to my emails, now that I've done his job for him, the workshy fuck.

Hi Rafe,

Great work with the algorithm.

I'll go out and sell it tomorrow to the press.

We've done great here,

Gavin

Thanks for acknowledging that I did all the work, you fucking piece of shit.

My foul mood is dramatically improved when I look over the results in the evening.

I see that all the chaps from Eton have got their grades and the state school people have been knocked down a couple of grades in certain instances, which is perfect. I've expertly trodden the middle way, making sure the right chaps get the right grades while ensuring grade inflation is kept at an all-time low so the right chaps' grades don't seem arbitrary. With my expert supervision, Alex has created a superb algorithm. This is a perfect testament to the value of working smart not hard and you love to see it.

I sit in a Côte Brasserie enjoying a Peroni aloni, relieved, happy and exhausted, knowing that I've truly done something worthwhile in education. It's been a tough old week in politics but it's moments like this that make it all worth it.

Thursday 13 August

I wake up to see that for some reason people are 'angry' and think the results are 'unfair', which I actually find offensive. I worked incredibly hard on that algorithm and I know it was good because I personally received an email from the provost of Eton congratulating me on what a great job I'd done. Sure, some people at Hull Academy might have missed out on a place at Sheffield Ring Road University because they were downgraded from a D to a U, but in the grand scheme of things that's not very important.

The stupid whinging woke elite on Twitter are totally slating the algorithm and the media seem to be whipping the whole thing up into a fucking shitstorm.

We all get called into Number 10, which is fucking annoying because I was going to eat out to help out in Nando's today (like Pizza Hut, this is another one of those ironic takes on a food bank).

'I think it's absolutely disgraceful. The incompetence!' says one of the more gammon-faced old Tories, great big juicy droplets of spit raining down on the table as he speaks.

His comments are met by plenty of 'hear hears' from other senior Tories gathered.

'Sorry, just to cut in,' I say, saving Blojo an earful. 'It wasn't actually bad for all the pupils. For independent school pupils the percentage of As actually went up 4% from the previous year.'

At this, the consternation of the senior Tories is replaced by a tranquillity the likes of which I've never seen before. This is short-lived, however, as within about five seconds they're spluttering loudly: 'Then why on earth have I been called into this meeting?!?'

At this point several of them leave, shouting things like: 'The woke left are taking over!' and 'My free speech is being attacked!'

Once the old Tories have filed out, Matt Cock-in-his-Hands breaks the silence to say: 'Listen guys, I think we should probably ditch the algorithm. I don't think it seems very fair t—'

We all unanimously cut him off at this point by shouting in unison: '*Shut the fuck up, Hancock.*'

Which is nice and, I imagine, rather like the feeling you get being in a choir.

'Look,' says Blojo. 'I think the results are robust and fair. I say we send Gavin out on the press tour and it'll be yesterday's news certainly by the time the weekend rolls around. All those in favour say "aye".'

Everyone except Hancock says aye.

'Right. That's passed then,' says Blojo, clapping his hands together in opposing vertical motions to imply he's just taken out the rubbish. 'Gavin, go out there and sell it old boy,' he adds.

Gavin doesn't answer.

We all look round and no one can see him. He's not here. He hasn't fucking shown up. He's trying to hide from the biggest day in his career. Given that I'm this fucking frenulum's spad, I'm tasked with finding him so he can face the UK's media.

On my way out of the office I jump into a lift with Poppy of all people. I'm definitely totally okay with her but I'm so absorbed in sorting this Williamson mess out that I don't have the energy to make eye contact or conversation with her and am forced to pretend to be on the phone.

I exit the lift and jump in an Uber Lux and get to his house in fifteen minutes. For the second time in a week, I'm doorstepping someone to intimidate them to do something I want. It feels like working for the Russian mafia or something.

His wife answers. She's wearing an apron and looks quite sweet in a sort of 'bake you a cake and discuss why immigration has gone too far' kind of way.

'Hi, my name's Rafe. I work with your husband. I really quite urgently need to talk to him. Is he in?' I ask.

'I thought he was at work,' she says, taken aback. 'He's always doing this,' she comments, an odd mixture of anguish, resignation and sadness on her face. 'Wherever he is, it's not here.' She gently closes the door.

For fuck's sake.

I jump back into another Uber Lux, racking my brains as hard as I can to think where on earth he might be. Then it comes to me. If anyone who isn't Gavin Williamson is going to know where Gavin Williamson is, it's Matt Cock-in-his-Hands.

'Where the fuck is Williamson?' I bark at Cock-in-his-Hands back at the Department of Health.

'I don't know,' he says, sweating and, for once in his life, refusing to make eye contact.

'Don't bullshit me, Hancock,' I say, grabbing him by the scruff of the neck. 'I need to know and I need to know now.'

'Alright, alright. I'll tell you,' he says. 'He's in the downstairs loos… Middle cubicle… Don't hurt him though, Rafe. He's my second-best friend after you.'

As I burst into the downstairs loo I hear Gavin's stupid voice softly say, 'Dammit.'

I bust through the central cubicle with a particularly high-end karate kick and see him fully clothed, PSP in his left hand.

'Ah, Rafe,' he says. 'Great to see you. I was hoping I might run into you. I've got a doctor's appointment now so I'll have to dash. But let's have a coffee tomorrow.'

He tries to push past me but I hold firm.

'Rafe, what are you doing?' he says. 'I'm feeling incredibly sick, Rafe. You wouldn't stand in the way of a sick man trying to see a doctor would you, Rafe? Let me go. I think I've got Covid, Rafe. Don't get too close.'

'You're not going anywhere, mate,' I say sternly and firmly. 'You're going to sit down and take some shit from the British press and I'm not going to let you leave until it's over.'

I sit Gavin in a side room in Number 10 and watch him get angrily shouted at by journalist after journalist.

Watching Matt Cock-in-his-Hands get bullied is classic because he reminds you of the kid in school no one liked getting pasted. The butchery of Williamson is satisfying in a different way, though. It's like seeing the supply teacher who was a massive twat and doesn't have a clue what he's talking about get ripped a new arsehole by your parents at a parents' evening.

Obviously, as I've said, I think the algorithm is great, but my desire to see Gavin Williamson get fucked extremely hard is greater than the desire to see something excellent I've done get praised.

Friday 14 August

The algorithm storm hasn't fucking gone away by the morning. I text Blojo about it but get the following back.

> Sorry, old boy, would love to help but on pre-holiday now so it would technically be illegal for me to work. Got to fucking holiday in Scotland for 'PR'. Hope the local brothel isn't just four cows...although that would be an improvement on some of my old flames.

God, I can't wait to be prime minister so I'm allowed to take a holiday in a crisis.

I arrive at my table in Yo Sushi to see a note. I go to throw it away but in doing so see it's addressed to me. It reads:

> Rafe,
>
> I knew you would be here based on my knowledge of the Chinese alphabet and Elon Musk's philosophy of engineering. Great work on the algorithm. The time will come when you should reverse it, but we must not do that yet. That would be too simple, too easy. When it is time it will be clear to you and

then Whitehall and the elites will come raining down from the sky like the apocalypse, Rafe. Classic Dom, classic Dom.

Conventional wisdom is for cunts,

Osama Bin Laden

As a fan of the algorithm, the produce of Yo Sushi and not having to work when it's not absolutely necessary, I don't need telling twice.

Saturday 15 August

I get a text from Will.

Mate, who the fuck was behind that algorithm? It's an absolute joke.

I reply:

I know mate. I've literally smashed it.

He immediately texts back:

It was you! That needs to get changed right fucking now, Rafe. I've got employees whose kids are missing out on Oxford places because of that algorithm. You've absolutely fucked the state sector. Change it. Now.

I'm not letting this fucking prick counteract my finest work in politics. Also, who gives a solitary shit about the state sector anyway! I reply:

> It's the weekend, mate, so I certainly won't be doing anything
> with the algorithm, which both I and Dom Cummings are very
> proud of, so you can get fucked.

I then turn off my phone for the rest of the day. Prick.

Sunday 16 August

I happen upon some scales in my bathroom in the morning.[28] I
weigh myself and decide there must have been a mistake. It says
I weigh 120 kilos. I'm a tall man but nonetheless I can't think
of a single professional tennis player who weighs that much…
It must be a mistake with the scales.

I go to the shops and buy some new scales, but the result is
the same.

Surely that can't be true.

I take a look at myself in the mirror. All my strong abs, my
lean chest and sculpted shoulders seem to have been replaced
by a somewhat engorged-looking midriff, rather like Blojo.

I wonder if this has anything to do with the 'eat out to help
out' scheme…

Monday 17 August

I've hereby stopped eating out to help out as part of my quest
to reclaim *le rig*. I'm just drinking black coffee and went for a
5K this morning, which I ran in twenty-seven minutes, but I

---

28 This isn't a euphemism for ejaculating on them.

wasn't really trying, so really I'd argue my fitness has probably improved.

Big Daddy Cum Cum has told me to put in place the U-turn on exam grades and the algorithm.

'Now the time is,' he says from under a long cloak (I wonder if the syntax might be a reference to Yoda).

'Why act now, though?' I say. 'Surely this isn't going to make any difference to the low-end state school pupils who've lost out on their grades? They'll have lost their places by now anyway.'

'Don't you see, Rafe?' he says, pulling his hood down. 'That's the point. This is how we're going to tear the elites down. We're going to send Gavin Williamson on an apology tour for something I'd planned all along. Why on earth would the government apologise for something it had planned all along, Rafe?! They won't know how to deal with this information.'

I swiftly leave Big Daddy Cum Cum's office and head to the Department of Education, where I collar Gavin Williamson with the same energy you'd collar a naughty dog that's just run into a farmer's field.

I get him to do some bullshit statement about how there was no way we could have known the algorithm produced unfair results until results day, even though we had all that information the day before. This isn't to say I think the results were unfair; I still support the fuck out of the algorithm but I recognise I have to move with the party. If it benefits me, I will trade in absolutely all my principles, ideas and beliefs for popularity and power. I learnt this one from Blojo.

This evening I'm in the gym for the first time in a vary, vary long time.

There's an absolute worldie next to me on the treadmill.

I keep trying to catch her eye but she doesn't catch mine. I wonder if women actually find men staring at them in gyms as flattering as we think it is. Perhaps they don't, but then all the guys I've ever spoken to about it say they do…

I eventually become disillusioned and sack off the treadmill.

I decide I've already run today so a nice dinner really won't hurt. I throw my wheatgrass and kale smoothie in the bin and instead make some dauphinoise potatoes and beef bourguignon; it is extremely delicious.

Tuesday 18 August

I wake up and get on my scales and see that I'm now at 121 kilos. What the fucking fuck? I literally spent most of the day running?!? And I've put on weight…

I realise it's probably muscle and I head into work.

The Gavin Williamson stuff is still raging today and Blojo's been told to cut his holiday short so he can come and take the helm.

We're debating whether or not Gavin Williamson should stay. The good thing is, given that Gavin Williamson hasn't shown up to the meeting, we can discuss him freely.

The difficult thing here is that Gavin has actually done so little work that it's very difficult to meaningfully assess how valuable he is to the Conservative Party and the government as a whole.

Matt Cock-in-his-Hands will occasionally chirp up to say that Williamson should stay because 'he's kind', and 'actually a ruddy good bloke'.

Silence falls as everyone sits considering.

'Right, Gavin stays,' says Blojo. 'If he goes, it'll be a fucking nightmare to get someone new. We can't just bend the knee again because a load of people want us to.'

From here, Blojo and I have to draft a statement to give to the fucking press.

We genuinely sit for about twenty minutes, throwing out positive adjectives to explain why Gavin Williamson ought to keep his job, but none of them seem right. The problem is, after the press annihilation he's just suffered, no adjectives implying skill or competence are going to ring even remotely true.

Eventually, we decide the best thing we can say about Gavin Williamson is that he's loyal, and just hope the public have forgotten about the fairly well-publicised affair he had a couple of years ago, which casts a great ironical shadow over the endorsement.

'Right, I've got to go, old boy – session with the personal trainer – sadly not a woman,' Blojo says, and flaps out.

Gavin goes out and says he's very sorry while also not really acknowledging it's really his fault (the politician apology special). He suggests that they acted as they did to protect the disadvantaged children (when in reality it's too late for them). I sincerely hope I never ever have to work with this prick again.

On my way back home I see that not only is Pret struggling, M&S (which I often think of as backup Pret, or Pret Poly) is also in grave danger and has cut 7,000 jobs. We really need to fucking sort out this virus. People are starting to get properly affected now and it's not funny.

Thursday 20 August

I have a session with Blojo's trainer this morning.

He's surprisingly posh for a trainer; I thought they were all mostly *Love Island* alumni and exclusively from Essex. This chap is from a private school and is vary, vary good. He puts me through my paces, gives me a diet and exercise plan and we agree to meet every other day. I am building my rig back better. The best thing about it is, we're just invoicing the sessions to the Treasury.

GCSEs are out today and, to prevent another massive public outcry, we've let all the shit schools have good grades. I'm a bit annoyed about this because it's going to make it harder for Oxbridge academics to discern between good candidates (Eton, Westminster, St Paul's, Scabby Abbey) and shit ones from budget schools, but I don't let it distract me too much as I'm well into my fitness journey.

It's mostly just juices and chicken breasts.

My trainer texts me to keep me accountable every half an hour. I'm feeling strong, *très* strong.

Saturday 22 August

I've sat on the spinning bike for four hours and I feel incredible.

I've got tennis with Blojo later as well.

I just love fitness. The best thing about it as well is not only doing it but getting to talk about it. I get to have two lots of endorphins: one from doing the workouts and the diet; the second from talking about them. It's brilliant.

This is what I'd normally do over the course of the day:

06:00 Wake up
06:15 Black coffee, smoked salmon and a Pret rice cake
06:30 Workout 1
07:30 Smoked salmon
09:00 Smoked salmon and a Pret rice cake
10:30 Rice cake
11:00 Workout 2
13:00 Smoked salmon and a Pret rice cake
15:00 Smoked salmon
16:30 Smoked salmon and a Pret rice cake
17:30 Workout 3
18:30 Smoked salmon and a rice cake
20:00 A protein shake made by blending up some smoked salmon and Pret rice cakes
21:00 Bed

It's an amazing lifestyle which everyone should take on. This is the thing about fitness, anyone can do it. Just invest in a personal trainer. It's not hard. Also, if poor people tried not to eat out so much and not to drink masses, they'd have more than enough money left over to pay for four or five sessions with a personal trainer per week and the sorts of high-quality foods you'd need to maintain an excellent rig. The reason they don't is just laziness.

Monday 24 August

I've already dropped five kilos since I started this fitness journey and feel incredible for it. God, fitness is so amazing.

Though the Gavin Williamson stuff has quietened down

by now, we've been called into a general meeting to discuss migrants boats and rising Covid cases.

I have to say, re the migrants coming over, for the first time in my life, I've actually changed my mind. Watching parents ferry their children across the Channel in the hope of fleeing war-torn countries and the prospect of being bombed is pretty grim. I mean, I know we didn't fuck up everything in the Middle East to begin with, so technically we shouldn't have to take responsibility for this, but surely you'd be pretty heartless to turn their lilos made out of recycled Fanta bottles and thread back around and force them to risk life and limb to travel back to Calais…

I wonder if Bully Patel actually doesn't have a heart, or that part of the brain required to feel empathy. She keeps banging her fist on the table when she's told she can't use the Navy to intercept the migrants.

The conversation moves to rising case numbers. I wonder if the initiative to get us all to sit in enclosed restaurant spaces together has anything to do with it…

'We absolutely must do something here,' says Chris Wetty urgently.

'What can we do?' I pipe up. 'The economy is going down the shitter. If we lock down again, Pret won't survive. If a thousand – or even several thousand – people have to die to save Pret, then that's what's going to have to happen. We have to be utilitarian about this.'

This draws murmurs of agreement from everyone (except the scientists) who would have done John Stuart Mill's *Utilitarianism* for their Oxford prelims and will have enjoyed the reference.

'None of this would be as much of a problem if we had a functioning Test and Trace system,' Wetty fires back.

My lip curls as he says this. My response is so ready, it jumps from my conventionally attractive lips before I even need to think of it. 'Yes, how is Test and Trace coming along, Hugo?' I say, applying all the new muscle I've acquired from all of my fitness to stop my lip curling.

I then watch Hugo get fucked by ministers for about ten minutes. It is glorious.

Thursday 27 August

Rumour has it that Bully Patel hasn't taken the call for compassion re migrants very well. Felix, who's working for her in the Home Office, says she apparently wants to start arming the Navy with tasers to deter refugee children from coming to the UK. She's also apparently been calling civil servants 'pussies' for suggesting that this is barbaric.

I wonder if Bully Patel would ever use a taser herself. I briefly imagine her in a PVC skirt using one on me.

For some reason I can't quite fathom, I feel very sexual at work today.

Monday 31 August

Covid cases are apparently rising so we've been called into a GM, which is a pain, but on the plus side the US Open tennis has begun and you absolutely love to see it, so yin and yang...

Today's GM is different from previous ones as we're joined for the first time by Carrie, sausage dog in the crook of her arm, Prada bag over her shoulder. Her presence greatly displeases Big Daddy Cum Cum, who tries to block Carrie's entry by putting his arm across the doorway and saying clearly and bluntly, 'No girlfriends allowed.' Carrie ducks under his arm (surely he would have predicted this?!) and slides both herself and her dog into the seat on Blojo's right-hand side, which is usually occupied by Big Daddy Cum Cum.

'Right. Everybody out,' says the Big Daddy, clearly incensed. 'I need to have a word with the prime minister alone!'

'What is it, Dom?' says Blojo, sounding agitated. 'Just say it here in front of everyone; we're not clearing the room.'

Dom looks absolutely furious and Lee Cain, sat next to him, is gripping the table so hard his knuckles have turned white.

'Prime Minister, we cannot allow unelected romantic partners to make big decisions; she has to go.'

Lee Cain barks and gnashes his teeth like a dog in agreement with the Big Daddy.

'You're not elected,' Carrie fires right back. 'Why should Boris listen to you anyway?!' Winston, Carrie's sausage dog, barks and gnashes his teeth in agreement with Carrie, also like a dog (he is a dog).

Both parties look at Blojo (also a dog, but in a completely different sense altogether) for some sort of decisive action, but unfortunately Blojo doesn't know what that is and he flounders. He appears to be stuck between two dominant personalities, both fighting for him. Rather than choosing a side, he waits ten seconds and then begins recounting an anecdote about the time he was writing at the *Telegraph* and got so drunk he free-wrote an article with no research or checking back over the sentences he'd written and the whole thing got published.

'That said,' he quips, doing his best to cut the tension with humour, 'I was still a right side better prepared than Matt Hancock.'

This does attract laughter, most notably from Matt Hancock,

who is now trying to laugh along with his bullies in an unsuccessful attempt to make it so that they're laughing with him, not at him. However, it does nothing to resolve matters. For the entire duration of the story, Big Daddy Cum Cum stares furiously at Carrie, who sits texting with one hand and showing him her middle finger with the other.

The meeting begins with applause for Rishi, whose 'eat out to help out' scheme has palpably boosted the economy by getting people to eat in mostly unventilated indoor spaces. Blojo then hands over to Dom for a speech on how, unrelatedly, Covid cases are majorly up and rising fast.

The Big Daddy embarks on a presentation, turning out all the lights in the room, leaving just the projector and Carrie's iPhone (she's still texting).

He begins by showing us a white square on the projector screen.

'What do you all think this is?' he asks, pacing up and down.

'I think this is fucking facile,' says one senior minister who is then swiftly and gruffly escorted out of the meeting by Lee Cain.

A few of the senior Tories mutter things about 'woke culture' and 'not even being allowed to sing "Rule Britannia" any more', but silence quickly resumes.

'It's the moon,' says Dom. 'As cases rise and we refocus on the herd, the moon is the way forth. We must listen to it, observe how it affects the tides and understand the unconventional wisdom it teaches to solve Covid and allow the herd to resume their normal conventional lives. That will be all,' he says and returns to his seat to some muted spad applause and a theatrical yawn from Carrie, designed to antagonise him.

'Yes, stupendous,' says Blojo, sniffing out the opportunity to not have to do any work.

'Good to see you moon-shooting over more than just women who write for the *Telegraph*, Blojo,' I say hilariously, like some sort of *Mock the Week* panellist. Blojo and everyone at the meeting (except Carrie) roars with laughter.

'Right, Is that it?' he says. 'I'm more desperate for food than an African.'

Bully Patel smirks – or that may just be her face. It's hard to tell.

'Very quickly,' I say to Blojo, 'there's an email I've just opened from a while ago from one of our chaps in the north asking if we can lift their lockdown because they think it's no longer necessary.'

'Not my problem,' says Blojo, as he and everyone else files out of the room.

I take that to mean we can unlock the northerners and, in classic Hubris fashion, delegate the task to Daniel, who we've all been calling Marcus since the Cock-in-his-Hands incident.

SEPTEMBER

Wednesday 2 September

I'm sat in work watching the Murray/Nishioka US Open highlights. Murray has come back from hip surgery, and from two sets to love down, to defeat Nishioka. He's definitely good at tennis, Murray, but with my serve I think I'd probably beat him. Obviously, I didn't go pro because I was always destined for the corridors of power. All I'm saying is, if it had been me in the Wimbledon final in 2013, much like every Tinder match I've ever secured, he'd have found me a handful.

I'm unceremoniously interrupted from the highlights by Marcus (Daniel) who says all the northern leaders are slating the decision to lift the northern lockdown. Apparently cases in somewhere called Bolton were up by 59 per cent last week. The man calling himself Mayor of Manchester (which for me is about as prestigious as titles like 'the Aristocratic Savage', 'the Giant Dwarf' or 'Stig of the Dump') has been slagging off the move all over Radio 4 this morning.

I tell Marcus to do what we always do when there's a big public outcry over something we've supposedly done 'wrong', and just U-turn. I usher him away from my desk and return to the highlights. Murray seems to be lobbing a lot, which is fine

261

if you're playing a short guy like Nishioka, but it just wouldn't fly against someone of my height and general athleticism…

Thursday 3 September

Unsurprisingly, given my talent and high birth, I've been selected to work on Operation Moonshot. I'm having to work with Cock-in-his-Hands in the Department of Health, which is definitely unfavourable but surely can't be as bad as what I've just endured at the hands of Gavin Williamson (who I still haven't seen since, the prick).

We all sit down, crushing Deliveroo (*merci beaucoup*, taxpayer) and brainstorm. I'm still guarding my excellent reclaimed rig so I'm nailing sushi; you love to see it. You've got to hand it to the Japanese: excellent cuisine and a history of empire; strong, *très* strong.

The problem with Operation Moonshot is that Matt Cock-in-his-Hands is now aware of how phenomenally unpopular he is and how badly he's done throughout this pandemic, so to compensate, is quite literally shooting for the moon and aiming for things not even a competent politician could deliver. He wants a system where a million tests are carried out every day and the people who test negative for the virus then get a passport which allows them to go out and mix with other people, while those with a positive test are made to stay inside.

This obviously entirely rests on Test and Trace being not only tangible but also credibly not shite; it is neither of these things.[29] We all know there are fucking articles all over the internet from contact tracers explaining how they just sit with

29 For non-Oxbridge readers who may have some difficulty with double negatives, by this I mean Track and Trace doesn't exist and is shit.

their feet up all fucking day because they have nothing to do. I suppose you could say the system is a Test and Disgrace (classic).

'Matt, you can't create an entire system based on technology which doesn't even exist,' says Emily.

'Shoot for the moon and you'll land among the stars,' he says, grinning madly like a fucking moron (what kind of a government official thinks this is a good thing to say?).

'We can't enact this, Matt. The app isn't ready and my guy at Google isn't going to have it for at least another three weeks,' says Hugo.

'You can have it ready, Hugo. I believe in you,' says Matt, glaring so manically it's as if he's high on ecstasy. I bet he's never actually done it though; he's such a wetty.

'You're so clever, my G, I think you're amazing. You got this, yeah?' Matt says in that appalling faux gangster accent he does.

With that, he departs. The man is a disaster. The man is a fucking disaster.

As a way of dealing with the stress, I create a WhatsApp chat called 'What the fuck is going on?!'

I spend the rest of the day creating various memes lampooning Hancock, which fly back and forth among the various ministers, spads and civil servants that have joined. By the end of the day the group has reached one hundred members…

Friday 4 September

I'm sat at lunch with Lettie and Hugo.

I feel like there's no point dwelling on the past with Hugo and who wronged who. There's no need to discuss it; we're not women. Like anything in life, it's best just not to acknowledge it, and that way it goes away.

Lettie is fresh off furlough and, classic as ever, she's smoking a Marlboro Gold in the canteen. The girl is genuinely a fucking riot.

'It's laterally a hundred miles an hour here, isn't it, Rafe? I've spent the whole morning doing interviews,' she says.

'What interviews have you been doing?' I ask.

'Oh just some stuff about BLM,' she says.

'Oh, the unconscious bias stuff?' I ask.

'No. Just how dreadful they all are,' she says coolly.

Hugo and I exchange a glance of suppressed mirth at this.

I return after lunch to see that Lettie has been re-furloughed.

Saturday 5 September

Tough loss for Murray at the US Open to the young Canadian Felix Auger Aliassime; I can't help but feel as though if it had been Hubris instead of Murray, it might have been a different result…

The 'What the fuck is going on?!' WhatsApp chat is now 500 members strong and has been renamed 'Matt Cock-in-his-Hands'™ Rafe Hubris, BA (Oxon). The group has been witness to some positively noumenal[30] levels of chat and seems to operate as a sort of therapy space where ministers, civil servants and spads alike can all come together to share how truly diabolically shit Cock-in-his-Hands is. Some other people refer to him as Matt Wankcock, which is definitely

---

30 In Plato's philosophy he distinguishes between the phenomenal realm (that which we experience through our faculties) and the noumenal realm (the higher world of ideas). When I say the chat is noumenal I mean it's as high-end as chat can be.

funny, but nothing will ever beat Cock-in-his-Hands.

I've thrown out some absolutely phenomenal meme work. Perhaps my best is a picture of Jack and Rose in the final scene of *Titanic* where Rose sits on the raft while Jack floats in the water. In this particular meme I've managed to superimpose Matt Cock-in-his-Hands' face onto Rose's and have written 'The British public' over Jack's face. As he sits while the British public drowns, Matt Cock-in-his-Hands has a speech bubble coming from his mouth saying: 'We're being led by the science.'

In fairness, this works a lot better if you can see it...and among those who did it was vary, vary wall received; even Govey reacted to it with a 'crying laughter' face.

Monday 7 September

Another Monday, another GM.

Today we're joined by former Australian Prime Minister Tony Abbott, who apparently is going to be advising us on trade. I've seen a couple of videos going round the internet alleging that the old chap is a misogynist. I'm sure, like all this stuff, there's way more to it than meets the eye though.

'I'm not going to say anything too controversial,' he says, introducing himself, 'especially because that'll give the women an excuse to start whinging.'

This opener is met by huge laughter from the chaps, though oddly, not the women. He then goes on to talk about Brexit and other boring shit I don't care about, and I zone out. I think it's pretty clear from this that he's not a misogynist though. He's just a natural comedian like Blojo or me, playing off stereotypes about women being whingy to entertain the court.

After Abbott has spoken for a bit, the conversation moves to furlough, which Rishi is putting pressure on Blojo to end, with the support of Big Daddy Cum Cum, who wants to re-divert spending to fund an intellectual Olympics for five-year-olds to find 'the next Warren Buffett'.

'We can't afford to keep propping up furlough, Prime Minister. The longer it stays in place, the longer we're just encouraging people to sit in zombie jobs. It keeps everything stagnant,' he says urgently.

Blojo plays with his pen (the writing kind) clearly trying to weigh the potential damage to the budget and economy against the massive public outcry if furlough was discontinued.

'Look, if Boris doesn't want to talk about this, he doesn't have to,' says Carrie, breaking the silence. Today her sausage dog is dressed in a miniature Burberry mac.

'Prime Minister, maybe if you stopped listening to your girlfriend and a little more to people who actually know stuff, we wouldn't be in such a fucking mess,' the Big Daddy snipes.

'My word is final!' screams Carrie and bangs her hand down extremely hard on the desk. She may have even dented it…

Bully Patel looks at Carrie's fist wide-eyed, clearly impressed.

'Come on, Champagne,' says Carrie, exhibiting her fairly nauseating habit of giving Blojo high-end food-and-drink-based pet names. She grabs Blojo by the forearm, saying, 'I've had enough of them talking to you like this.' And with that she leads him out of the room and the meeting.

I've never seen anything quite like it.

Tuesday 8 September

Today, Cock-in-his-Hands has palmed me off with having to do a Zoom with Stig of the Dump, or as he's labelled himself, 'the Mayor of Manchester' (the arrogance!). His name is Andy Burnham and he's one of the Leninist choppers left over from Corbyn's cabinet.

I apply the anger I feel at Cock-in-his-Hands tasking me with something this menial into making an absolutely savage meme where his face is imposed onto the line judge whose throat Novak Djokovic slapped a ball into during yesterday's US Open. People fucking love it. I'm fairly sure everyone in government except Hancock is on the group now.

'Thanks for joining us, old boy. I didn't know you chaps had WiFi in the north,' I say, welcoming Burnham to the meeting. With literally anyone else on the planet this would have positively shattered the ice, but Burnham doesn't flinch. His lip doesn't even curl.

'Is there not going to be a minister joining you?' he asks tersely.

'I'm afraid not, old chap. You'll have to put up with me,' I say, pretending I need to justify myself to this idiot when I'm going to be prime minister before long.

Relations between Stig and me go from bad to worse as the Zoom progresses.

'We need our own Test and Trace system if you lot have been too lazy to sort one,' he says.

'Listen, Andy,' I say, deploying my seductive charm (in the social not sexual sense). 'We love what you're doing and just yesterday everyone in Number 10 was talking about how excellent you are at whatever it is you do. We're definitely committed to making a Test and Trace system work for everyone in the short- to mid- to long-term future. So how about we put all this northern-only Test and Trace on ice for now and reassess i—'

At this point he logs off the call.

I'm furious at his audacity to waste my incredibly important time for about ten seconds before I realise his logging off means I don't have to do any more work on it and immediately I feel completely chill.

Wednesday 9 September

The cases are looking like they're rising *très* fast this week (we're up to 3K new cases a day. Obviously 3K in and of itself is nothing, but sadly this stuff does all add up). Given this, Blojo, Rishi, Govey, Raab, Cock-in-his-Hands, Big Daddy Cum Cum, Carrie, Wetty, Van-Tam and I are all sat on a Zoom, talking about what to do.

'Right chaps, we have a simple choice to limit this virus,' says Blojo, looking tired and stressed, Carrie at his elbow. 'We can either limit the number of people mixing to eight or to six,' he says.

Most of the ministers argue in favour of eight people, as does Carrie, since she's planning to have a *Sex in the City* night with six of her best friends plus Boris. She then goes into immense detail explaining what she has planned and how her friend Tash is so uncannily like the Miranda character.

She gets cut off halfway through this speech by Big Daddy Cum Cum who mutes her and Blojo's Zoom.

Chris Wetty then puts forward the case for limiting the people mixing to six – appallingly wet stuff. The decision, as ever, rests ironically on perhaps the most indecisive man in the world: Blojo.

There's a long silence and eventually he says: 'It's going to have to be six, chaps. I will not have the virus overwhelm and fuck us hard like Jennifer Arcuri.'

We all get to see Blojo's face slowly drain of colour as he realises he's just made a gag about an old flame in front of a current girlfriend. Before we get to see what she does to him though, we all get thrown out of the meeting.

In the afternoon I sit with Blojo in his office, drafting a speech about all the new restrictions, to deliver to the people of the UK. He looks a tad despondent, presumably from having been banished to the doghouse after the Jennifer Arcuri comment.

'What's the situation with Operation Moonshot, old boy?' he asks.

'Mate, it's moonshite. Cock-in-his-Hands is trying to create something for which the technology doesn't even fucking exist.'

'Fuck,' he says, running his hands through his hair. 'I was fucking banking on that. We need it to make the public think we've got a fucking plan.'

'Well, why not just mention it, mate, but just really vaguely?' I say in one of the most Oxbridge moments of my entire life.

'That is brilliant, Rafe,' Blojo says, which makes me feel a little bit warm inside in a non-gay way. 'Let's do it,' he says.

I put in some vague crap about how 'work is under way – and we'll get on at full pace until we get there'. We then chuck in a few vague promises about Christmas being totally normal, which seems perfectly plausible, and we're done.

'Top work, old chap,' Blojo says. 'See you next week. I'm off for a mini-break to Italy over the weekend with Carrie and Wilfred.'

'Anything to get yourself out of the old doghouse, eh?' I say.

'You're not wrong, old boy,' he replies and flaps out.

I suppose that's what you have to do if you're a man in your late fifties romantically involved with a woman in her early thirties – and fair play to Blojo. If that were me I would literally do anything she said; I'd staple my foreskin to my scrotum if it made her happy.

Thursday 10 September

I watch Matt Cock-in-his-Hands announce Operation Moonshot to the Commons – to open laughter from ministers gathered.

People are actually openly laughing at the proposal, it's so fucking ridiculous. Cock-in-his-Hands even starts laughing himself halfway through delivering the speech. Blojo has joined our 'Matt Cock-in-his-Hands' WhatsApp group and has started calling him 'Hopeless Hancock'. A part of me sort of hopes Cock-in-his-Hands never finds all the WhatsApps we've sent about him, but another part of me very much hopes he does. That part would like to film his reaction and project it onto the Houses of Parliament every night for a year.

Friday 11 September

I'm sat in the canteen with Hugo. The old chap is explaining the whole situation with Test and Trace, which still isn't fucking done.

'Lee Cain is chasing me like a rabid dog, mate,' he says, anxiously fiddling with his signet ring. 'I've had to officially announce the app is "coming soon" to take some of the heat off myself.'

'And is it?' I ask.

'Of course it fucking isn't. I've got no why idea why the

fucking tech drone at Google can't do it fucking quicker. This is literally his fucking job.'

I look sympathetic but the reason is obvious. This is Hugo's fault: he sacked off Apple and Google in the first place to try and make the app himself, then I picked up the pieces and reconnected with Google but by that point we were a long way down the line and a long way from an app being created.

We chat a little about the tennis but he's not really with me and slips out of the canteen because he thinks he can 'hear Lee Cain coming'. It's a vary tough predicament for the old boy and one you'd hate to find yourself in. Luckily, it doesn't affect me at all so I'm able to stop thinking about it as soon as the old chap ducks out of the canteen.

Monday 14 September

Everyone is assembled for the GM but Blojo and Carrie are nowhere to be seen.

'If he doesn't turn up in fifteen minutes I'm pretty sure we all get to go home,' I wryly comment, but the only one who laughs is Matt Cock-in-his-Hands, who desperately tries to catch my eye as he does so. I resist his attempt. I refuse to start my week with something so very low-end.

After about forty-five minutes, Blojo and Carrie arrive. They both look tanned; Blojo is wearing an open linen shirt and some suede loafers (which look *très* strong). Carrie is also in linen, and is wearing Dior sunglasses and a great big summer hat. Under her left arm is her sausage dog (in linen too) and under her other arm is a big panettone tin.

'So sorry we're late, guys,' says Carrie. 'There was a headwind on the way back from Italy… Big delay vibes,' she says, taking her seat at Blojo's right-hand side. She opens the panettone tin, cuts it and offers everyone except Big Daddy Cum Cum and Lee Cain a slice.

'This is actually a traditional Italian dessert,' she says, sunglasses still on. 'I saw it and thought I must have it and bring it back to you guys. You are literally my tribe.' I'm fairly sure it isn't a traditional dessert but I don't say anything about it for fear of crossing her.

Carrie then explains that they were away getting Wilfred baptised 'the non-chav way' by an Italian priest and, in very long-winded fashion, explains quite literally every detail of their trip. For the entire duration of this story, Big Daddy Cum Cum sits with his fingers in his ears whispering under his breath, like he's muttering some sort of incantation to make her stop talking. When Carrie eventually does stop we discuss business.

'Test and Trace – do we have an app yet?' asks Blojo.

In characteristic fashion, Matt Cock-in-his-Hands is incredibly slow off the mark and can't shift attention onto Hugo before Hugo can shift it onto him.

'Well, I think Matt is in charge of this,' says Hugo so quickly it's almost incomprehensible.

This triggers another mass ten-minute character-assassination of Matt Cock-in-his-Hands from everyone gathered.

'Well, that was cathartic,' says Blojo. 'Lovely. Is that everything?' He motions us to get up without looking around for a reply.

'Not quite, Truffle Oil,' Carrie says to Blojo, pushing down on his forearm and forcing him to stay put. 'Remember?'

'Ah yes,' says Blojo, remembering. 'So, we're going to be launching a White House-style press briefing…uhhh…thing,' he says, clearly desperately trying to remember the conversation he'd rehearsed with Carrie before the meeting. 'And we're going to appoint someone to be head of handling all the media malarkey, et cetera. Ipso facto, we need someone to step into the role. Does anyone know of anyone good who could do it?'

This is quite literally my dream job. Goodbye Rafe Hubris, spad, hello Rafe Hubris press secretary; the man with the tongue as silver as the spoon in his mouth at birth.

But before I can raise my hand I see Carrie's is already in the air.

'Yes, Carrie,' Blojo says.

'My friend Allegra would be perfect for the job,' she says smugly.

'Wonderful. That's decided then,' says Blojo. 'Thanks everyone,' and with that he takes the remains of the panettone and departs.

This was clearly an inside job. Carrie had this planned all along.

The old girl is a political operative…and a very wily one at that.

Tuesday 15 September

There's a clip going round of Bully Patel on Kay Burley saying if she saw her neighbours breaking the rule of six she'd call the police. This is absolutely hilarious on two levels. Firstly, because it's absolutely believable: I can vary vividly picture Bully Patel in a stab vest (or maybe a leather corset), surrounded by armed policemen storming her neighbour's garden, smirking gleefully as the seven people breaking the rules are being roughly pinned to the ground and arrested. I can also imagine her following up on this by forensically cross-examining the ancestry of everyone in her neighbour's garden and finding an excuse to deport them all. Secondly, the contradiction represented by Bully Patel encouraging people to dob others in is almost beyond irony. This is the woman whose favoured aphorism around the workplace is 'snitches and little bitches get stitches'. Indeed, anyone who has been found to 'rat' is either fired on the spot or ground so hard into the floor that they resign. We then have to fucking organise financial settlements out of court for the wetties. Luckily it's only taxpayer money so it doesn't matter how we spend it really.

I and the rest of the spads have a good laugh at the clip. It's absolutely classic.

Wednesday 16th September

I'm enjoying a Pret flat white with coconut milk today (rogue but actually *très* strong; Pret never misses). I haven't allowed myself to think about what would happen if Pret went under. I'm just doing what I can to be there for it and support it, and I pray every day that it pulls through. Pret to me is like a seriously ill relative.

Word on *el vine de grapes* is that the police are currently inundated with calls from people snitching on their neighbours for breaking the rule of six after the Bully Patel interview. Though the interview was classic, I send a WhatsApp to Blojo to tell him he needs to go on record and correct what she said:

To get the police off our fucking backs.

Because I don't actually think it's a vary good idea for us to be preaching a message of transparency and accountability for people breaking rules. If we did do that and half the stuff we've done comes out, we'd be absolutely *fucké*. This means, when the bullying allegations against Bully Patel inevitably stack up, if we go on the record to explain that it's important not to call people out for breaking the rules, we get a wonderful excuse to not be transparent at all and therefore protect the Pritster.

Given how badly neighbour-snooping fucked Blojo in 2019, anything we can do to counteract that culture is incredibly important.

I get Blojo to say something about going easy on 'sneak culture' and unless someone's having a great raucous house party with hot tubs and the like, to sack off dobbing them in.

The thing is, fundamentally, you shouldn't dob someone in for something. I'm aware that's what I did with Hugo and Poppy but that was a long time ago now, and also it stood to benefit me. We will also all unanimously and unequivocally be dobbing Matt Cock-in-his-Hands in at the inevitable Covid inquiry in a heartbeat, but again this benefits us. If it benefits you that's a different issue, but if it's just for the purposes of woke virtue-signalling, dobbing in is incredibly poor form.

Friday 18 September

Quel surprise. I see that Oxford University has been voted university of the year once again. Rather like matching with a girl you've super-liked on Tinder, it would be an egregious wrong for it not to happen but nonetheless it's vary nice when it does. I make sure I sign off all my emails today with 'From a proud alumnus of the greatest university in the world', just in case people don't know that I went to Oxford, which of course I did.

We won best university for our 'response to the virus', which has obviously been *excellente*. From scientists coming up with vaccines to cure this virus to politicians crafting shrewd and robust policy, Oxfordians excel everywhere...except Ghislaine Maxwell, who, of course, is sadly still in prison.

Without Oxford, where I studied, I simply do not know where we'd be today.

I studied at Oxford.

There's mounting pressure from scientists, civil servants and ministers alike on Blojo to enforce tougher sanctions against the virus but he's off giving some sort of interview dressed in a hard hat and a high-vis jacket on the BBC.

People are starting to get incredibly bemused. I join a throng of civil servants and medical guys watching the interview huddled around a laptop in Number 10. They all look exhausted, angry and on the verge of breakdown.

We watch Blojo describe the second wave as 'inevitable', which causes immense uproar.

'He can't just call the second wave inevitable as if there's nothing we could have fucking done,' screams one of the civil servants.

'You've got to wonder whether we need to go further than the rule of six,' Blojo continues.

'Oh really you've got to wonder, have you? Maybe if you stopped fucking wondering and did a bit more fucking working, the cases wouldn't be rocketing, you feckless cunt,' the civil servant shouts even louder this time. He looks as if he hasn't slept in weeks.

I notice Chris Wetty stood next to me, a single tear slowly sliding down his cheek.

This is starting to feel like it did in April again...

Sunday 20 September

I wake up in the middle of the night in a cold sweat.

I keep having this recurring dream that I'm in work and everyone's bottom half is on fire. Chris Wetty and an army of civil servants keep trying to reach fire extinguishers around the office but Blojo has locked them all to the wall.

'Don't worry, everyone,' he says. 'I'm opening the doors to air out the fire. That should get rid of it in no time.'

But it doesn't get rid of the fire. It just spreads it and it spreads up all of us and we're all burning and dying, and as I'm about to pass away amid the wailing of everyone gathered, I hear him say, 'You've got to wonder whether we should go further than opening the doors to air out the fire.'

Monday 21 September

Hugo, sensing another enormous group fuck in the GM, given that he still hasn't got a Test and Trace app sorted, has sacked off work today.

The old boy needn't have worried though, as we don't actually even get onto Test and Trace. The majority of the meeting is just minister after minister unloading on Blojo.

It's vicious.

For every attack on Blojo, Carrie comes back with a harder, crueller counterattack.

Everyone is tired, anxious and angry and acutely aware of the impending tsunami of shit that's coming our way.

'You could have done something about this, Boris, but you were too busy swanning off in Italy with your girlfriend,' says Big Daddy Cum Cum.

'Don't you dare come for my mini-break!' Carrie screeches back.

'Shut up, Princess Nut Nuts,' he snipes back.

'What the fuck did you call me?' she says with a cold fury.

'Princess Nut Nuts,' he says defiantly.

Blojo has to do everything he can to stop Carrie from launching herself at Big Daddy Cum Cum right there and then.

It takes several minutes to calm them down.

The meeting is then adjourned until after lunch.

I'm not really sure about the nickname 'Princess Nut Nuts'. It's certainly no 'Matt Cock-in-his-Hands'. I'm not even totally sure what it means. Is it some sort of allusion to Carrie being a squirrel? Surely not. I suppose the 'Princess' part signifies that she's a bit princessy, but 'Nut Nuts'?! Also, why 'Nut Nuts' and not just 'Nut'? Is this a reference to the fact she has control over Blojo's balls? She's the princess of his nuts? Or princess of his nut nuts, I should say. Whatever it means, it has clearly struck a nerve with Carrie.

When we all return from lunch the tension has hardly dispersed.

Chris Wetty passionately stresses that something has to be done to get ahead of the curve, not behind it. Matt Cock-in-his-Hands suggests applying a 10pm curfew to stop people from mixing in pubs as much and cut down the rising cases. Rishi immediately protests against this:

'We can't do that, Prime Minister. The economy is struggling as it is. We can't let it shrink even further.'

But Blojo can't deal with the hatred of the rest of his party and waves his hand at Sunak saying: 'We'll have to fucking do the curfew. We're doing the fucking curfew.'

'But prime minist—' Rishi protests.

'He's made his mind up,' Carrie knifes at Rishi.

This attracts even more uproar from the ministers who accuse Blojo of ruling by decree rather than by democracy but, clearly sensing another mass unloading, he ends the meeting there and then and flaps out of the room with Carrie.

I'm starting to feel like we're not really in control of this.

My day goes from bad to worse when, on the way out of the office, Lee Cain bundles me into a store cupboard.

'Where the fuck is Test and Trace?' he says gruffly, inches from my face, aggressively gripping my sartorial shirt.

'Lee, you know I don't work on that any more. It's Hugo's job.'

'Well, Hugo's not turning up any more so now it's your fucking problem. Either you get this to me by the end of the week or you're going to get fucked extremely hard,' he says, stinking of brandy.

What fresh hell is this?

Tuesday 22 September

I've WhatsApp-called Hugo forty-eight times in the last twelve hours but the fucking slippery prick hasn't got back to me. I truly am living a fucking waking nightmare.

Blojo and I sit in his office drafting another speech he's going to go and present to the British public. Neither of us are totally focused today; I'm dividing my attention between the speech and constantly checking my emails to see if Alex (Google drone) has got back to me. Blojo is dividing his attention between the speech and Carrie, who is sat with us in the meeting room, still infuriated by yesterday's GM. The old girl is venting furiously, as if she's on a particularly heated episode of *Made in Chelsea* about how Big Daddy Cum Cum 'is actually not okay', is 'stopping her from living her best life', and how he should 'laterally be fired'.

I spin Blojo some vague language about how, because of rising cases, we're taking the incredibly serious and decisive action of closing pubs one hour earlier than they would have normally closed and how, if people follow that, it'll definitely mean we can get a handle on the virus.

I also use words like 'hope' and 'dream' to describe the prospect of mass testing because, owing to the complete abandonment of Operation Moonshot (everyone has seemingly just given up on this and just doesn't say anything when you mention it now), hope and dreams are really all we have.

I finish up with Blojo, still having to listen to Carrie whine, and phone Hugo another three more times but he doesn't fucking pick up.

Thursday 24 September

By the evening, having had nothing back from Hugo or Alex at Google, I'm forced to go back round to the old chap's flat just like I did to get the results algorithm. I arrive and hammer on the door but the person that comes to it isn't Alex. It's a different guy altogether.

I soon ascertain that Alex doesn't live there any more; he moved out at the end of August. I have absolutely no way to find this guy's new address and I think I might be fucked. As I drift past the Famous Cock tavern in Islington, and the enormous droves of people tightly packed together on the street at the same time because of the curfew (great move, Cock-in-his-Hands), I play out various different scenarios involving Lee Cain pasting me in front of the entire office, each more unpleasant than the one before it.

I have my recurring fire nightmare again, except this time Lee Cain is setting me on fire and everyone in the office is watching and clapping.

You hate to see it.

Friday 25 September

I walk into work with a feeling of calm resignation about my fate.

I've experienced proper dressing-downs from Will and the older boys at school before. The trick is just to close your eyes and think about something else that isn't so horrible until it's over.

But as I log onto my emails I see one right at the top of my inbox, from Alex, the tech drone!

Rafe,

Hope you're well.

Sorry for the delay here. It's been an extremely intense last few weeks. I can now say the app has passed the trials we put it through and will be ready to go out on Monday.

Best wishes,
Alex

Fucking yes. I knew God was a Tory, I've ~~got away with it~~ used my natural talent and intelligence to produce a desirable result once again.

I present this to Lee Cain, who looks for a moment as though he doesn't viscerally hate the world, and I slide into the weekend.

Rafe Hubris lives to tell another tale.

I celebrate in the evening by indulging in some naughty salt with the chaps from school. Christ, I'm fucking elite.

Monday 28 September

This morning's GM is dramatically better than those of previous weeks. Everyone is in much better spirits, given that today we're finally launching the Test and Trace app.

There are a few cries from naysayers that just launching an app isn't fucking good enough and that all the celebrations are premature, but Blojo hushes them.

Carrie has bought some Cristal (today her dog is dressed as a little waiter) and we all stand around drinking. Hugo is back in work (the spineless prick) but I make sure he can't swan in and fucking claim all the glory as if he was the one who made this happen.

Six million people download the app on the first day. I genuinely think this might be the end of Covid and it's all down to me…and obviously the chap who made the app. But I employed him so, technically, mine is the glory.

Wednesday 30 September

Today is the biggest daily rise in cases at 7,108, but I'm certain this amazing new app will resolve all that imminently. Given this, Blojo and I draft him another vague speech recognising the importance of the virus as an idea but not actually practically putting much else in place (relative to the start of September) to fight it.

I get the feeling this winter is going to be a good one.

'Listen old chap,' Blojo says. 'Something Tony Abbott has said has upset Carrie; you don't mind sorting it do you? Just a gentle rap of the old knuckles. Nothing too severe…'

I'm not thrilled about running errands, given how important I am, but in the very small pause I leave before answering, Blojo says: 'Thanks Rafe. Really appreciate it.'

I ascertain that Abbott called Carrie 'a gold-digging, jumped-up PR girl', which, though almost certainly true and very funny, is the sort of thing we have to be seen to reprimand.

I decide to write the old chap an email conveying both our no-tolerance policy on misogyny in the workplace and my appreciation of his excellent chat. It reads:

Dear Mr Abbott,

It has come to my attention that you called Ms Symonds 'a gold-digging, jumped-up PR girl'. While this sort of thing might be funny in Australia (it's also funny here) you can't go round saying that here (you can; it's classic; please continue to do so).

This is your first written warning (recognition of your excellent

283

wit) and if you continue to commit similar transgressions (tell such excellent jokes) you may be summoned before a professional tribunal (what we call the Tory chaps' drinking club).

Yours sincerely,
Rafe Hubris, BA (Oxon)
Senior spad and proud alumnus of the greatest university in the world (Oxford).

Job done and done vary wall.

I spot Big Daddy Cum Cum in his office on the way out of Number 10. From what I can see he appears to be giving Chris Wetty some sort of lecture; he's gesturing at a whiteboard with a diagram on it of a stick man (labelled 'Dom') with an arrow pointing to a planet (labelled 'Mars') with lots of zeros and ones underneath and then underneath that the infinity symbol.

I catch Wetty say: 'I'm really sorry Mr Cummings but I just don't follow.'

And I hear Dom reply: 'Isn't it obvious?! The code allows me to transport myself to Mars…' before they're out of earshot.

Poor Chris Wetty. The bloke just seems to get dominated by everyone. Even though he can be a bit of a wetty, he surely deserves for people to lay off him a bit…

OCTOBER

Friday 2 October

Busy day in Number 10 today as it's the party conference. Sadly, it's having to take place over Zoom this year rather than at Rupert Murdoch's house like it normally does. It's an exhibition in brown-nosing (rather than the normal white-nosing we get up to), as everyone spends a good ninety minutes patting each other on the back for their 'formidable' and 'excellent' work in the pandemic. Obviously this is completely disingenuous, but there are journalists on the call so we need to keep up the front that we're doing a bloody good job and everyone is the best of pals. Blojo and Carrie sit on a rainbow background doing a lip sync battle to 'Fight Song' by Rachel Platten. The rainbow background is supposed to show off our party's solidarity with the ~~tank-topped bumboys~~ LGBTQ community, who we've always made a concerted effort to pretend to get behind (not literally, obviously). I imagine this was Carrie's idea…

Govey then does impressions for about ten minutes of all the different ministers but none of them are very good and he hasn't workshopped any of the jokes, so about 70 per cent of them fall flat.

Finally, Dominic Raab gets up to give an embarrassingly

wet speech about coronavirus and how he 'worried for Carrie, pregnant with Wilf' back in April. This exotic display for the media ends without anything being said about Matt Cock-in-his-Hands or Gavin Williamson; clearly the powers that be have decided if you don't have anything nice to say in front of the media, don't say anything at all.

I think Matt Cock-in-his-Hands' exclusion has really affected the old chap. He appears to be at breaking point and snaps hard at some minister in the House of Commons for simply pointing out that residents of Slough are having to drive miles to get a test. The obvious thing, which anyone with a cool head would do, would be just to ignore this question, as it concerns Slough, which simply doesn't matter. Hancock doesn't do this, though. He loses it and says he will not tolerate 'divisive language' in the chamber. There's obviously an enormous irony to this given that Matt Cock-in-his-Hands being incompetent is pretty much the only thing we're united on as a government and nation right now. If anything, language coldly demonstrating his incompetence is ultimately unifying, not divisive…

Saturday 3 October

I sit reading the papers in the morning and see that Donald Trump has been diagnosed with Covid. I'm not sure whether I really give a shit about this. I'm by no means a Trump fan, so wouldn't really care if he died, but I also definitely don't hate him because sometimes he can be quite classic (see Stormy Daniels encounter).

I'm soon distracted by a story about some absolute fucking chopper called Margaret Ferrier, one of the Scotch Egg's

286

associates, who travelled on public transport after receiving a positive Covid test. Somehow this isn't the stupidest thing I read this morning, as I stumble across an article about how the north seems to have been placed under a blanket lockdown while the south hasn't – as if that's a novel discovery. I'd venture one of the Tweenies could have written something more insightful. Obviously, the south is more important and exempt from the rules that apply to the north; that's how the world works. If you had a choice between a GAIL's seeded sourdough loaf and a mouldy Tesco's own-brand one with human shit smeared all over it, which would you choose? Christ, journalism has gone downhill.

Monday 5 October

I've been told to sack off the GM this morning to deal instead with Baroness Dildo Harding, who has fucking lost a week's worth of Test and Trace data. Why the fuck is this even happening?! She's in charge of mass government technology and she was storing all the Test and Trace data in Excel – in FUCKING EXCEL!!!! She lost the data in Excel!!!! Not even a fucking intern would do this. Not even a fucking Year Ten on work experience would do something so fucking stupid.

Her great friend Matt Cock-in-his-Hands (perhaps they bond over a shared case of not having a fucking brain) sits with us to try and resolve the issue. Dildo looks distressed, red-faced and embarrassed.

'Do you think I'm going to have to resign?' she asks, looking panicked.

I want to reply saying: 'Yes you are going to have to resign, Dildo, and for the sake of the rest of the human race you shouldn't ever be allowed to work in tech ever again, you clueless fuck.'

But I don't say that; I let Matt Cock-in-his-Hands speak. Using his weird, creepy, over-attentive soothing voice he says: 'Don't worry, Dido, no one has to resign. We'll just blame Public Health England. I ruddy hate those homeboys. We'll say it's down to them and then we can just brush it under the carpet, alright?'

Dildo starts to look a little more upbeat and takes a Cath Kidston napkin out of her purse and wipes her eyes. I've never wanted someone to not cheer up more.

I sit reflecting that evening, looking out over the Clapham Riviera, and remark that perhaps we ought to just lock down everyone over fifty-five and let the young chaps roam free. Frankly, it's not as though anyone who is going to actually die from the virus is going to contribute anything to society, so I reckon let people live and get herd immunity. I've got the antibodies, my body is bursting with them in fact, so I'd be fine and it's really fucking my mental health not to be able to do whatever I want all the time. I might put this argument to Blojo. It makes a lot of sense…

Wednesday 7 October

Shit is really starting to hit the fan now and it's caking everyone in an ever-thickening veneer of the stuff. The cases have jumped by about 10,000 every day this week. Although it may actually be even worse than this if Dildo Harding has been involved in the gathering of the data…

We're being called into GMs pretty much every day. Chris

Wetty is only a couple of stages above pleading with Blojo to take action to mitigate the virus rather than just slapping it on the back on its way through, but Blojo doesn't want to budge until things are so bad he's absolutely forced to take action. Carrie isn't with him today – she's meeting an interior designer she's had flown in from Milan to zhuzh up their flat.

Wetty and the assembled scientists keep coming up with different ways of presenting lockdowns to try and entice Blojo into cautiousness, but caution isn't in the old boy's blood and should we be surprised, given his attitude to contraception?

'The fact of the matter,' says Wetty seriously, 'is that Test and Trace isn't doing what it needs to do for us to get a handle on this.'

I sense that he might be directing this at me so quickly chip in: 'Yes, I think unfortunately Dildo Harding was trying to solve a Mac problem with 1943 ENIAC.' A bit of a niche computer reference but some of the older people present smirk slightly at the comment.

'Be that as it may,' says Wetty, 'we need to act – and act fast. There are two options. The first is what we're calling a circuit-breaker lockdown.'

At this point Blojo, who is doodling on the meeting notes, mutters, 'Circuit gayker lockdown,' which attracts some sniggers from those present.

'What this would involve,' Wetty continues, 'is a short-term total lockdown to "break the circuit" and press cases back down.'

'I'm not having a fucking lockdown,' says Blojo definitively, still without looking up. I crane my neck and I'm fairly sure I can see he's drawn a picture of himself surrounded by naked women on a throne with the words 'World King' written on it.

'Well, the second option,' says Wetty, trying to remain

positive, 'is to impose a tier system where, relative to the status of cases within an area, we tailor limitations to fall into one of three categories or tiers.'

Almost before Wetty has stopped speaking, Blojo hastily says, 'That one. We go with option two. I'd sooner circumcise myself with wooden scissors than lock down again.'

This is actually a vary good strategy as it allows us to just formalise what we've been doing up to this point, which is locking down the north to keep open the places of greater renown. You love to see it. I take the opportunity to squirrel this zinger down in the notes of my phone in case it comes in handy for a Blojo speech some time soon.

That evening we all receive an email from Matt Cock-in-his-Hands saying he's seen the group on WhatsApp we've made about him and asks if we could please stop calling him Matt Wank Cock and Matt Cock-in-his-Hands because 'it's actually really hurtful'.

I'm lobbied into deleting the group, which I eventually, reluctantly do. Fucking cancel culture.

I spend the rest of the evening reapplying my insatiable desire for meme work to creating memes out of the images of Donald Trump swaying all over the place with Covid (which are absolutely fucking hilarious). Constructing them isn't quite as satisfying as the Cock-in-his-Hands stuff but it still goes down vary wall on the main spad chat.

Friday 9 October

Carrie's friend and the thief of Rafe Hubris's rightful position as head of government press briefings, Allegra Stratton, starts her new role today. I briefly set eyes on her (she looks like a thief) as Carrie shows her around Number 10. I also notice Poppy following Allegra around, and glean that she's now risen back up the ranks after the exile period in the Department for Digital, Culture, Media and Sport she endured because someone (I can't for the life of me remember who) made a rumour up about her and Hugo banging in the store cupboard.

I'm actually completely fine with Poppy being around the office more; it actually makes me happy to see the old girl doing well in a way that doesn't threaten my position. At the end of the day we're both adults and we don't need to dwell on who might have called who fat and who might have dumped who after who poured large amounts of love and care into a meal for who, which who didn't even have the decency to appreciate. What I'm saying is, I'm totally moved on and can tolerate Poppy being around.

I hear Carrie say, 'So this is the water cooler but like, to be honest babe, the water in here can be really skanky so you're better just buying Fiji before you come in,' before I get pulled into a meeting.

Hancock, Sunak and I are sat on a Zoom with Stig of the Dump again. The nerve of this man is truly unbelievable. He sits in his glasses and dark linen shirt like someone from a minor public school. It's fucking embarrassing. He doesn't engage when we try to get a bit of banter going at the start, which is phenomenally fucking rude. Instead he just dives into quietly and clearly explaining his demands like a fucking prick.

He says that if Manchester is going to be put under restrictions which close pubs and stop people from going to work, the furlough scheme (which is scheduled to finish by the end of the month) must be extended. He explains to us that if financial provision isn't made for the people of Manchester, he'll take us to court.

Rishi explains that he can offer them a 67 per cent furlough compensation but Burnham says it's 80 per cent or nothing. He then logs off the meeting.

What an arsehole.

I look at Rishi and Cock-in-his-Hands. Rishi looks arrogant and stand-offish back at the screen, which is absolutely fair enough – the guy's wife is a billionaire; he doesn't need to answer to anyone. He could actually probably kill someone and get away with it. Cock-in-his-Hands, by comparison, looks terrified and he probably should – he'd fold like a Plasticine Buzz Lightyear in a microwave if cross-examined by a barrister.

Over lunch I reflect on Stig of the Dump's demands while I watch Poppy, Carrie and Allegra tuck into a couple of Joe and the Juice salads they've ordered in (I don't think any of them have done any work so far today).

It's a bit fucking rich for a northerner to tell us that he deserves loads of fucking money. I've obviously never been up there but one of my mates, who missed his grades for Cambridge, ended up at Manchester and he said you could literally buy a house there for like £400. The idea that we would somehow give the northerners as much as 80 per cent of their normal money is absolutely fucking ludicrous. He'll do well to win against us in court, too; both my godfathers are QCs. Stig can come at us all he likes but he won't win.

Saturday 10 October

For the first time in a vary long time I find myself on a date with a girl. She's actually invited me to her flat (also in Clapham) and you love to see that forthrightness from a girl. Her name is Sophie and she's definitely fit although she is also northern – from Manchester actually, and I haven't worked out whether I like it or not. On a level it feels friendly and a bit dirty, which is great, but on another it feels a little bit common…

She's a lawyer and actually took legal action against Bully Patel's crushing of asylum seekers, which for me is a bit too far. It's obviously not good what Bully Patel was doing but actively suing someone for something like that just smacks of virtue signalling for me.

She keeps asking me about my work and I tell her about the whole fucking northern situation and Andy Burnham being such a fucking prick.

'Oh I love him,' she says. 'Andy is great, He really cares about the people.'

'You don't like Stig of the Dump, do you?' I ask.

She looks so appalled at this that she looks like she might be about to spit her wine all over the floor.

We get into a heated debate about the importance of London and the old 'locking the north down to protect areas of renown' policy. The more I say, the more morally outraged she seems to become.

Yet, rather than throw me out, the old girl keeps pouring me more wine and pushing me for my beliefs on other topics. We cover Marcus Rashford, whose MBE I think undermines the British Empire, and the MP pay rise, which I think doesn't go far enough (except in the case of Dildo Harding, Williamson and Cock-in-his-Hands). Just as I'm about to explain how I haven't ever seen Piers Morgan miss, she launches herself at me. But rather than launching herself to punch me, she kisses me passionately. I experience passionate kissing for the first time since Poppy.

The Hubris masterful techniques of seduction have worked once again. I have no idea what the techniques were, but they've definitely worked and you love to see it.

Monday 12 October

Hubris, spring in his step in the wake of a shag, is back on Blojo speech-writing duty today. Allegra Stratton is supposed to be joining us but she's off in Blojo's flat with Carrie having a palm reading with a Chelsea-based mystic who Carrie read about in *Tatler*. I imagine Poppy will probably be with them – not that I mind either way.

I throw Blojo the zinger I've squirrelled away in my notes out about 'locking the north down to protect southern areas of renown', but sadly Blojo doesn't take it.

Halfway through writing the speech to set out all the tiers, Blojo is presented with a letter, which he tells me is a group letter written by northern Tory councillors imploring us to reconsider our attitude towards the north.

'More stuff on the circuit gayker lockdown,' he says, scrunching up the paper and throwing it in a perfect arc into the bin.

The speech is pretty easy to put together. We finish it in fifteen minutes and spend the rest of the afternoon playing bin golf. Blojo ends up sneaking me on the eighteenth hole par five but I'm not too annoyed about losing; the game is played in really good spirits. He'll say 'Well done, son' when I sink a particularly good shot and sometimes he'll give me technical pointers and let me take the shot again if I've messed it up.

It's probably one of my happiest afternoons in government – absolutely (and I cannot stress this enough) not in a gay way though.

I text Sophie in the evening.

She asks me what I've been up to and I explain how Blojo and I spent a few minutes on his speech but mostly played bin golf at work. She then writes me a long message about how I'm arrogant and complacent and that my inaction has caused masses of needless death. I then tell her she doesn't know anything about politics and imagine this means she's cut me off or some feminist bullshit.

Yet fifteen minutes later she tells me to come round and we make passionate high-end love again.

It's so confusing but so enthralling. Normally I'd have lost interest with a girl by now, just like I did with Poppy, but here I'm completely captivated.

Wednesday 14 October

I arrive at my desk this morning to see a chocolate bar with a note on top of it from Big Daddy Cum Cum. The note is written in the style of Willy Wonka and reads:

Spad,

I have included five golden tickets in chocolate bars that I have placed on the desks of all of you this morning. Winners of the golden ticket will win a special prize.

I open the chocolate bar to see no golden ticket, which is a shame, but I imagine the prize will just be one of Dom's essays so I'm not very disappointed at all. I bite into the chocolate but immediately spit it out because it tastes disgusting.

I spit it into the bin and throw the bar away and am forced to swill my mouth out with Pret Still Water (750ml).

I turn Big Daddy Cum Cum's note over and see he's written:

Fool!

There were no golden tickets and I made the chocolate with salt instead of sugar in my basement.

TRUST NOTHING.

Conventional wisdom is for cunts.

I'm starting to think Big Daddy Cum Cum might actually just be a bit unhinged…

Thursday 15 October

I am beyond bemused to see images of Stig of the Dump outside some building in Manchester whinging about Manchester being made to be 'canaries in the coal mine' – presumably some reference to where all the northerners work – for an 'experimental regional lockdown strategy'. He's still wearing the same budget linen shirt and shit glasses. At the end of the day he can whinge all he likes but it's not going to change our minds. The fact is Embargo's, Annabel's, the bulk of Britain's cocaine, Wimbledon and attractive blonde women are all in London and not Manchester, so London is always going to be our priority.

I learn after lunch that plans have been put in place to put London into tier two, which makes me absolutely furious. What on earth are they thinking doing this?! Lock down literally everywhere else in the UK if it means London gets to stay open. This move fundamentally violates one of the Tory key principles: 'If you live in the South West and your family has a crest you get treated best.' I can't believe the government are basing policy relative to the number of Covid cases in an area when it makes way more sense to lock people down relative to their annual incomes.

Chaps on shitty incomes like 50K and below would be under the toughest restrictions, then chaps who bring in 80K and below under the middling restrictions, people below 100K would be on light restrictions and everyone earning more than that should be able to do whatever they fucking want. It's simple economics!

I furiously text Blojo with this solution but like with any message that doesn't directly benefit him, he just leaves it on 'Read'.

What next if London prioritisation goes? Are we going to start taxing the wealthiest 1 per cent more now? Are we going to start actively encouraging non-Etonians to become prime minister? Are we going to stop providing complimentary chang at the Conservative Party over Christmas? These are all obviously extreme examples which we'd never actually let happen but I'm sure you can understand how much of a slippery slope this is.

I storm to Sophie's house and rant to her about the whole issue for ten minutes straight. She launches herself on me again, which initially I think is a bit much, given I'm actually properly upset about something, but I soon change my mind. During sex she keeps asking me to say what I think about universal basic income.

'I think it's a total waste of public funds,' I say honestly, and she orgasms right there and then.

I start to feel like maybe I kind of like this girl.

She's amazing. She has sex with me loads – amazing. I think I might be able to even look beyond the northern thing.

I'm also feeling a lot calmer about the restrictions, which are phenomenally intrusive and difficult to bear – if you intend to follow them ;) Just like every other chap, for my 'mental health', I'm afraid I'm just going to have to carry on living my life as normal.

Friday 16 October

We're hitting back against Stig of the Dump today by firing a message to him in a press conference of our own. If he's going to slag us off to the media and not politely invite us onto a Zoom, he can get fucked. The prick is still refusing to accept tier three and the vary generous 67 per cent furlough we're offering, which is phenomenally stupid as, if he keeps forgetting his manners like this, we've got the power to knock it down to 50 per cent. Beggars (which I think is an apt description of all northerners) should not be choosers. I get Blojo to imply that the longer Stig waits, the more death he causes and that if he doesn't take what he's given, Blojo will be forced to intervene anyway. This is really spicy stuff – a bit like the good old days of tennis press interviews where McEnroe would slag off Connors and then Connors would slag him off right back (unlike now, where they all seem to be set on politely circulating their desire to wank each other off).

As we move into the weekend, though, Stig still isn't playing ball and Blojo tasks me with writing him a letter.

For the first time in my life, I take my work home with me. I obviously wouldn't do this if it were something unimportant like Test and Trace or whatever, but this – an opportunity to exhibit Hubris's supreme penmanship – is frankly essential. I'm fully aware that this letter could, and quite frankly should, go down in history.

I write it with the most Oxbridge part of my brain and it is superb. It reads:

Dear 'Mayor of Manchester',

I do hope this finds you amicable.

Or at least more so than over Zoom anyway!

Let's cut to the chase. I can see very clearly what you're trying to do here. You're creating an image for the court. We all do it – no one more so than our prime minister. I see you trying to cultivate the image of Manchester's martyr to boost your own career. I see the self-interest that belies the serious exterior as you protest against Manchester being made canaries in the coalmine, when underneath it all you're the cat who ate the canary, smug and self-satisfied as you ascend the greasy pole. I respect that. It's Populism 101. But you've had your time in the sun (metaphorically and in print). You've had your PR. Now is the time to do the honourable thing and roll over.

Well done on Cambridge by the way – I had no idea you went there. You must have been so surprised to get in!

(I was at Oxford.)

Rafe Hubris, BA (Oxon)

I print two copies of the letter – one to frame and one to sign with the official Hubris wax seal. You absolutely love to see it.

Sophie is over for dinner tonight. I've bought us a meal from M&S along with her favourite wine. She seems different tonight, though – a bit off with me…

I ask her about her day and stuff but she looks very disinterested for some reason.

After dinner she reads my letter and launches herself at me again.

This woman is genuinely an enigma. I don't think I could ever get bored of her company.

'So what are we?' I ask tentatively afterwards.

She laughs and looks slightly disgusted when I say this and leaves shortly afterwards without staying the night.

God, she's so mysterious.

It drives me wild.

Monday 19 October

Despite receiving possibly the greatest letter ever constructed, Stig of the Dump is still refusing to play ball. It's just boring now from him and you hate to see it. He's whinging about a £75 million deal for Manchester's businesses, which is just fucking greedy. We've told him he can have £60 million if he asks nicely, but he just comes angrily back explaining that £65 million is the absolute bare minimum that Manchester would need. We all decide not to waste any more of our precious time on him and tell him via Twitter that unless he's going to adhere to the (actually fucking generous) demands we've sent over, they're getting put under tier three by noon tomorrow.

Tuesday 20 October

Last chance saloon for Stig, who sits on a Zoom with all of the big boys at midday.

He's still not budging below £65 million. We all find him incredibly irritating and have taken to openly mocking him in front of his face, mimicking his incorrect accent.

'Manchestoh needs more muneh,' says Blojo, to raucous laughter from everyone gathered.

'This is your last chance, Andy,' says Hancock. I've never seen him look down on someone like this. 'Ask politely for £60 million and we'll give it to you,' he says.

'You're playing a poker game with peoples' lives,' Stig says venomously.

'Right,. That's it,' says Blojo, slamming shut the laptop we're all gathered round.

'No fucking deal,' he shouts triumphantly and we all cheer.

Blojo produces some champagne and we stand drinking it to mark our crushing of the northern rebellion. Spirits are absolutely in the sky. We order a shit-tonne of food from Deliveroo (I won't say the exact number but the figure comes to more than the MP wage increase) and everyone spends the rest of the day drinking and celebrating except Lee Cain, who sits drinking in the corner by himself looking violent and on the verge of a breakdown, like one of those damaged detectives you see in crime dramas, or someone processing having been made to watch all of their immediate family being brutally murdered.

I rock up to Sophie's flat *extrêmement inebrié* and also *un peu coké*.

I tell her I'm on cloud nine after what we've done for the north.

She keeps asking me to talk about the whole thing while we're having sex, but I don't really want to and I stop halfway through.

'Why did you stop?' she asks.

'It just feels a bit weird you constantly asking me for my opinions on stuff,' I say.

'But Rafe, that's what makes you so hot. You're so problematic,' she says.

'I'm what?'

'You're one of those dreadful floppy-haired posh boys with mummy issues and the type of public-school entitled arrogance to think the position you've been over-promoted into is actually where you belong. Your public schooling means you pretty much totally lack empathy, which means you not only actually believe all of the cruel establishment-preserving right-wing narrative designed by elites to manipulate the working classes, you actually see it as your moral duty to enact it, and it's so fucking hot,' she says, launching herself at me again, but this time I push her back.

As I digest this it feels a little bit like my heart withers and

302

shrinks in my chest. It's like she only wants to have sex with the idea of me and not the actual me. I tell her I'm not doing this any more and put on my clothes and leave.

I don't think Sophie is a particularly nice person – profiling someone for their gender, race, class, background, lifestyle and demeanour is genuinely so horrible, I can't believe someone would do that.

Thursday 22 October

The stupid northern idiot footballer, Marcus Rashford, has chosen today, of all days, to start his virtue-signalling Twitter 'Feed the children' shite again, just because we've pretty much unanimously voted to end the free school meals scheme over the Christmas holidays (or as I've been calling it, the 'eat nowt to help out' scheme). I literally have no idea why he's being so fucking difficult about this. We already fed the children back in June; they should be full!! What does he want? For us to feed poor children forever?! Also, we voted for it; it's fucking democracy. You can't just change something we voted for if you don't like it. Just as we crush one northerner, another one raises it's fucking head. It's like a never-ending game of Whack a Mole for people with stupid accents.

I decide to act pre-emptively on this one and call on my unerringly excellent penmanship to save the day.

Dear Mr Rashford 'MBE',

I do hope this finds you reasonable.

Or at least more so than over Twitter anyway!

Let's cut to the chase. I can see very clearly what you're trying to do here. You're creating an image for the court. We all do it – no one more so than our prime minister. I see you fighting for the oppressed because you've probably done something dodgy you want to offset. I get it. I'd do the same in your position. But you've had your time in the sun (metaphorically and in print), you've had your PR. Let's not let the British Empire, of which you are now nominally a member of the order, down. Now is the time to do the honourable thing and roll over.

Well done on the football by the way, I've always been more of a tennis and rugby man, but I YouTubed some of your goals and they were actually quite impressive. You must have been so surprised someone like you made it professionally!

(I was at Oxford.)

Rafe Hubris, BA (Oxon)

10 Downing Street

(This is like Old Trafford but for politics.)

Once more I print two copies, seal one with the official Hubris seal and get it sent off. Top work from me – extremely strong.

I do hope he knows how to read…

Friday 23 October

I wake up and see, for the second time this month, that my supreme penmanship hasn't resolved an enormous shitstorm.

It doesn't matter though. Rashford is going about feeding the children himself. The brilliance of this is it means we don't have to. We can just let him do the hard work and sit back. This way everyone wins. The greedy poor children will be happy because they get to have more food, which means Rashford will be happy and stop whining, which means we're happy because he'll stop causing a massive scene and trying to make us look like shit and we don't have to do anything.

Blojo is furious about Rashford when I get into work and vows to 'fight him until the dying hour', but when I explain that he's doing our jobs for us, Blojo seems a lot more amenable.

Big Daddy Cum Cum has taken to creating quite offensive satirical cartoons of Carrie and Blojo, which he's photocopied and stuck up at various points around Number 10, the Home Office and the Department of Health.

Today he's circulated one of Carrie (labelled Princess Nut Nuts) holding a leash attached to a collar round Blojo's neck. Blojo is on all fours and Carrie is wearing a cone-shaped hat with the words 'conventional wisdom' on it (I wonder if Bully Patel ever makes people follow her around on a leash…).

Unsurprisingly, this has not gone down well with Carrie, who has tasked her army of supporters with removing all the pictures. Carrie is also particularly venomous, as it transpires that Lee Cain has found her booze stash and has drunk his way through all her Clase Azul Ultra-Extra Anejo tequila (£3.1K a bottle) in an afternoon. I think this means war.

Wednesday 28 October

We're sat in GM, as the tier system isn't fucking working so Wetty *et* Van-Tam are pushing for a lockdown.

'No fucking lockdowns,' says Blojo, like an obstinate child.

'Prime Minister, there's no other way,' pleads Wetty.

'My friends, I would sooner let the bodies pile high in their thousands than close everything down again. We will not have a fucking lockdown.'

Eventually, we peer-pressure Blojo into doing it; we push for Friday but Carrie (who has talked through the whole meeting with Allegra, who I still haven't seen do any work yet) pipes up to say that Friday isn't going to work because she and Allegra are having a girls' night with some of her old friends from Godolphin and Latymer.

Wetty tries desperately to get Blojo to move it forward but Blojo gives him the hand.

What a fucking mess.

If Blojo doesn't step up soon, this winter is going to be absolutely fucked.

Friday 30 October

I'm pulled into Big Daddy Cum Cum's office on entry into Number 10 this morning. He pushes another of his satirical drawings towards me. This one is a visual account of how he imagines Carrie's 'girls' night' will play out. In the picture Carrie, Allegra and six other identikit women all sit in a circle round a fire with Blojo spinning on a stick over it.

Carrie has a speech bubble coming from her mouth with the words: 'OMG. I literally love groupthink.'

I don't really understand what he's trying to say with this one…

'It's genius, isn't it?' the Big Daddy says, looking unhinged. 'But that's nothing, Rafe. That's just an introductory exercise to what I've got planned. I'm going to break Boris and Princess Nut Nuts up,' he says, breathing frantically. 'I'm going to fly one of the drones I've bought from the dark web and pump pheromones into the office and lock Boris in there with a sex worker I've hired. His relationship with Princess Nut Nuts won't last five minutes and then, Rafe, Number 10 will be mine again. It'll be mine.'

'Dom, I'm really not sure this is the right thing to do,' I say.

'Don't you see? This is how we're going to overthrow the elite, overthrow the media and its spiritual queen, Princess Nut Nuts,. Then we can rule the government together, with me as emperor ant and you as deputy ant.'

'I can't get across this, mate.'

'Then you are useless to me,' he says and banishes me from his office.

I'm all for employing sex workers and bringing them into work – that's absolutely classic (see *The Wolf of Wall Street*), but not like this. I really think Big Daddy Cum Cum might have started to properly lose it now.

On my way out of Number 10, I hear raised voices, which I recognise to be Carrie's and Rishi's.

Rishi, trying to get access to Blojo's office to discuss furlough, seems to have been intercepted by Carrie.

At five foot seven, Carrie absolutely towers over Rishi, who's wearing a cashmere tracksuit with gold trainers.

'It's not economically viable to continue to extend furlough. It's going to completely ruin us,' says Rishi.

'I don't give a shit about that,' Carrie says. 'It's what Boris wants so it's going to happen. I see you, you know, thinking you're laterally the prime minister, trying to knock Boris out of his job. That is laterally not okay. If you don't make furlough happen I will personally fuck you up,' she says, her voice dripping with venom.

'Are you threatening me?' Rishi asks.

'Oh my God, that's so toxic. I can't believe you'd accuse me of that when I'm such an empath,' she says and turns on her heel and leaves.

Fucking hell.

Saturday 31 October

It's Halloween and rather than dressing as something horrible and unpalatable (last year I was Jeffrey Epstein: classic) I'm living something horrible and unpalatable: the prospect of another imminent lockdown.

Blojo and I sit in work on a Saturday, both feeling phenomenally depressed at being locked up for another fucking month. The speech is easy enough to write and we rattle through it without the usual jokes or breaks to look at 'girls with excellent knockers on my Tinder'.

He presents the whole situation as something that totally blindsided us as if there was no way we could have predicted this coming and as if it wasn't thanks to a cocktail of incompetence and arrogance that led us here, but rather a medical inevitability. I can't help but feel as though this isn't quite right from Blojo.

As he goes out to deliver it on BBC One on Saturday night I feel gripped by a powerful melancholy. For once it's not because of me. It's because of something greater and bigger than myself, something that all of us periodically rely on in our desperate moments – one of the impactful inventions of the twentieth century for British society, something without which, life as we know it could not be lived: Pret.

Pret, in its understated majesty, its culinary profundity, the provider of metropolitan jocundity, will surely have to face a challenge greater than any of us will have to face in the coming months. Already on its last legs, having been forced to make 400 of its key workers redundant, we must all think of Pret.

When I think about Pret, it puts all my suffering into context.

I would sacrifice so many northerners so it wouldn't have to die.

When I think about Pret, I feel like I could cry. Obviously I don't actually though, because I don't cry. I am really cut up about the whole thing though – we all are.

NOVEMBER

Monday 2 November

Big Daddy Cum Cum doesn't seem mentally very well.

This morning's GM begins with him dressed in a hooded cloak made of a hemp-like material, telling 'the tale of the leader ant's girlfriend who ruined everything'. Lee Cain provides musical accompaniment to Big Daddy Cum Cum's tale, playing 'Greensleeves' on a keyboard, but keeps fudging the tune and smashing his fist down on the keys, which makes several of the more timid spads jump. The whole performance is obviously just a very thinly veiled dig at Carrie, who attempts to throw some of her Fiji water over the Big Daddy at several points during the speech.

Today, we are without the old Tories – who have reignited the 'libertarian squadron' and are uniting against the concept of lockdown, which they argue 'harms the most basic freedoms of humanity'. Although surely the most basic freedom of humanity is the freedom of not being dead, which, for many people, unlocking would surely take away. Obviously I don't give a shit if some people die but their position is hardly reasonable.

'There's got to be something we can fucking do here,' Blojo keeps saying, desperately.

'If Operation Moonshot's testing can take place then we can get rid of the lockdown,' says Poppy, who I'm totally fine with being in the meeting.

'Yes, that's wonderful, Poppy,' says Blojo, agitated, 'but that relies on Operation Moonshot actually fucking existing – and we all know it doesn't.'

'Hang on a second,' I say, preparing the floor for a pearl of Oxbridge wisdom. 'What if we stopped looking at solutions and just…blamed the public for the rise in cases?'

Then, slowly, something incredible happens. Blojo starts applauding, then Carrie starts, then Govey; soon everyone gathered is applauding. They're applauding me – they're applauding my brilliant suggestion.

Blojo looks me straight in the eyes and says: 'Rafe, that is genius.'

When he says this I get a wonderful warm feeling. It's like how I feel when Blojo gives me a high five but times a thousand. In that moment it kind of feels like, even if I didn't achieve anything for the rest of my life, I'd still sort of be enough. None of this is in a gay way though…

Wednesday 4 November

There's yet more tension in the office today because Blojo has promised Scotland a shit-tonne of furlough cash and has reinstated Universal Credit without consulting Rishi.

The word on the grapevine is that apparently Carrie absolutely fucking loves the Edinburgh Fringe – hence the furlough cash – and she has a struggling artist friend from her Warwick Uni days who needs Universal Credit to keep producing her 'important interpretive dance pieces', which she performs exclusively across the allotments of Stoke Newington.

This is much more than just a demonstration of Carrie's ownership of Blojo's testes though. It's a power move which sends a clear message out to Rishi and anyone standing in her and Boris's way: if you do not move, we will crush you. It's Power Politics 101. You've got to send out a clear message about who is boss and who is dross, just like they do in the hood. That really is a good comparison actually; Carrie does seem to operate vary much like a gangster. I don't think Rishi will be getting in her way again any time soon. *I* certainly wouldn't. (I wonder if Carrie ever dresses up in a PVC skirt and zaps people with a taser.)

The office is divided into three groups at the moment: Carrie's supporters (Allegra, Poppy, pretty much all the girls), Big Daddy Cum Cum's disciples headed up by Cain (calling themselves 'The Cumquats' and calling Carrie 'Princess Nut Nuts'), and the floating voters headed up by Blojo. As with anything of this nature I sit very firmly in the floating voters' camp and will make my decision on who to side with moments before it becomes apparent they'll be victorious. There's a showdown brewing with Carrie and Big Daddy Cum Cum. I can feel it in the air. One cannot live while the other survives.

Given that it's lockdown tomorrow, like a bird going south for winter, I go to Tinder for birds from South West. I change my bio to 'Here to break the law as well as your heart. 25. Clapham. Conventionally attractive' and swipe for the best part of twenty minutes before Tinder presents me with Emily's profile. A shiver travels through my spine as I look upon her conventionally unattractive face and my mind flashes back to railing her in the downstairs loos at Chequers. This thought is then followed up by a feeling of guilt, like it's bad to be physically repulsed by someone who's butters, which I suppose on a level it is. Nonetheless, I will not be swiping right, and throw her, along with all my previous old flames, resolutely in the bin. Tinder isn't playing ball though, and stays frozen on her profile even after I've restarted the app several times. I'm forced to sack the whole thing off.

Friday 6 November

The phone rings at my desk. Normally with something like this I'd let it ring out, or let someone less important deal with it, but against my better judgement, I decide to answer it.

I immediately regret this decision.

The voice I hear is young and northern and asks to be connected to the prime minister. The prime minister! The prime minister of the United Kingdom!!! As if the prime minister just sits around all day waiting to have a good old chinwag with a northerner as if this is fucking LBC!

I tell him I have absolutely no desire to buy whatever it is he's selling and put the phone down, not before getting a fucking earful of virtue-signalling bollocks about the children and feeding them for some reason.

That's the last fucking time I'll be answering the fucking phone in the office.

Lunch is particularly delicious today.

Great big, fat thick-cut chips, lovely delicate fish in a nice batter, mushy peas and tangy tartar sauce. The best thing, as well, is that the food in the Number 10 canteen is so heavily subsidised it's basically free. Even the most low-end people could eat there…although obviously they'd have to be employed and I'm pretty sure there aren't any spaces going among the cleaning staff, so while theoretically they could eat there, practically there's not a civil servant's chance in Bully Patel's office of them actually doing so…

My phone lights up with a message from Poppy. I get this weird feeling like my stomach is about to fall out of my arsehole when I first see this; the fish must have been undercooked. On a closer inspection I see Poppy hasn't directly messaged me, but rather the entire spad group to say: 'Can someone clear Saturday for Boris to talk to Marcus Rashford? I just spoke to him on the phone. He said he'd been trying to get through all morning but someone had told him they weren't interested in what he was selling… Let me know.'

Oh my God.

I put the phone down on Marcus Rashford.

I treated Marcus Rashford like a man asking if I'm happy with my broadband provider.

That is fucking hilarious.

This has to be one of my most classic moments of the last year. This is my Bluebird anecdote now.

Jokes aside, there's absolutely no way Poppy is going to get Blojo to give up his Saturday to talk to a footballer who hasn't just won the World Cup – especially not a northern one!

Sunday 8 November

I'm agog to observe that not only did Blojo sacrifice his Saturday night to talk with Rashford, he's fucking U-turned on the free school meals shit. He's become such a fucking wetty since Carrie has started exerting more influence over him. He would have never done this before. He's pledging £170 million for it as well, for fucking fuck's sake. This is what happens when you're weak and spineless like Blojo: you let people control you and it fucks everything up. It's why getting into a relationship is invariably a bad idea. They invariably make you let your guard down, then women get into your brain and make you think it's important to look out for fucking weak people.

I see Biden has won the US election. He seems intolerably woke and yet he's so fucking old (surely a contradiction), he genuinely looks like a light jog would see him off. But I suppose liberalism is in now and whatever Trumpism was is out. Then it dawns on me. Blojo hasn't reinstated free school meals out of compassion, he's done it to ride the wave of public opinion. He's not a compassion-led wetty, he's a scholar of the public mood, currying favour by playing off popular sentiment... For perhaps the first time in my life, I've been wrong about something. Mad.

I don't think Biden is actually that bad either, to be honest. I understand he's a fan of bombing the shit out of the Middle East so there's definitely something to get on board with there. That's the thing about all these wokies: it's always a front.

Monday 9 November

Carrie has had the GM moved to the afternoon today as she's got a crystal expert coming to assess Wilfred's chakras and has insisted Blojo accompanies her.

I arrive at my desk to see a scroll sitting on it with an East India Company wax seal which I recognise to be Rees-Mogg's.

I open it and see it appears to have been written with a quill on old-style parchment.

It reads:

Dear Hubris minor,

I do hope this finds you in similar form to that which I understand you enjoyed on the tennis court at both Eton and Oxford.

Though I derive great pleasure from writing to you, I'm afraid the matter at hand is comparatively displeasing.

I'm sure you will have seen the dreadful political stunt by our prime minister feeding the children. I'm equally sure that, like any good Conservative, you share my firmly held belief that this is neither right nor proper.

Accordingly, I am gathering all those opposed and we shall be setting out a counter-case to the prime minister just before supper on the day of our lord Tuesday 10th November. It would be an honour to welcome someone as accomplished as yourself to proceedings and indeed, without you, the movement would undoubtedly be a lot less than it otherwise could be.

Kindest wishes and greatly looking forward to welcoming you to the chamber some day very soon I have no doubt.

Floreat Etona!
Jacob Rees-Mogg

What a lovely chap.

Obviously I'm never going to oppose Blojo, but he's so charming and politely insistent it's almost enough to make me change my mind.

'Good morning everyone, how is it actually going?' Carrie says, to begin the afternoon's GM. 'So I've been talking to a lot of the girls and we've all said there's a lot of nasty laddish energy in Number 10 which really needs to be cleansed, so I've spent lunchtime today burning sage around the office. You're welcome. I've also decided the best way to reset the energy is to show you guys the absolutely gorg renovations I've made to my flat.'

All Carrie's followers, led by Allegra and Poppy, clap at this. Big Daddy Cum Cum looks appalled.

She must show us at least forty before-and-after photos of the same room.

Just as she is saying: 'So that's the atrium and, like, we spent like pretty much all the budget on that, but that's okay because we got a new budget, so this is the champagne cel—'

'This is fucking bullshit,' Big Daddy Cum Cum interrupts, turning to Blojo to protest as he does. 'Don't you see? She's using you, Boris, to get what she wants. You don't need her.' He then brandishes a large assortment of papers in front of Blojo's face. 'I've modelled out your relationship and it's going to end on the 4th of April 2026 anyway!!!' The pictures he's brandishing are just squiggles on paper…

'How fucking dare you meddle in my relationship? You're not even a member of Soho House!' Carrie screams back at him.

'Fuck off, Princess Nut Nuts,' he fires right back.

It's so tense it feels like the air has become one great big solid.

Carrie and Dom pace back and forth at opposite ends of the table, Carrie still with her dog in the crook of her arm and an oat flat white from GAIL's in her hand, Dom in a hooded cloak.

It's like *Made in Chelsea* meets *Revenge of the Sith*.

'I'm laterally not like other girls. I've actually been so tolerant of him – like I'm such a tolerant person, aren't I, girls?' she says.

Allegra and the rest of her supporters aggressively murmur in agreement.

'She has led you away from unconventional wisdom, Boris. 'Can't you see that?' Big Daddy Cum Cum barks at Blojo, who is staring into the middle distance and looks like he's experiencing the worst family Christmas argument of his life.

'I'm such a good person,' she says, 'which is why I have to do this.'

Carrie then takes her GAIL's oat flat white and launches it at Big Daddy Cum Cum, but he's already predicted this and dodges the jet of coffee, which instead hits Matt Cock-in-his-Hands square in the forehead.

I see the whip of Big Daddy Cum Cum's cloak disappear round the door and a few moments later, Lee Cain, messily clattering into things on his way, bringing up the rear. The Cumquats slowly file out, leaving the rest of us with Carrie, who's being softly told by all her supporters, 'You're so strong,' and, 'Babe, I'm so proud of you for being such a good person,' while Matt Cock-in-his-Hands rolls around on the floor in agony.

I have never seen Blojo look so very shaken in all my days – not even when he had Covid.

Wednesday 11 November

Number 10 is a confusing place at the moment, beset by so many rumours it's hard to decipher what is and what isn't true.

Some spads are saying that Big Daddy Cum Cum will surely resign.

Others are saying Blojo and Carrie have broken up.

Others still claim that Big Daddy Cum Cum has got Blojo to make Lee Cain chief of staff.

When Carrie comes out to address the office at 4pm you could hear a luxury lapel pin drop on a plush carpet.

She stands in the middle of the room speaking into a gold-studded microphone that she's twisted Blojo's arm to buy.

'Hey everyone, how is it actually going?' she says.

This is met by a few murmurings of 'Yaas qween' from her followers.

'So guys, really sad news is that Lee Cain is resigning. Boris was going to make him chief of staff but I just felt really worried about him not being his best self in the role,' she says.

This is gargantuan. Lee Cain out. I knew Carrie would get him back for drinking her tequila.

At this point we all hear a monumental series of bangs from Lee Cain's office. It's hard to tell, because the door is shut, but I'm sure I hear him ripping his computer from his desk before bludgeoning it with his keyboard some fifteen times, screaming the word 'CUNT'. Lee Cain rams open the door, holding only a Japanese peace lily and leaving behind him the smouldering remains of a monitor and an office which looks like it's been hit by a small bomb.

'Ohhh, there he goes. Look everyone – so sad – say goodbye to Lee Cain,' Carrie says in mockingly sentimental tones.

Cain doesn't look at any of us; instead, he slowly staggers out of the office and, as he passes the water cooler for the final time, gives it an almighty thump and completely breaks it for good.

Carrie tuts and says, 'How classless. Anyway, onto stuff that is actually high-vibe and matters. Boris and I are having the loo painted gold, lol. It will actually look so good. Who wants to help with a little charity project to fund it?'

Allegra raises her hand.

'Amazing. Thank you Allegra,' Carrie says. 'Right. Things are going to be changing a little bit round here. No more jokes about willies. If you're going to be a sexist pig you can do it in your own time. I'm going to be issuing a list of banned words. If you say them, you'll be fired on the spot. They include the terms 'cock', 'balls', 'shaft', 'bell-end' and 'Princess Nut Nuts'. She says this so furiously she almost looks like she might shatter the Fortnum and Mason champagne flute she's holding.

'Finally, there are a lot of people in here who need to pour a bit more effort into their look. You know who you are,' she says, pointing very deliberately and clearly at a handful of bedraggled civil servants. 'Get yourselves suits that don't make you look like chavs because I don't want to create the sort of environment that encourages people to think it's okay that they look fucking gross. Thus from this point, nothing lower-end than Whistles for girls and Ted Baker for boys can be worn in the office, and that is final.'

And with that she leaves.

Fucking hell.

What Carrie has just said is absolutely fucking crazy.

I mean, obviously she's absolutely right about the clothes some of the civil servants wear – they look fucking butters – but I can't believe she's scalped Lee Cain!

Thursday 12 November

Word on the grapevine is that Carrie is lining up her godsister to replace Lee Cain as chief of staff. She's called Fluffy or Muffy or something and also has a background in PR apparently. I'm not sure this is a good idea at all.

I haven't seen Big Daddy Cum Cum since Monday, but surely he won't be happy about this…

Just as I'm thinking about him, as if by magic I hear his voice whisper in my ear: 'Rafe, meet me in the cupboard in ten minutes.'

The cupboard Big Daddy Cum Cum has chosen is particularly small and smells of old piss and we are sat on top of each other in it. There is also no light.

'Rafe, tomorrow Princess Nut Nuts will be forced out of the hive. I've been preparing all week to trigger this by reading TS Eliot and Robert Taylor, and I will release her stranglehold and return to the important tasks this country needs…like sucking all the CO_2 out of the atmosphere and putting the brains of rats into randomly selected children. I've lured her in by playing her at her own game, using conventional time structures to arrange a meeting with her and the prime minister at what normallos call 9am. When Princess Nut Nuts has been banished you will know, Rafe, and you must come to me then,' he says urgently. 'Until then you must be gone and I must leave lest she sees me.'

With that he pushes me out of the cupboard and back into the office.

Friday 13 November

It's 9am and I stand practically shaking with excitement outside the room Big Daddy Cum Cum, Carrie and Blojo have entered. Pretty much all of Number 10 are stood with me, listening in.

It's hard to make out a lot of what's being said for the first ten minutes of the meeting but soon, voices are raised.

I can hear Big Daddy Cum Cum shouting: 'It's her or me. You've got to choose. You don't want to be with her. Think of everything we've done together.'

'He doesn't want to be with you, you sad man,' says Carrie cruelly.

'Is that it, Boris? You're going to choose dates over data?' That is an absolute fucking zinger from the Big Daddy, I must remember to whack that in a fucking speech.

We all hear Boris prevaricating and umming and ahhing and saying something like: 'Oh come on, Dom, can't we all be friends?'

'No!' both he and Carrie scream in unison.

'You're gonna regret this, you know,' Cummings says as he moves closer to the door. Hearing this we all scurry back and pretend we weren't listening in.

'I can ruin you.'

'What are you going to do? Write a blog?' asks Carrie mockingly.

'Never underestimate the power of my blog, Princess Nut Nuts.' With that, he launches himself out of the room.

About an hour later in the office Big Daddy Cum Cum gathers the spads and gives a speech.

It's odd to see him address us all without the threat of Lee Cain there to back him up. He looks tired, dejected even.

'As the less intellectually rubbish among you will know, it has always been my plan to depart from Number 10 today. I always said it would be today that I leave on my blog and if you go back and read my blog you'll be able to see that.'

He then writes on a whiteboard behind him:

Conventional wisdom = for cunts
Prime minister's girlfriend = conventional wisdom

He then gathers the reams of printouts from his own blog and the bulk of his Lego, puts it into a great big box and leaves Number 10.

Holy shit.

Big Daddy Cum Cum is Big Daddy Go Go.

This is the end of an era.

It kind of makes me feel sad. I'm not sure Big Daddy Cum Cum ever really did anything other than wreck stuff and reel off incomprehensible riddles but in a way (definitely not a gay one), I'll miss him.

Sunday 15 November

Carrie is throwing a 'Dominic Goings' party at hers and Blojo's flat – all socially distanced of course…;)

The place looks like a cross between an extremely high-end brothel and Annabel's, Mayfair (although perhaps the two aren't mutually exclusive). She is quite scary but Carrie is also an absolutely fucking excellent host. She presents me with a champagne flute on arrival and I grab a few canapés from the essential workers who are milling around.

From talking to Carrie I glean that her godsister can no longer fill the role of chief of staff. Oh my word, this could be it. This could be my opportunity to fill the role, like a worldie I've picked up from Infernos….

I mull over the prospect of Rafe as chief of staff, shouting at people and firing them on the spot, hair and clothes like Jordan Belfort; it would be perfect for me and I am perfect for it. I can practically taste the smoked salmon at the congratulations party my parents will throw for me in Virginia Water and it tastes strong – *très* strong in fact.

I'm then brought back to earth by Carrie giving one of her

speeches to everyone assembled.

'Hey guys, how is it actually going? Thank you so much for coming. It is laterally so good to see you. You're all looking gorg,' she says, blood diamonds glittering in the light. 'As all of you will know, I've had to cut some really toxic people out of my life recently but now I've done that I'm laterally on such a high vibe. So let's all cheers to how strong I've been and to me and Boris and our amazing flat!'

Everybody toasts them.

Cheers to Boris and Carrie and cheers to Rafe Hubris, chief of staff – or as I think I'll change the name to, Rafe of Staff. Classic.

I sidle over to Blojo to try and put a good word in for myself but the old boy is absolutely smashed. I've never seen him this hammered. He is steaming. Carrie tries to stop him as he grabs one of the trays of nibbles that are circulating and quite literally hoovers it up.

I keep trying to put myself forward for the chief of staff role but Blojo isn't with it at all. He's just babbling incoherently all over the place. Then, in a moment of clarity, he grabs me and says: 'Rafe, I'm going to be too fucked for work tomorrow. Cover for me, old boy.'

'You want me to do this as chief of staff?' I ask, desperately trying to feed him the words, with the desperation of a sixteen-year-old trying to lose his virginity on an exeat, but it's no use. Blojo is just dancing all over the place and looking at the women now.

I look at this as an opportunity to prove myself and secure the role, crafting an ingenious plan to help the old boy out.

I leak to the press that he's been pinged on the Test and Trace app so is going to have to isolate. That way he gets to stay home and nurse the ol' hangover and we make the Test

324

and Trace app look good even though it isn't; it's an extremely strong move.

I cast my eyes across the bar and see Poppy getting chatted up by some older married spad.

It doesn't bother me in the slightest though, because I'm going to be one step removed from prime minister in a matter of hours and I won't even be able to see Poppy from where I'll be sitting. I drift home and dream dreams of congratulatory parental smoked salmon all night.

Monday 16 November

With Blojo and Carrie 'isolating' after last night, the GM is called off.

I once watched a talk a guy gave on networking and he said the two major techniques you need are reaching out and touching base. Really insightful stuff.

I apply both this morning and text Blojo to follow up on the night before:

> Blojo, nursing a sore head this morning in more ways than one I imagine. Don't suppose you recall the ol' chat re Rafe as chief of staff. Think I could be *très* strong. Shall we lock it in?

All I see on his WhatsApp is 'Last seen at 01:31'. He's clearly still asleep.

With Big Daddy Cum Cum gone, the boycott of *Good Morning Britain* and Piers Morgan has come to an end and some complete moron has decided to send Cock-in-his-Hands in to talk to him without any sort of prep.

I sit watching, ferociously running my hands through my

hair (Susanna Reid is looking fucking phenomenal as ever this morning but, if anything, that makes me even more on edge).

They cover in immense detail all of Cock-in-his-Hands' appalling gaffes from April until now. Somehow though, gloriously, he manages to slither out of all of it. He still looks a bit like he's a nonce filming a confession tape but way less than usual.

He even sidesteps a question from Morgan about Big Daddy Cum Cum. Christ, he's come on. I'm so fucking relieved about this.

I decide not to tell him he's done a good job though, as it's imperative that we keep him small and therefore easy to manipulate, so giving him praise is always a bad call.

At midday, which is when I think he's woken up, Blojo texts me to say:

Rafe! Thanks for covering me last night, old boy. You are a gentleman and a scholar. Listen, there's a report on my desk about Priti Patel and some 'bullying' nonsense I haven't got round to sorting – and I thought you'd be just the man to make it go away. I'm sure we can look into the chief of staff role if you do well.

Holy shit. This is the biggest moment of my life.

I hurtle into Blojo's office and find his in-tray. The papers on it are so high they nearly come up to my chest. I rifle through them; they're mostly bitterly angry letters from civil servants telling him that never in their time have they ever seen a prime minister so entitled, incompetent and arrogant. Eventually, I find the dossier. It's extremely thick and takes me several hours to work through. I decide to work through the dossier in Blojo's office rather than returning to my desk, given that he's not working there and it makes sense for me to get comfortable, given that all things being unequal I'll be calling this place home vary soon indeed (seven to eight years' time).

The dossier has a very large number of very detailed accounts of Bully Patel's bullying of civil servants.

I read:

24 February 2020
Ms Patel ran up to me while I was having fifteen minutes off over lunch to eat a salad. She then upended the salad so the dressing spilt all over my clothes but refused to let me go home and change. I was forced to spend the rest of the day working covered in Caesar dressing. It was extremely humiliating.

1 August 2020
Ms Patel threatened to stick the heel of her boot in my mouth unless I rescinded on blocking an immigration bill which I perceived to be particularly barbaric. When I did rescind she still tried to stick the heel of her boot in my mouth anyway.

12 September 2020
Ms Patel poked me in the chest so hard and called me 'a fucking dumb bitch', causing me to cry. She then told me if I didn't stop crying I'd lose my job.

I decide the best way to deal with this is to send Bully Patel a written warning. That way we can be seen to be doing the right thing and because it's a written warning it'll mean she'll definitely stop bullying people.

I decide not to go too hard on the 'don't ever do this again' stuff because the bullying is classic so I say:

Dear Home Secretary,

I hope this finds you well.

Seventy-three complaints have been made against your behaviour in the workplace. Multiple civil servants have complained that you are 'violent', 'aggressive' and 'intimidating', and that your conduct makes them feel uncomfortable.

If you could try and reduce the bullying that would be great but do what's most comfortable for you. Maybe try and cut back a bit and not bully every third civil servant or something, but no worries if not.

Best wishes,
Rafe Hubris, BA (Oxon)

(I went to Oxford University.)

Moments after sending the email Bully Patel replies with a crying laughter face and that's that.

I swiftly put the folder of wetty complaints in the bin and sit with my feet up on Blojo's desk, confident that I, Rafe Hubris, BA (Oxon), am now chief of staff.

I, Rafe Hubris, BA (Oxon), ROS (Rafe of Staff).

I immediately email my brother, Will, Mummy and my father, the provost of Eton and the rector of Exeter College, Oxford (I went there) to inform them of the news. I know I haven't had it confirmed for definite yet but it's as good as mine. I then post on my LinkedIn a picture of a ladder and the caption 'big development being announced tomorrow…'

I decide it's time for a slightly different look in this new authority role and buy myself a light-blue suit with a light-pink tie (Eton colours; if you know you know) and a black suit with a dark pink tie (Exeter College colours; if you know you know). Perhaps this is what I'll be known for: *Rafe Hubris, the most stylish chief of staff, occupying the role for nine months before becoming the longest-serving prime minister in UK history at just twenty-six...*

Wednesday 18 November

I wake up to a text from Mummy telling me both she and my father are absolutely thrilled and that I must tell her when the news is going to be officially out so we can arrange a congratulations party. I am going to get so much fucking smoked salmon at this party it's going to be offensive.

I also get a text from Will in which, for the first time in his life, he tells me he's proud of me, which is a bit gay but I actually don't mind it.

I'm practically glowing when I get into work. I can't stop smiling. All that's left now is to get Blojo to say the magic words. We're sat on a Zoom first thing in the morning; I keep dropping hints about confirming the Rafe of Staff role but he doesn't pick up on them. We're trying to change his Zoom background ahead of PMQs; it's currently a picture of Priti Patel's face imposed onto a dominatrix (which gives me this odd twitchy feeling in my lower stomach) whipping a naked submissive with Matt Cock-in-his-Hands' face superimposed. The submissive also has a micro-penis: classic, very classic. I spat out a particularly big mouthful of Evian when I first saw it. Sadly though it's not right for Parliament; Lindsay Hoyle would have a shit fit.

Blojo manages to change it in the nick of time before PMQs and just before he's about to log off says: 'Listen Rafe old chap – bad news. They've given the chief of staff role to Eddie Lister. Completely out of my hands I'm afraid. Sorry.' He then immediately ends the meeting.

The half-smile I tend to wear in Blojo's company falters and is slowly replaced by a look of disbelief then pure fury.

I quickly and quietly pick up my laptop and take it to the staff loos and close the cubicle door behind me and smash it to pieces. I smash it so hard I break the loo seat I smash it on. I smash it like Andy Roddick smashing a Pure Drive Roddick after a double fault. I imagine the laptop is Boris Johnson's stupid fucking arrogant self-serving face and smash and smash again and again and again.

At this point I'm fairly sure I hear someone leave the cubicle next to me and depart from the loos, the faint sound of Grand Theft Auto's soundtrack following them out.

Once the fury eventually subsides, a bitter resentment takes its place. Boris Johnson is a fucking cunt. When he needs you he's all charming and charismatic but he doesn't give a shit about helping anyone that isn't him. He's a nasty, spineless, self-serving little cunt and I fucking hate him. I hate him with my guts. I will never be okay with him after this. All he had to do was make me chief of staff after he'd fucking promised he would, but he hasn't. He's pathetic and weak and he's not even clever or funny and he looks like shit and Carrie isn't even that fit. Boris Johnson is a cunt.

Friday 20 November

I'm tensing my conventionally attractive square jaw so hard my teeth are aching, but it's all I can do to stop myself from smashing another laptop or someone's head into a desk.

I refuse to meet Boris Johnson's stupid fucking gaze in the GM or listen to his stupid fucking jokes to distract everyone from the fact that he's a shit politician who has absolutely no sense of duty and doesn't even give the tiniest fraction of a fuck about any of the rising cases and puts off acting until it's too late on everything. The man is a cunt.

Now Big Daddy Cum Cum and Lee Cain have gone, the vibe of the GMs is very different. Carrie makes everyone sign a logbook on the way in and out and has a Pret sandwich platter in the middle of the table for us all to help ourselves. None of this does anything to calm me down and I spend most of the meeting imagining Boris Johnson walking the wrong way down the M25. I'm so angry I don't touch a single Pret sandwich.

In the few moments where I'm not imagining Boris Johnson's mangled innards being rolled into tarmac by Range Rovers, it registers that Bully Patel is being sent out to give a public apology after the media aren't buying the 'please stop being a bully approach' I employed earlier this week.

'We've got to form a circle around the Pritster, chaps,' says the cunt.

He then embarks on a stupid speech about how bullying is unacceptable. While he's saying all this, my eyes find Matt Cock-in-his-Hands, who's hanging off Boris Johnson's every word. As Carrie is finishing off the speech with the words 'as an empath, I think you should be kind', I briefly fantasise about how truly thrilling it would be to flush Matt Cock-in-his-Hands' head down one of the Number 10 loos.

I slide my hand into his open rucksack and retrieve his lunchbox. After I've signed the logbook to leave the meeting I calmly enter the loo and spoon the couscous from Cock-in-his-Hands' cool box into the urinal.

While this is happening I flick on Bully Patel making a statement on ITV, where she apologises if people felt upset at her actions rather than actually apologising for the actions themselves. Absolute bread-and-butter politician apology. In exactly the same way I'm very sorry if Matt Cock-in-his-Hands feels upset because I'm spooning his lunch onto a pissy urinal cake but I don't for one moment regret doing it. I then spoon the couscous back into the lunchbox. This definitely makes me feel a bit better but I am still extremely angry and punch a wall very hard on the way out of the bathroom. It dents the wall. Is this how Bully Patel feels all the time?!

Saturday 21 November

I get a text from Will with the words 'Oh dear' and a link to an article, the headline of which is: 'Lord Edward Udny-Lister is made chief of staff.'

I don't reply and spend most of the weekend drinking.

Monday 23 November

In the morning I learn that the AstraZeneca vaccine from Oxford University (where I went) is performing very well in clinical trials. For the first time in nearly four days my quiet fury lifts a little. You absolutely love to hear it; obviously it's what you'd expect, but nonetheless it's lovely to hear.

I'm so buoyed by this I even join in with the chant of 'Oxford! Oxford! Oxford!' started by one of the spads in Number 10.

Lifted by this experience I decide to put my anger behind me, not because Boris Johnson isn't a cunt, but because sometimes you have to navigate your way through cunts in politics to achieve a greater good, like ensuring restrictions are relaxed enough so as to allow the Christmas corporate party scene to go ahead. As anyone who has ever been to a Christmas corporate party will know, they are the places where the very best people come together to drink the best booze, have the best conversations, eat the best food and do the best coke off other people's spouses' genitals in the best loos. To ensure that they take place, if that means working closely with a man I hate, then that's what I'll do.

As I sit with Boris Johnson writing his speech it transpires Christmas parties are completely off, which is fucking shit. The supposed 'coming out of lockdown' is basically just a continued lockdown; all the shithole places that Stig of the Dump presides over will stay locked down and the nicer places will be under revised 'tier two' restrictions where the best thing people can do is meet in groups of six outside. All the Christmas corporate parties will almost certainly have to be on Zoom now, which is a fucking disgrace; how am I supposed to seduce women over Zoom?! Invite them to a private room and give them a striptease?!

I manage to lift my mood by producing one of the best zingers in their long and decorated history: 'Tis the season to be jolly, but 'tis also the season to be jolly careful.

Boris tells me I'm on fire today. He's not wrong.

Maybe he's not that bad after all; he is great fun and I guess, enjoyable as they are, Christmas parties can't go ahead as the cases are higher than Govey in the Nineties…

Wednesday 25 November

I'm a bit bummed out about all the tiers so I invite a couple of the chaps from school round for some post-work nose beverages. Though technically this isn't allowed, it is permissible on the Isle of Wight, which is incidentally what I always call my flat when we're having a cocaine taster, so I'm pretty sure that makes it in line with the rules.

I've never previously done cocaine on a Tuesday evening when I have work the next day. I've done it on all the other days, just not ever a Tuesday, so there's something particularly exciting about traversing unchartered territory. Chang is truly the best. I sit with the chaps talking about how we could probably all become doctors if we wanted and how we would expand London's CBD to engulf the whole of the capital.

When the chaps have gone, my brain is feeling so fucking high-end, I'm bursting with ingenious ideas. Pulling a piece of paper towards me I decide to pretend to write a letter to Boris from the perspective of an eight-year-old who is looking for clarity on Christmas. It's fucking brilliant. I complete it in about twenty seconds. I don't even need to make my handwriting look worse because I'm so unbelievably high, all my writing is a scrawl anyway.

I immediately screenshot and send it to Blojo. He replies within five minutes.

Brilliant, Rafe. People will definitely believe that's been written by an eight-year-old. Really top work.

He then follows up (he never does this) telling me:

It's got the thumbs up from Carrie too. Let's call him a believable name like Monti.

I text back almost before Blojo has sent me his message:

Perfect

I let out a war cry like I'm Jordan fucking Belfort (which in a way I am) and spend the rest of the evening aggressively ironing all of my shirts four times over.

Friday 28 November

Classic one at work today.

The tier-two restrictions, which come into play from Monday (1 December), state that to have a drink in the pub you need to have a substantial meal with it. Carrie has made this into a little bit of a food testing event. She's had a caterer come in and make different food items which can't be easily defined as a substantial meal or not and it's our job as spads to taste and vote to inform policy.

'Sorry guys, this one can't go to a vote – it's definitely in,' says Carrie, chomping on some cheese and Parma ham from a charcuterie board. 'I laterally love cheese. Somebody take it away from me or I'll laterally eat the whole thing!'

We're pretty much in unanimous agreement on all the food items she's had made for us, except for one: the scotch egg. Ben, Daniel and Poppy are insistent that it's a snack, not a substantial meal, whereas I, Carrie and Hugo think it's a substantial meal and should definitely count.

'The thing is, chaps,' says Hugo, finishing off a mouthful of an exceptionally gourmet scotch egg, 'if we say yes to this, it sends out a fucking great message re the union. It shows we give a shit about them. It's free PR.'

'Oh my actual goodness, yaas qween,' says Carrie. 'Protect the Fringe at all costs, I laterally love it. Right. That's on the list.'

I guess that is a good point. I think I would have made it better but fair play to Hugo I suppose.

Monday 30 November

Today's GM is pretty intense.

The 'libertarian squadron' are back and are accusing Blojo of 'ambushing them', promising a tiered system which is really just another lockdown. The thing is, there's nothing the old chap can do. The deaths are up to 75K now, which we'd all admit is a decent graduate starting salary, so he can't just do nothing.

Predictably, when people come to Blojo's defence, the libertarian squadron all run out of the room as if acid has been poured on their faces, screaming: 'I'm being cancelled.' They don't sign the logbook on their way out, which is not lost on Carrie, who looks furious.

When the libertarian squadron have gone, conversation moves to vaccines. With the Oxford AstraZeneca Oxford vaccine from Oxford University (I went there) soon available, we need to decide who gets priority access.

I immediately and sensibly say: 'Well surely it makes best sense to do it by income. That way the people who do most for the economy and are therefore most important get to roam free and then, if the poor people get Covid, it won't matter too much. Also, no one votes Tory who's poor anyway.'

'We have to be cleverer than that,' says Blojo. 'There'll be a fucking outcry if we do that. But,' he adds with a renewed energy, 'if we prioritise the oldies first and vow to vaccinate everyone over fifty before we do the rest, then we'll have looked after our chaps and protected the most vulnerable.'

'We'll also need to put people with underlying health conditions and care home workers first to make up for Matt's history with them,' says Poppy, who stares at Hancock as she delivers this line. He looks back with his usual manic and moronic grin.

'Yes, yes, fine, fine,' says Blojo, half-listening.

'What about vaccinating black people like Marcus Rashford?' asks Poppy, who seems to have swung back into the realms of intolerable wokery since she spoke to him on the fucking phone. Several people audibly groan when she says this.

'I'm not siding with the fucking Lefties in the culture war,' says Blojo gruffly.

'BAME communities are dying in much greater numbers from this virus, so we should surely prioritise th—'

But Govey cuts her off and says: 'I think they've had a good year already, sweetie.'

This is surely the right move. If we're going to prioritise protecting black people over white people, what next? An entire society unfairly advantaging black people over whites?! That sounds a little divisive to me.

The meeting ends with Carrie explaining how she's organised a Secret Santa this year and that everyone is to pick a name out of the Louis Vuitton bag as they leave.

'It's not a big spendy sitch, guys, so no one spend more than £500…unless you get me,' she says with a smug smile.

I rustle around in the bag and the name I pull out is none other than fucking Matt Hancock.

Fuck my life.

DECEMBER

Wednesday 2 December

I'm on my way into the office. It's a crisp, cold, still winter morning and yet, despite the lack of wind, I hear rustling from a bush as I walk past it. On closer inspection it looks like someone is trying to set the bush on fire while also hiding within its branches. On closer inspection still, I see this is Big Daddy Cum Cum. He must be trying to recreate the Moses burning bush scene from the Bible… I hear him whisper 'This is the revolution' a couple of times but soon leave to go inside. I don't have time for his weirdness any more.

I've found a pub where they're selling soup as a substantial meal. In this instance, it's one of my favourites: *la crème de la San Miguel*; absolutely delicious and goes down a bloody treat. You absolutely love to see it.

Friday 4 December

I've got my feet up on my desk after a big lunch and am mentally preparing myself for a chill weekend by dozing. Just as I'm about to drop off, a horrible thought crosses my mind. I jack-knife hard out of my doze and scrape half the contents of my desk onto the floor as I do, for I've just remembered something we've forgotten. This isn't something small either – like forgetting to buy your mate a round at Queen's club bar or buying PPE in March. We've forgotten about fucking Brexit. Why the fuck isn't Boris Johnson across this?! I can't believe I'm having to pick up the pieces for this flapping sexually persistent Honey Monster again for no thanks or extra pay!!! Nonetheless, I rush to his office to tell him he needs to get it together, not because he deserves it but because of a sense of duty.

As I push through the door, I see Boris Johnson is cuddled up with Carrie Symonds watching *PS I Love You* on a projector. Carrie looks extremely miffed that I'm taking Blojo away from her.

'Boris, Brexit,' I say urgently.

What follows is like the opening scene from *Four Weddings and a Funeral*.

'Fuck,' says Blojo. 'Fuck. Fuck.'

'Fuck.'

'Fuck.'

'Fuck.'

'Fuck it.'

'Fuck.'

He buffers for a good twenty seconds and then says, 'We're just going to have to tell people to prep for no deal. That's what we're going to have to do. We'll present this as the product of an uncompromising negotiation strategy rather than not having done anything on it since March. Yes, that's it!' he says. 'You book me in an interview and I'll say all that. Thanks for covering me, Rafe. All otherwise okay?' he adds, clearly trying to check in with me just so he can fucking manipulate me again.

I pause and, after a moment, smile and say: 'Never better.'

Sunday 6 December

Marcus (Daniel but we're still calling him Marcus), who was supposed to be briefing Matt Cock-in-his-Hands ahead of Piers Morgan tomorrow, has told me he's been pinged on Test and Trace and is feeling shite after a positive Covid test so I'm having to cover for him. The only thing fucking worse than working on a weekend is having to work with Matt Cock-in-his-Hands on a weekend.

He tries to FaceTime me but I decline and call him on the regular phone instead. He tries to change the call to FaceTime four times throughout the course of the conversation but eventually gets the message and gives up.

The interview is first thing so I don't have the time to properly brief him with anything.

'What if I just went in totally crazy? Like really off the wall,' he says, and then proceeds to do a sort of ham Brooklyn accent: 'I could be like "Hey Piers, how you doin'? I'm the Health Secretary. I'm ready to answer your questions…"'

'Hancock,' I say after a moment's pause, 'I need you to promise me that you will never do whatever that was ever again.'

'Sorry,' he says and starts to sound wet and emotional. Then a thought from my Oxbridge brain comes to me. That's it! Emotion. We've spent all this time trying to get Cock-in-his-Hands to be something he isn't by laughing through interviews or by trying to be statesmanlike, and it's been appalling precisely because he's awful at taking on those roles. But if we got him to lean into the role that comes most naturally to him – that of a snot-nosed Year Six who's tearfully explaining to his parents that he's just bombed all of his SATs, I think we might just be able to make it work for us.

'Hancock,' I say.

'Yes, buddy,' he replies, which still makes me throw up in my mouth slightly when I hear it.

'I need you to go into Morgan tomorrow and try to cry.'

'Why would you want me to do that?' he asks, nonplussed.

'Think about it, Hancock: if you go and cry there's absolutely nothing Morgan can do to make you answer his questions. He's just going to sound uncompassionate. Thus, crying equals no scrutiny, *capisce*?'

'I love it, Rafe. You're a bloody genius,' says Hancock. 'But what am I going to cry over?'

I scroll through the notes Marcus has emailed over and see that Morgan and Susanna Reid (I would shut my bollocks in a doorway just to go for one drink with her) are going to be talking about the vaccine. Then I see something that we can work with.

'I've got it,' I say triumphantly. 'They're going to show you images of a bloke called William Shakespeare who's going to get the vaccine; you're going to need to watch that and pretend it's making you really well up.'

'But Rafe, I'm not sure that totally makes sense?'

'I know it doesn't, but if your acting is convincing enough and you really fucking sell it, people will go for it. Just remember, Hancock, this is an open goal for you. All you need to do is lean into your natural persona as a floppy wet lettuce.'

'Sounds great, Rafe. Can't wait to make you proud, buddy.'

He then tries to get me to stay on the line and chat about stuff but I put the phone down straight away.

Monday 7 December

I watch Cock-in-his-Hands pretend to cry in front of Morgan and Susanna Reid and for once in his life he actually fucking nails it. Sure, it's not Oscar-worthy, it's not even BAFTA-worthy, it's not even drama scholarship at a low-tier private school-worthy, but in the right lighting to the sufficiently unintelligent observer, it's just about believable.

I know it's not a good idea to text Cock-in-his-Hands praise but today I'm so pleased with him, I do it. I tell him he's done a great job and has really turned a corner with the whole speaking to the press thing.

About ten minutes later he sends me back a picture of his red puffy face, eyes streaming with actual tears. He follows this haunting image up with an essay, which I don't read for fear of regurgitating my Pret breakfast all over my sartorial shirt.

In the evening I get a text in from Boris Johnson which reads:

> Rafe, dinner in Brussels tomorrow to fucking win round Ursula von der Lemon. You are coming for alcoholic and anecdotal support. Train at 12:30. We are going to get rEUined. BJ

I don't know what to make of this. On the one hand I fucking hate the idea that my going would mean Boris Johnson had won me round in some sense. I still haven't forgiven him for promising me chief of staff and not delivering.

On the other hand, missing out on the corporate Christmas party scene was really bumming me out and this would be an opportunity to let my hair down and get binned and there might be fit women there. Technically speaking, Boris is also my boss, so I can't really say no.

I decide to go but vow that I won't totally let my guard down with him.

Tuesday 8 December

We sit on the Eurostar at 12.30 and *el Estrellas* doth flow. The problem is, it's very hard to keep your guard up around Boris Johnson because he's so funny and classic. We keep ordering Estrellas and chatting. It's great – just like old times.

By the time we arrive in Brussels we are absolutely *fucké*. As soon as I arrive in my room I immediately pass out on the bed.

I wake up about ninety minutes later to Blojo hammering on the door and shouting in a high-pitched French accent: '*Monsieur Hubris, c'est cinq Euros pour une heure. Je sais que t'es un villain garçon.*'

(Mister Hubris, it's five pounds for an hour. I know you're a naughty boy).

I fling the door wide open to see Blojo in a white robe. He's somehow managed to produce a bottle of Lanson and two glasses and says loudly: 'Say hello to my lil friend.'

Whatever sobriety I'd reclaimed by dozing off, I lose by finishing the bottle off in fifteen minutes with Blojo.

We turn up to the dinner stinking of booze that the scent of my Chanel Bleu and Blojo's Creed Aventus aftershave does little to mask.

In the lift Blojo smacks himself in the face a couple of times to try and sober himself up. I do it to myself a couple of times too but I literally can't feel my face. Nonetheless, I just get this feeling that we've fucking got this dinner.

Ursula von der Lemon and Michel Barnier meet us and

invite us to sit down at the table. Blojo goes in for four kisses with Ursula von der Lemon so I do the same with her and wonder very briefly whether we might get off with each other, but we don't.

Very excitingly, von der Lemon and Barnier are accompanied by a young woman. I don't know whether it's because I've had about ten pints of Estrella and half a bottle of champagne but I think I might need to marry this girl.

'*Enchanté*,' I say and kiss her hand.

She looks incredibly taken aback by how flirtatious and attractive I am.

We go to sit and Blojo and I absolutely pile into the bread like a pair of gluttonous, glutenous hogs (notice how truly exquisite this wordplay is). I am so fucking hungry for some reason. We keep asking for them to bring out more bread baskets.

I let Blojo chat to von der Lemon and Barnier while I crack on with my future wife.

Her name is Brigitte.

I tell her I could be her Mark Darcy. She doesn't get the reference… I'm not sure they have Oxbridge in Belgium…

After about fifteen minutes of scintillating flirtation that I direct at the old girl she tells me in heavily accented English: 'You'll have to excuse me' – and she doesn't fucking come back.

Fucking women. I don't let it get me down though. I just pile into more booze – more winter reds. I'm practically shotting them.

Just before I pass out fully clothed on my bed back in the hotel room, heart thumping like a mallet in my ears, I reflect that this has been one of the greatest nights of my life.

Wednesday 9 December

I wake up still feeling totally rat-arsed from the night before, which is absolutely classic. I sit up in bed and see a great big presence in the bed next to me. It's Blojo; we must have gone to bed together.

I briefly nearly have a panic attack worrying we might have done something gay but see the old chap is fully clothed. He looks pretty out of it. His skin looks pale – almost yellow – and he's lying on his back with his mouth open.

'Blojo,' I say, but he doesn't answer.

Fuck. What if Boris Johnson is dead? What if it was I who killed him in his sleep? I wonder how I'd feel about that if I had murdered him… A part of me thinks it would be terrible, but another part thinks it would be good, but then another part still feels guilty for thinking that. If Boris Johnson died would I be prime minister? Would I be better? Would I be worse? Would Boris Johnson not being prime minister any more mean we'd deal with Covid better? Or is he the best man for the job?

I start wondering whether, if he started choking, I'd resuscitate him or just leave him and let his common sense see him through…

Then Blojo splutters into consciousness. He sits up in bed and gathers himself.

'I was worried about you for a second there, old boy,' I say, grinning sheepishly.

'Fucking hell. I don't think my head has ever felt this Bruged in all my life,' he says, and sinks back down into bed.

My head throbs on the Eurostar back; it feels like Bully Patel is skipping on top of my temples in her stilettos (I wonder if she ever puts on a pair of stilettos and tramples on people…).

Just as our third English Breakfast is on the way, Blojo clasps his forehead and says: 'Fuck! The fucking meeting. The fucking meeting. What happened, Rafe? I can't remember any of it.'

'Oh God,' I say, as little bits of the night before come back to me.

'Do you remember going in for four kisses with Ursula von der Lemon?' I ask.

'Fuck,' he replies. 'Please tell me I didn't grab her thigh.'

'No you didn't do that, mate,' I say, picturing the worst thing we did last night from all the hazy details floating around in my brain.

'What? What did I do? There's something, isn't there?!' he says.

I think for a moment and then the image comes to me. Blojo and I were so hammered we ended the dinner by doing a full act-out of Blojo's cherry-pie anecdote with Thai accents and me playing the ping-pong girls and everything.

I tell Blojo this and he looks absolutely mortified, then like he's going to laugh very hard, then mortified. He then looks very seriously at me and says: 'Well I think if a no-deal Brexit wasn't going to happen before, it's definitely going to fucking happen now.'

He then sidles off to the loos – I imagine, to vomit.

Thursday 10 December

I text Blojo as I sit slumped at my desk:

I'm still hanging worse than Saddam Hussain in '06, mate

Blojo doesn't reply though. I think he's in the doghouse again because he didn't bring Carrie back a present from Brussels and the old girl is furious about it. In my hungover haze I see her at several points explaining the situation tearfully to Allegra and some of the other girls in the office.

I slaughter about five Pret bacon baguettes and two litres of orange juice but it does nothing to return me to my usual high-end self.

At lunch I'm forced to bin work and go home to sleep the hangover off.

Friday 11 December

I return to Number 10 to learn that Blojo is getting sued by all the fucking civil servants' lawyers because he cleared all their bullying charges against Bully Patel. This would obviously be fine and not my problem but Blojo has texted me to say:

Rafe old chum,

Since you sorted this to begin with and it's gone to shit, I'm afraid you're going to have to get me out of it – it's only right.

BJ

I immediately phone both of my QC godfathers but they're both fucking busy.

I then work my way steadily and calmly through the 300 lawyers I have on LinkedIn but hardly any of them come back to me and the ones that do are charging ridiculous fees.

I realise there's only one option: to call Sophie, the northern lawyer I used to rail.

I pile out to Pret and call her. I know that what I'm about to ask her is going to go completely against her morality and the only way to push it through is by appealing to her sexual predilection for 'problematic' men.

Accordingly, I decide to lean into the most obnoxious version of myself and call her.

'You need to meet me in Pret in ten minutes.'

'What?' she says aggressively.

'Pret in ten minutes.'

'You're a dick,' she replies.

I put the phone down and then proceed to walk around outside for fifteen minutes to keep her waiting.

When I arrive in Pret, she's there looking furious.

'I can't believe you'd turn up late to your own meeting. It's so fucking rude,' she says.

'I haven't got time to hear some obnoxious northern woman shout at me,' I reply, which I can tell is absolutely driving her insane with sexual excitement.

'What do you fucking want then?' she asks.

'We're getting a lot of legal cases flying in because of how we dealt with Priti Patel's bullying. I need you to make these go away and I need you to do that today,' I say, looking around Pret, refusing to give her my full attention.

'You want me to defend someone who I morally object to so you can hush up claims of abusive behaviour in the workplace using public money?' she says, her face covered in disgust.

'Who said I'd be paying you?' I say and get up and leave.

I don't look back at her but I'm pretty sure I've fucking nailed that encounter.

By the afternoon I get a text telling me work has been put in place to offset the claims. I smile. I've just used my sexuality to get what I want; I'm like a beautiful woman!

This evening I get a knock on the door.

It's Sophie.

She barges in and is all over me.

She gets me to tell her I don't even think she's done a good job with the legal claims and I won't be paying her for the work as our trade deal on my Moroccan rug is well under way. This causes her to climax three times in the space of a minute – a Holy Trinity, if you will (as opposed to a Michaelmas, which would be one orgasm, or a Hilary, which would be two[31]).

I feel a little bit dirty afterwards and I want to give her a hug but as soon as I do she pushes me off and says: 'Don't fucking look at me,' and leaves.

I guess I'm Jennifer Arcuri now…

Monday 14 December

Carrie has seemingly forgiven Boris Johnson for not bringing her back a present from Brussels, and appears to be sporting a very impressive ring with a blue sapphire on it in the GM this morning.

Though the Bully Patel legal claims are gone (I'm still feeling a bit dirty for how I managed to get rid of them if I'm honest), we're having to sort boosting her image today to 'plaster over the wound'. We agree the best thing to do is to get her to publicly financially compensate the victims of Windrush, although not the dead ones, obviously: sadly we've just been too busy over the last forty-nine years to get round to them. Unsurprisingly, she's absolutely furious about this but

31 Here I'm alluding to term names at Oxford University, which is where I have a degree from.

eventually, she grudgingly agrees to go and do it.

We then move onto Christmas.

Cases are up to 20,000 a day now and the scientists are urging Boris Johnson to rescind his 'three households meeting up over five days' ruling issued in November, projecting that it will cause at least 100,000 deaths. Boris, on the other hand, keeps replying, 'I'm not going to be the Grinch who stole Christmas,' trying to make light of the whole thing so people bend to his will.

Eventually he breaks a heavy silence and says definitively: 'Look, I'll encourage people to have a small Christmas but I'm not changing the ruling. Right, we need a good joke to announce the policy, chaps. Who can come up with something about having a merry little Christmas? Shit, that's it! Have yourselves a merry little Christmas.'

He then gets up and leaves. All the spads at the GM exchange grave looks. It honestly seems like Blojo doesn't actually give a fuck about resolving the Covid situation, or being prime minister, or the UK in general. I'm all for sacking off work when you've got something more important to do, but the water's up to our fucking necks with this now and Blojo genuinely doesn't seem to give a shit about stopping the flood. I never thought I'd say this about him, but he's being a fucking chopper.

Wednesday 16 December

London is locked down once more.

No more *crème de la San Miguel* in pubs. No more anything good. I feel a bit like the world is swallowing me at the moment. It's not depression or anything – I'm not a wetty – but nonetheless it is *très* shit and you hate to see it.

Thursday 17 December

To pull myself out of feeling less than classic, ahead of Secret Santa tomorrow, I've decided to get Matt Cock-in-his-Hands the largest dildo I can find on Ann Summers – the King cock ultra-realistic girthy suction-cup 8.5-inch dildo, to be exact. It does mean I'm having to part with £45.00 of my money that I own but it'll be worth it for the humiliation it'll cause him.

Just as I'm paying I'm presented with a scroll with the same Rees-Mogg seal as before.

I open it and it reads:

Dear Hubris minor,

I hope this finds you recovered from the supper I understand you were forced into having with the savages of Brussels. What a nasty business having to break bread with people so ghastly. I think your stoicism in the face of such a dystopian predicament was admirable.

Further, as chair of the Eton politics association, I am now looking into booking speakers for the new year and would be overwhelmed with happiness if you would be so kind as to come and talk to the prime ministers of tomorrow. I would be delighted to invite you to speak on the day of our lord, Friday the 15th of January, and will eagerly await to see if you'd be agreeable to the prospect.

I'm afraid there is another matter I must broach which brings me far less pleasure than Eton societies and their distinguished guests.

I was so shocked and angered on hearing that UNICEF have been feeding children in London that I very nearly had one of my servants break some of my crockery on my behalf.

I'm sure you will agree with me that this nasty political stunt from UNICEF, who are supposed to exist to protect children who aren't languishing in the luxury of food bank provision, is appalling and should not go unchallenged.

I would not only welcome but relish the opportunity to pledge a mind as fine as yours to our cause as we protest this appalling injustice tomorrow to the prime minister.

May UNICEF's floccinaucinihilipilification of our very charitable efforts to provide food banks with the gallons of gruel we currently provide not be left unchallenged.

Eagerly anticipating your reply.

Floreat Etona!
Jacob Rees-Mogg

I think once again about whether I want to oppose UNICEF feeding starving children and though it does seem like a bit of a political stunt, I'm not sure I can really be bothered to do this. I'm not even sure I can be bothered to do the Eton politics talk either. I just don't really see the point.

Friday 18 December

I watch after lunch as Matt Cock-in-his-Hands unwraps the enormous dildo I've bought him. There is a small smattering of applause when people see this is what he's been given and he looks confused, embarrassed and a bit red. I feel a lust for life I haven't felt for a good while take hold as I watch this spectacle unfold, but it soon evaporates away again.

I'm pulled into an emergency meeting with Boris, Wetty and some of the main players: Gove, Raab, Carrie, etc. Carrie seems extremely pissed off because whoever got her in Secret Santa has bought her a small candle from the White Company rather than the deluxe model.

Matt Cock-in-his-Hands, though not actually invited to the meeting, has turned up anyway, a bit like a partner you've told you don't love and don't want to be with any more but who keeps following you around all the time. He's stashed the dildo in a rucksack he's carrying around but the bulbous bell-end of the item doesn't fit within the bag and rides high enough in the air so that it sits above his head, making him quite literally a dickhead.

Wetty shows us a particularly depressing graph, which basically shows the cases going up in a practically vertical line. Who would have thought a Test and Trace system that doesn't fucking work, no vaccine and a government telling people to continually mix would have caused this?

Boris Johnson spends the meeting scrabbling around trying to find a way to cover his arse and defend what has effectively been a 'slapping the virus on the back and saying "jolly good luck"' policy since cases started to rise again.

'What can we blame this on?' he thinks aloud.

'That woman who was so fucking rude to me when I was trying to buy that crystal to repel negative ions in Space NK?' Carrie suggests.

'That's the right sort of ballpark,' says Boris, sensing that to tell Carrie she'd come up with a simply moronic suggestion would not be a good idea.

'What do people in this country like to blame things on...?' Then he snaps his fingers and says, 'That's it: immigrants. An immigrant mutant virus washing up on our shores, infecting us with its foreignness and compromising our values! Tell me that's theoretically possible, Chris!' he says energetically.

'It's perfectly possible that a foreign variant could have come over and be driving up cases.'

'Perfect! That's that then,' says Boris.

'Hang on a second, Prime Minister. It is possible, but if I'm honest I think the dramatic rise is probably more to do with the fact that cases spread more in the winter and we've been allowing people to mix in pu—'

But Wetty is cut off by Carrie, who says: 'Ummmm, excuse me, but he actually said that's that then, were you not listening?'

Wetty just tails off at this point under Carrie's glare.

'Right. Christmas,' says Blojo, a heaviness in his voice. 'It's got to go, hasn't it?'

Wetty looks back at him and nods gravely.

'What would you advise?'

'I think we need to reduce the number of households mixing to two, only on Christmas day and only in areas where Covid cases aren't the highest.'

This causes Carrie to erupt in front of us. It's been brewing for hours after the White Company incident and now it all comes out. Pure volcanic South West London fury.

'Carrie, calm down,' says Blojo, desperately trying to stem the flow of anger.

'Don't you fucking tell me to calm down. I'd planned for Mummy and Allegra and my godparents and Focaccia from Wilf's playgroup to all come over and now that's all ruined because another bald man is coming in and trying to ruin my life,' she says, pointing at Wetty. 'I got rid of the other two baldies and I'll get rid of you too,' she says venomously, looking directly into Chris Wetty's kind eyes, which narrow slightly in sadness as she lays into him.

We all take this moment as our cue to leave, as none of us want to be there when Carrie's is full-on losing it, and quickly slither out. Matt Cock-in-his-Hands brings up the rear but the dildo in his rucksack falls out on the way out of the door and he has to pop back to pick it up.

Saturday 20 December

Clearly not even Carrie has been able to convince Blojo to go back on this one and I watch the old chap explain that Christmas is very much cancelled for many, given the new rules.

I get a text from my mother telling me that they've decided to bubble up with Will at Christmas because he's had such a good year and they think it's right for Jonty's first Christmas to be with his grandparents as a family.

Tuesday 23 December

I'm in the canteen eating a decidedly BTEC Christmas dinner. The turkey is dry and the potatoes are incredibly low-end. I leave half of it and go to stack my tray. As I'm doing so I lay eyes on Boris Johnson.

'Rafe,' he says. 'Just the man! I need you for something, old boy,' and probably because it feels too effortful to say no, I let him lead me into a side room in Number 10. He closes the door behind him and looks at me and says, 'Rafe, we need to finalise Brexit. I need your help. I promise it won't take long. Let's just bosh the whole thing out in half an hour.'

At this point he slaps a Monster energy drink down on the table before us and says, 'Have some of this nectar, old boy. It'll make you think like the fucking ancient Greeks.'

We share the drink and I can confidently say I've had less potent lines of chang in my life. It's like someone has aggressively pulled up some Venetian blinds that had been half shut over my existence.

I'm so tired but also simultaneously so fucking wired.

I want to focus on everything at the same time, which simultaneously means I can't focus on anything at all.

This means we just end up going round in circles. The problem here is that I'm not very interested in Brexit at all so haven't really kept up with the ins and outs of it and Boris, though aware of the ins and outs, is too lazy to formulate specific and exact parameters that we need to form the basis of the deal.

By midnight we are no closer to having it finished.

There's a knock on the door; it's Carrie.

Boris excuses himself and says he'll be back in a minute but an hour goes by and he doesn't come back and when I call his phone it just goes straight through to answerphone.

Boris Johnson has fucked me over again. He's drugged me and forced me to do something he's been too fucking lazy to do. Why the fuck do I continue to let him back into my life?! I hate him, I hate him with all my Oxbridge brain and conventionally attractive features. I'm too simultaneously exhausted and alert to focus on this though and decide all I can do is just get the job done and then I can fucking sleep, maybe forever… I try to read a little bit around the deal and look at meeting minutes and notes and emails but my brain is in a different solar system, making me woefully inefficient…

In the end I just wing it. I'm not sure whether what I end up with is good or not, but it is at least done and I think that's all that really matters. After all, the slogan was 'Get Brexit done', not 'Get Brexit done well' or even 'Get Brexit done adequately'.

On the deal it looks like it'll be harder for Britain to sell services to and travel through, work and settle in EU countries. There'll also be checks on British exports that didn't exist before but I've made absolutely certain that we retain the sovereignty of our fishing waters. In other words, it's good news for salmon, which is good news for smoked salmon, which is good news for Pret, which is good news for everyone in government, and at the end of the day I don't think you can expect much more from me than that.

I travel home and collapse into bed and don't wake up until the evening. When I do wake up I see Boris Johnson hasn't even sent me a text. He hasn't even texted me to say thank you after he wilfully shafted me. I have no words for him any more. Other than one. Cunt.

My bemused frustration and resentment of Boris Johnson is replaced by a hollow emptiness when I realise it's Christmas day tomorrow and I have no plans, no people to see and no food.

I immediately put on my coat to go to the shops to get food ahead of tomorrow but of course everything is shut. Even Deliveroo isn't running because it's too late.

I sit drinking and finish a whole bottle of wine in about forty-five minutes and fall asleep on the sofa.

Thursday 25 December

In a cruel twist of fate, because I was asleep for most of the day the day before, I'm wide awake by 5am this morning. Even though there's quite literally nothing for me to get up for, I can't not get out of bed.

I half-hope Santa will have visited in my sleep and left a sack in the sitting room but he hasn't. I know he doesn't exist really, and in fact he couldn't exist in the current climate as the MeToo movement would fucking cancel him on some trumped-up charge.

I try with all my might to pass the time.

I have a shower, I make a coffee, I clean my French press, I make another coffee, I clean my French press again. By this point it's still only 6am.

I log on to the News Channel but they're just slagging off my Brexit deal, which makes me feel even more shit, so I turn that off.

By eleven o'clock I remember about lunch and look through my cupboards to see if I have the food to make a semblance of a Christmas dinner but there's only some Jacob's cream crackers, ketchup and chia seeds from when I was reclaiming the rig.

I text Mummy, asking if she wants to FaceTime but I don't get a reply.

I start drinking about midday and carry on into the afternoon and, in perhaps the most shameful moment of my life, order McDonalds on Deliveroo. Even the delivery driver looks embarrassed for me when he delivers it. That's how low I've descended in the social strata: I'm being looked down on by someone little better than a manual worker!!!

I sit eating the McDonalds, which is disgusting but in a sort of dirty nice way, like having sex with someone who is butters but extremely filthy in bed.

I get a notification on my PayPal mid-afternoon from Will, who has sent me £30 with the note 'Go and buy something nice', but rather than cheering me up it just makes me feel more alone.

I drink about four beers and a couple of bottles of wine and I lie on the sofa and think about my life.

I text all the girls I've known in the Shakespearean sense, asking if any of them want to come over but none of them do. Not even Emily wants to come and spend time with me. Even more crushingly, Sophie tells me she has a boyfriend now and that she'll be blocking my number.

I wonder if I will ever reach a point lower than this…

Friday 26 December

I've sent out a few feelers among the chaps from school who are in the Clapham area to see if they want to table ski. A good seven say they'll come but it gets to the evening and none of them do.

My mother replies to my text from the day before saying she doesn't have the patience to work the technology to FaceTime so it's better if she and I catch up anon.

For some reason I can't stop thinking about Poppy tonight. I've drunk a lot again and I find myself looking back over a photo of me and her that's still on my phone; I must have missed it when I'd aggressively tried to scour all existence of her from my digital life back in July. I don't know whether it's because I'm drunk or because I'm alone, but I miss her. It's not even a sex thing. I miss the way her eyes used to crease as she smiled and her sense of humour and just knowing there's someone who understands you and cares about you. I miss knowing there was someone gentle in a world full of the pressure to be high-end all the time.

Before I have time to think about it, I've unblocked her number and I'm calling her on WhatsApp.

She answers.

We talk.

I tell her I'm sorry for starting the rumour about Hugo and she tells me she's sorry for how the relationship ended.

'You know I never stopped caring about you, Rafe. Through all of the shit, I never stopped,' she says.

In that moment, for the first time in my life, I hear the muffled drop of a tear on the sofa cushion I'm hugging to my chest. For the first time in my life, I'm crying.

'Rafe, I think it would be really good if you saw a therapist,' Poppy says gently.

'I know,' I reply.

Wednesday 31 December

It's New Year's Eve and nearly five days since I spoke to Poppy.

It was definitely good to clear the air with the old girl as no one wants bad blood with old flames. I think I got a bit carried away when we were chatting though. At the time I definitely thought I was crying, but in hindsight I realise I was just trying to give the old girl what she wanted to hear, so wasn't actually crying at all. I also emphatically do not need to go to therapy: I'm not a wetty or a nutter and there's no good reason to spend a load of money on someone to talk about emotions with when I just don't really feel them.

I'm sat in my lounge with Matt Cock-in-his-Hands, who is at the bottom of the list of people I'd choose to spend New Year's Eve with but no one else got back to my texts. We're drinking IPA shandies he's made us and he's playing 'Shut Up' by Stormzy on repeat, which he asserts is 'dank'.

'You know there's no one I'd rather be seeing the new year in than with you, buddy,' says Cock-in-his-Hands.

Though this makes me cringe horrifically, maybe spending New Year's Eve with Cock-in-his-Hands is just what I need. Maybe in actual fact a great big rip-roaring high-end party with chaps, chang and ridiculously fit women wouldn't actually bring me more happiness than just sitting with someone who's been there for me through the hard times, waving goodbye to the old year and ushering in the new one.

At this point my phone buzzes in my pocket and I'm invited via group-text to a rip-roaring high-end party with chaps, chang and ridiculously fit women, by Rupert, a chap from school.

Without a second thought I put down my IPA shandy and change into my most high-end outfit and shout to Cock-in-his-Hands: 'Sorry mate. Got a better New Year's offer. Let yourself out.'

The door slams and my phone goes off again.

This time it's a text from Boris Johnson.

I briefly consider ignoring it but ultimately decide to read it:

Rafe,

Absolutely blinding work this year. Keep up the brilliant stuff and you'll be in my shoes one day, I have no doubt.

BJ

I can't believe this. I can't believe Blojo thinks I'll be in his shoes one day!

That is so fucking strong!! I can't wait to see what we do next year together.

He's right, of course. I will be prime minister – and one day soon, I have no doubt, especially after a year like this. And what an excellent year it's been:

I've shagged *beaucoup de* worldies, organised a Brexit party, organised Brexit, helped Blojo duck out of Cobra meetings, got a *Shrek* quote into an official government speech, learnt that PPE can mean personal protective equipment and not just

Philosophy, Politics and Economics, procured a load of PPE and helped my mates out in the process, successfully risen above peer pressure and not clapped for carers, abused Matt Cock-in-his-Hands, dealt with the fallout from Big Daddy Cum Cum's Barnard Castle antics, not taken the knee, intimidated someone, sat through Matt Cock-in-his-Hands' endless conveyor belt of gaffes, helped create a world-beating Test and Trace system and a results algorithm which ensured our schoolchildren got the grades they deserved, helped protect the union, written countless speeches and pithy zingers for Blojo, eaten out to help out, got fat for a joke and then lost all the weight again, maintained a square jaw, done some phenomenal meme work, generally kept levels of WhatsApp chat at a level Aristophanes would have been proud of, crushed a northern rebellion and was just generally classic.

I look up at the sky and smile.

For the first time in a long time I feel vary, vary wall.

ACKNOWLEDGEMENTS

Writing this book has been a meaty, challenging and emotional undertaking. Accordingly I have a long list of people to thank, starting with Andy Murray, without whom I might not have a career. His decision to share a clip of me gently mocking his voice gave me the PR boost that started me on the route to becoming a professional comedian.

I'd like to thank the team at Union Jack Radio (specifically Ian and Donnach) for taking a financial risk in backing me to produce funny content for their station when I was twenty-one and much less funny than I am now. I'm not saying I wasn't funny. I was. I'm just trying to be self-effacing. I'd also like to thank Rob Brydon, who gave me some very good advice early in my career, which has paid off.

Thanks also to everyone who has grown Rafe (like bacteria) over the years on social media: Owen Jones, Femi Oluwole, Lorna Luxe, Gary Lineker, Hugh Grant, Omid Djalili and many more (what an eclectic list!). My book agent, John Baker, who has been tirelessly supportive, attentive and dedicated to this process, as well as my editor, Simon Edge, whose deft understanding of the character and eye for detail added a lot of value to the manuscript. I'd like to thank Dan Hiscocks at Lightning Books, who, along with Simon, believed in this book when everyone else in the industry didn't want to pay for it (cowards).

To Bo Burnham, Steve Coogan and Sacha Baron Cohen in whose shadows I will live for the rest of my career.

To my mother, brother and father, whom I love very much and who had to listen to me whinge at various points throughout the process about what a difficult artistic journey I was on. To Lucy Spicer, who was very supportive throughout the process. To Archie Manners, whose uniquely effervescent mind is a rare gift and who helped me grow the character beyond the confines of forty-second Twitter videos. To Ross Ashcroft who is a mentor and a scoundrel in equal measure.

But most of all, and at the risk of sounding like one of the very worst of my generation, I'd like to finish by thanking myself. I was the one who stayed up until four in the morning writing this fucking book and to be perfectly honest I think the bulk of the praise ought to go to me. Josh, you are incredibly talented, hard-working and clever. Although it must be said, given how clever you are, it's curious how desperate you are for other people to recognise and praise you for it. Regardless, I'm sure whatever it is you do next will be just as artistically significant as mocking a slightly exaggerated version of yourself across a 100,000-word book.

If you have enjoyed *Staggering Hubris*, do please help us spread the word – by putting a review on Amazon (you don't need to have bought the book there) or Goodreads; by posting something on social media; or in the old-fashioned way by simply telling your friends or family about it.

Book publishing is a very competitive business these days, in a saturated market, and small independent publishers such as ourselves are often crowded out by the big houses. Support from readers like you can make all the difference to a book's success.

Many thanks.
Dan Hiscocks
Publisher
Lightning Books